G000166270

1 MONTH OF
FREE
READING

at

www.ForgottenBooks.com

By purchasing this book you are eligible for one month membership to ForgottenBooks.com, giving you unlimited access to our entire collection of over 700,000 titles via our web site and mobile apps.

To claim your free month visit:

www.forgottenbooks.com/free79285

ISBN 978-1-5285-6933-0
PIBN 10079285

A SOCIAL THEORY

OF

RELIGIOUS EDUCATION

BY

GEORGE ALBERT COE

PROFESSOR IN THE UNION THEOLOGICAL SEMINARY, NEW YORK CITY

NEW YORK

CHARLES SCRIBNER'S SONS

1917

TO
HARRY F. WARD

WHO SEES
AND
MAKES OTHERS SEE

FOREWORD

WHAT consequences for religious education follow from the now widely accepted social interpretation of the Christian message? The present work is an attempt to answer this question.

The answer is not simple. For the social message does not require us merely to insert this or that new duty into our present scheme of living, but also to judge every detail of conduct from a higher point of view. We are required to organize the whole of life upon a different level.

It would be strange indeed if the new meaning that this gives to every-day affairs did not change our outlook upon child life. If we are to be logical and practical in our social Christianity, we must revise our policies with respect to children at least as much as our policies with respect to adults. The chapters that follow undertake to show the directions that this revision will need to take.

As we proceed, it will appear that the whole perspective of religious education undergoes a change. The central purpose, to begin with, grows more specific because the nature of goodness is seen to be as concrete as the neighbor who lives next door. Christian experience comes out of the clouds, because in our dealings with our brother whom we have seen we are dealing with the Father whom we have not seen—yes, we here come into relation with what is deepest in his character and purposes. To Christian ears these statements do not sound strange, perhaps, yet when they are applied to the religious life of the young they do sing a new melody. A profounder significance attaches to the will of a child, and especially to his relations with persons, whether children or adults.

All the plans and methods of religious education have now to be reorganized with reference to these social relations and

vii

experiences. A new measure is provided for the material that goes into the curriculum of instruction. Organizations that undertake to educate, whether the family or the church, meet a different test from that which has been traditional. Theological and ecclesiastical types take on new meaning, and they encounter demands that they have not always foreseen. The educational relations between state and church, likewise, have a different look when we approach them from the standpoint of a thoroughly socialized religion. Not less true is it that emphasis now shifts from one part of educational psychology to another.

Through my whole discussion there runs a conviction that within Protestantism there is, or is coming to be, a distinctive religious principle, that of a divine-human industrial democracy. "My Father worketh even until now, and I work." I believe that here the Christian religion contains a permanently progressive element, and therefore a motive for self-criticism as well as for criticism of "the world." Religious education, consequently, is here thought of not merely as a process whereby ancient standards are transmitted, but also as having a part in the revision of standards themselves.

Another conviction that controls my discussion is that educational organization and methods are not static tools, like saws and hammers, which are indifferent to the structures that they build, but living and moving parts of the collective life. A democracy cannot afford to use in its public schools the methods that an autocratic state finds adapted to its purposes. When the purposes of society are transformed, education must be made over. Protestantism cannot make Protestants of its children by the methods of Catholic teaching. A divine-human democracy cannot grow up through educative processes that have in their nostrils the breath of autocracy.

These are themes of high intellectual interest. They are also religious issues of the greatest import. They have a direct bearing upon even the ordinary duties of religious educators. The humblest worker will do better work if he knows the why and the whither of it than he will if he merely follows some prescription. Therefore I hope that this book of mine will be found practically helpful by those who bear the heat and the burden of the day in the schools of the church, as well as by those who guide congregations or whole communions.

As my study of this theme has progressed, I have been more and more conscious of the magnitude of the problem, and of its unending ramifications. I cannot hope to have said the last word, nor to have escaped error, but I dare to hope that others will be stimulated to face the issues and to declare their own convictions. I trust also that my faults will be judged in the light of the fact that this is the first attempt to work out in a systematic way the consequences that will follow for religious education when it is controlled by a fully social interpretation of the Christian message.

While these chapters have been in progress the wail of children in the lands at war has been in my ears, a wail for the fathers of whom they have been bereft, a wail for bread, a wail for a decent world in which to grow up. To my thinking it is a cry from all the children of the world for the sort of education that faces, and understands, the great madness that is abroad, and not only understands, but also knows the resources of human nature and of religion. Even while I have been writing about educating children in the love that loves to the uttermost, I, as a citizen of the United States, have gone to war! I am so bound into one with my neighbors that I cannot, if I would, act as a mere individual; and my neighbors and I, who constitute the United States of America, are so bound up with neighbors beyond our national boundaries that our moral destiny is intertwined with theirs. We and they must rise together, or we shall not rise at all. Forward, out of nationalism, with its limitations upon brotherhood, into world society! But we are partly of the past, "red in tooth and claw," and only partly of the ideal future. With our hands we fight our brothers; with our hearts we abhor fighting. 'Wretched men that we are! Who shall deliver us out of the body of this death?'

The future of society depends upon the sort of social education that we think it worth while to provide.

FOREWORD

Any reader who is familiar with present movements in educational thought will perceive, as this work proceeds, how much I owe to writers who have had in mind the public school rather than religious education. I am indebted most of all to John Dewey, who is foremost among those who have put education and industrial democracy into a single perspective.

GEORGE A. COE.

GLENDORÀ, CALIFORNIA,
    May 12, 1917.

CONTENTS

PART V

INTRODUCTION

hemmed and hawed, and finally replied: "Well, what do you think it ought to be?" The simple fact is that we are doing a great many things because they have been done before rather than because we have a reason for doing them. If we are asked for a reason we commonly give one that is so general as to be without point. We say, for example, that our aim is to make our pupils Christians, but if we are then required to say whether we aim to make all of them Christians immediately, on the present Sunday, or only by and by, and just what we mean by a pupil-Christian, it turns out that our apparently clear end is foggy after all.

Nor is the case any better with our notions of the means to be employed. Which is the most certain and the most economical way to produce such or such a change in this or that Sunday-school class? Are you pursuing your present methods because you have any reason to suppose that they are the most effective possible? And when the work of a year or of a series of years is done, how do you definitely know to what extent you have attained your purpose? Questions like these answer themselves. Our work is famishing, and our pupils are perishing, because we have not enough theory.

Ineffective practice produces defective theory, and perpetuates ineffectiveness thereby. It is no more true that a poor theory leads to poor practice than that poor practice leads to poor theory. Theories of education have all arisen within practice; they are attempts to think out what already exists. The reason why we stop to think is, indeed, that we are not altogether satisfied with things as they are, but yet we do not invent a better state of things "just out of our heads." No, we make improvements by mixing a little that is new with much that is old, and this mixing occurs in our thinking as well as in our practice. That is, more or less of yesterday's practice is always taken into to-day's thinking as a presupposition, or not-yet-analyzed premise, and then this thinking is used to justify the very practice from which it is derived. Now, some of yesterday's faults always escape attention; some of them are ever being accepted as virtues. For example, methods of family discipline that defeated their own aims have dominated theories of such discipline. Many a parent has conscientiously made goodness unattractive to his children, and then recommended that all parents go and do likewise! Many a progressive-minded Sunday-school worker unconsciously bends his standards to fit Sunday schools as they are. He has a theory, but it is not sufficiently critical.

The consequence of this is that the cause of religious education requires the repeated reopening of matters that seem to be already settled. The reason is not that revolutions are desirable, but that our thinking, being under the influence of our own defective past, never reaches a point where it can properly say: "Here I have reached finality; here revision will never be necessary." This is the pride that goes before a fall. The spirit of true theorizing is humble. It says to itself: "In all probability my present views of religious education are a mixture of truth and error. Let me, then, scrutinize them once more, and may the succession of scrutinizers never fail!"

The main problem is how to make Christian education sufficiently, as well as efficiently, Christian. We should stumble into a total misconception if we were to think of a theory of religious education as an attempt to control religion from outside itself, as, for example, by mere speculation. No, it is an attempt to judge our religious performances from within religion. Christian education is to be thought of as through and through the Christian religion in operation. Its methods are to be scrutinized and revised from the sole point of view of religious effectiveness. Its aims also are to be weighed in religious scales, and no others.

Not only do old methods come to us bringing hay, wood, and stubble along with precious metal, but the same is true of old purposes. They, also, as well as methods, have to be "trued up" from time to time, partly because we forget something that came to us in the hour of spiritual vision, partly because insight into the meaning of life does not attain fixity in any generation. There are depths in the Christian message that our fathers' plummets did not sound; there are depths that will remain unknown until generations yet to be born shall ask their own fresh questions. Accordingly, when we reflect upon the existing aims of Christian education with a view to revising them, we are engaged in an attempt to make them more Christian. We are not satisfied to become more efficient upon yesterday's religious level; we aspire to raise the level itself. Our problem is to make Christian education as Christian as possible.

The application of this remark to the situation of the churches to-day is unmistakable. The aims and methods of Christian education, as of church life in general, that this generation inherited were predominantly individualistic. We have been so taught as to think of the great salvation as a rescuing of individuals, each by himself, from the guilt and the power of sin, and of establishing them, each by himself, in the way of righteousness. When Canon Fremantle gave us the phrase "*the world* as the subject of redemption" we had to think twice before we could see just what it meant. For most Christians were still thinking of the increase of Christ's kingdom in terms of a mere census, a mere count of individuals rescued out of an evil world. But our generation has come to see that the redemptive mission of the Christ is nothing less than that of transforming the social order itself into a brotherhood or family of God. We are not saved, each by himself, and then added to one another like marbles in a bag or like grains of sand in a sand pile. A saved society is not made by any such external process. We are members one of another in our sins, and we are members one of another in the whole process of being saved from sin. I cannot go alone either toward or away from the kingdom, for it is my relation to some one else, a relation of help or of hinderance, that determines the direction that my own character is taking. "In this the children of God are manifest, and the children of the devil: Whosoever doeth not righteousness is not of God, neither he that loveth not his brother. For this is the message that ye heard from the beginning, that we should love one another." For us of the present generation the duty of making Christian education sufficiently Christian will mean bringing it into line with this social message.

Love as an inclusive law for education has not been worked out in theory or tried in practice. This is an astonishing thing to say, but it is strictly true. We have endeavored to include love within education as one item among many, but we have not taken it as the higher and inclusive conception by which to determine our aims and by which to test our methods. We have been accustomed to start the educative process outside of the act of loving, say in some dogma or religious rite, expecting somehow to get inside love at some later time. We have not thought of method as systematized love producing its like, that is, as the divine social order, already started on earth, and here and now giving children a place and an incentive to grow within itself. We have not conceived religious education as itself a part of the campaign for the social righteousness that the law of love requires, or as an actual initiation into the social relations that belong to the citizens of the kingdom. Rather, we have assumed that the campaign for social righteousness is an affair of adults exclusively. We have even hesitated to bring it to church with us lest it should disturb reposeful contemplation of God. As if we could contemplate the Father without thinking about that upon which his heart is set, or as if he himself could have peace of mind only by taking a vacation from the rest of the family!

Here and there, in fragmentary ways, we have begun, it is true, to experiment with lessons that touch upon love in action. Social-service activities, moreover, have here and there become a regular part of the educative procedure. But as yet these are additions to presocial religious education, or palliatives of it, rather than an attempt to socialize the whole control. Thorough socialization will require a fresh approach to the curriculum as a whole. It will require us to re-examine the organization of religious education in order to see whether the social relations in which the child is here already placed do themselves train him in active love and in methods of co-operation. It will require us to scrutinize every detail of teaching method to see what sort of social relation it involves between teacher and taught, and between pupil and pupil.   Here, surely, is need for a theory of religious education.

The theory of public education is undergoing a transformation that is of the utmost significance for the churches. The old assumptions of public education, like those of religious education, were individualistic.   The day school was expected to put the pupil into possession of certain tools (as reading and writing), and to impart a certain minimum amount of useful knowledge (as geography), all of which was thought of as preparing him to live as an individual.   To-day we cannot think of the public schools as having any smaller task than that of preparing young citizens for living *together*.   Moreover, we are engaged, in both theory and practice, in bringing school training closer and closer to the every-day occupation of a citizen, his labor for a livelihood.

The growth of the social idea and of the industrial idea in public education is significant for the churches in several ways. In the first place, humanitarianism is getting a new organ, one that promises to become immensely efficient.   The state can hardly train its citizens in the art of living together without teaching, more or less, the brotherhood that is of the heart. Nor can this teaching go very far before it awakens thought upon the ancient injustices that persist in society.   Moreover, when the school, with this growing social outlook and inlook, is brought close to the industries, it is bound, sooner or later, to interpret to our whole people, either intentionally or otherwise, the meaning of "the food which perisheth," the significance of labor, of income, and of wealth.   All these are ancient interests of the Christian preacher, and they are present, vital concerns for Christian teaching, whether of adults or of children.

What shall the churches do, then, with respect to these new developments in the theory of public education?   How can we be unmoved by what is going on?   If we really believe in the axioms of Christian living, we cannot be indifferent.   Nay, we whose consciences are just now being pricked by the neglected social elements in our religion, if we have even a moderate amount of practical sense, must take our place as citizens beside those who have seen a social vision in public education. We must try to understand what the vision saith; we must support and encourage the reformers in their hard task, and we must gladly tax ourselves for public education as we have never taxed ourselves before.

But we shall not empty out of the church into the state school the whole function of social education. Rather, we shall define and realize more definitely than ever before the educational implications of the old faith that God himself is love. Gladly co-operating with every one who endeavors to put the love of one's neighbor into education, we shall go on to probe the educational significance of the two great commandments in the Christian faith. For us there must be a theory and a practice in which the love of God to us and our love to him are not separated from, but realized in, our efforts toward ideal society, the family or kingdom of God. Such a theory of Christian education we have not as yet.

Four components of educational theory. The divisions adopted by each writer upon this subject are likely to depend more or less upon his notion of convenience in exposition. But the following components will be found in one or another form in any broad analysis:

(1) An indication of the *kind of society* that is regarded as desirable.

(2) A conception of the *original nature* of children.

(3) A conception of the *sorts of individual experience* that will most surely and economically produce in such children the kind of sociality that is desired.

(4) A statement of at least the more general *standards and tests* by which one may judge the degree to which these sorts of experience are being provided by any educational institution or process.

All four of these parts of a complete theory will be found in the following pages, though not in this precise order. In a general way, Chapters II to V, inclusive, concern the first point; Chapters X to XIII, the second; Chapters VI to IX and

Chapter XIV, the third, and the remainder of the book the fourth. But I have made no effort to schematize my treatment. Rather, I have endeavored to be concrete, even though thereby problems crowd together somewhat, and even though the same problem appears more than once.

PART I

THE SOCIAL STANDPOINT IN MODERN EDUCATION

CHAPTER II

GENERAL EXPOSITION OF THE SOCIAL STANDPOINT

Various uses of the term education. Education, in the broadest sense of the term, takes place wherever a plastic mind acquires a set of any kind. It is often said, for example, that a child receives much of his education from contact with nature—from falls and bruises, obstacles and achievements, and the beauty of natural scenery.

In a less broad sense, education lies in the contribution made by society to the set of a mind. Again and again has it been pointed out that only through association with his elders can a child attain to civilized life at all. The total difference that such association makes in the organization and outlook of his mind may be regarded as the education that he receives. The ways in which society forms an individual are, however, in large measure unsystematic and even unintended. The "social inheritance" of an American child, for example, includes the influence upon him of all such things as sights and sounds upon the street; newspapers; public amusements; political contests; business and social customs; waves of public opinion; home conditions—indeed, the influence of every man and of every "man way" that he meets.

As far as these things—any of them—are controlled *for the purpose* of giving a set to young minds, we have education in the third and strictly technical sense.

It is with education thus technically understood that the present book is primarily concerned. Often, indeed, we shall find ourselves analyzing the unintended influence of men and women upon children, but always for the sake, ultimately, of more clearly defining our deliberate purposes. Deliberate

13

educational purpose underlies many undertakings besides schools. A family is an educational institution. The same can be said of certain phases of the public library, the art museum, and the natural history collection of to-day. For they arrange their possessions and advertise them in part with the young in mind, and they even provide trained instructors. The children's room, the children's adviser, and the story hour in the modern library are educationally eloquent. The playground movement likewise is educational in the strict sense, for it accepts the axiom that facilities for play should be so organized that the players will form socially valuable habits.

The position of the churches in this constellation will have our attention after a time. But even this partial and merely representative list of the educational institutions of modern society would be defectively representative if it did not mention juvenile courts and new types of law concerning children and youth. When a child violates a law or an ordinance, an enlightened legal system no longer merely inflicts pain and deprivation upon him because of his past, but considers how to form him into a good citizen. To this end, physical, mental, and social diagnosis is employed to discover the causes of the delinquency, and then the offender is *sentenced to be educated* by the most skilful methods that science can devise! This blending of the conception of justice with that of education is extending itself to various parts of law. The abolition of child labor, and the restriction of labor in the adolescent years, have an avowedly educational motive, as have ordinances that regulate the relations of children to the streets and to public amusements. We are, in fact, moving toward the notion that society, wherever it is in contact with children and youth, should be a consciously educational force—in short, that the young should be constantly at school merely by virtue of their presence in our civilization.

Society is not merely one educator among many; it is the prime educator within all educational enterprises. If teachers, parents, librarians, story-tellers, playground directors, judges in juvenile courts, and legislators who press for child-labor laws will but reflect upon their educational enterprise, they will perceive that it is not their own. They act as agents for society. This means not only that they labor toward social ends, but also that the power that does the work is one or another social influence operating through them. This is obvious in the case of all who are employed by state or church, but it is true of the others also. A parent teaching his child a grammatical form, or manners at table, or a standard of moral conduct, is himself at the moment under the control of his group in respect both to what he teaches and to the fact that he teaches anything at all. Moreover, the effectiveness of his teaching depends in large measure upon the existence of a social environment that backs it up. In a profound sense, then, the educator in all education is society. This proposition is not invalidated by the incompleteness of our social integration —our divisions into parties, social classes, and churches— with the resulting ambiguity of the term "society." For in each of these groupings the educational worker is moved by his group consciousness, and he endeavors to give effect to the things that bind him to his fellows, be the fellowship narrow or broad.

"Unfolding the powers of the child" is an inadequate conception of the work of education. Since society is the educator, we may ask next, What is society about when it educates? It is dealing, of course, with unfolding powers or growth. But every child has many powers, better and worse. It is the essence of education to discriminate between them, and while promoting the growth of some, to prevent the growth of others. The same distinction has to be made when we meet the statement that the aim is to help children toward "self-realization," for behind this statement lies the unexpressed assumption that there are different sorts of self that an individual may become, and that education must give the advantage to some of these as against others.

What education does is, in a word, to bring the child and society together. It increases one's participation in the com-

mon life. It puts a child into possession of the tools of social
intercourse, such as language and numbers; opens his eyes to
treasures of literature, art, and science that society has gradually accumulated through generations; causes him to appreciate such social organizations as the state, and develops habits
appropriate thereto; prepares him to be a producer in some
socially valuable field of labor, and evokes an inner control
whereby he may judge and guide himself in the interest of
social well being.

Education aims at "social adjustment and social efficiency." This phrase represents the strong reaction of recent years against all formal conceptions of education, that is,
conceptions that involve no notion of guiding the young in the
social *application* of the powers that education brings out. To
define the aim of education as the unfolding of children's
powers is like saying that the purpose of a railroad is to cause
cars to move from one place to another. What the cars carry
and whither they are going are the important considerations.
The strains that have developed within our industrial and civic
life since the coming of machine manufacture, steam transportation, and the massing of the populace in cities have compelled
us to see that the attitudes and the outlook of children with
respect to their fellow men are the prime concern of schools.
At the same time, poverty on the one hand, and the increasing specialization of occupations and of industrial and commercial processes on the other, have convinced educationists—that
is, those who investigate education and promote educational
standards—that every child ought to receive assistance in the
selection of his occupation, and also specific preparation for
skilful work in it. The more democratically minded among
us are coming to think of the future in terms of industrial democracy, an organization of producers governed by producers.
Hence it comes to pass that progressive schoolmen are largely
occupied at the present moment with problems of occupational
training and vocational guidance.

Scarcely more than twenty-five years ago educationists were
still disavowing industrial ends, which they distinguished from

those of "general" culture. Manual training was in some of the schools for the sake of formal mental discipline and the teaching of numbers, but avowedly not as an introduction to fundamental processes in manual industries. I remember a time when college heads turned up their noses at "bread-and-butter education." If the blindness of some efforts at the "practical" partly justified this scorn, it in turn was blind in that it saw not the social-ethical significance of earning one's living by daily toil in one's trade or profession.

To-day we think of education as a way of getting the human energy of each new generation effectively applied to the maintenance and the increase of human welfare of whatever sort. Keeping children well, and teaching them how to keep themselves and their community well; showing them how to manage a home, with its need for many sorts of skill; introducing them to the civic, industrial, and philanthropic institutions of their community; acquainting them with the machinery of government and with the duties of citizens; opening the way to skill in an occupation, and revealing the riches of play as well as of literature and the fine arts—all this, which the schools of yesterday left largely to chance, is being incorporated into an education that deserves to be called "new."

The reason for mentioning these things in a discussion of religious education will appear fully in later chapters. Already, however, it must be evident that the relations of the church to the child as well as to the adult are going to have their setting in a new world. Religious education is bound to be judged from fresh standpoints. "Imparting" certain "subjects of instruction" is becoming thin and threadbare as a conception of teaching. "Inciting" to "virtue" in general will seem flat to children who are accustomed in their daily schooling to the enrichment of concrete social experience and to participation in important specific social enterprises. Moreover, when the schools become an agency for applying human energy, instead of providing a merely general or unapplied culture, they move in the realm of life purposes in which religion has a vital interest. In particular, education that aims to pro-

duce devotion to the social weal touches at its very heart the
religion that has set out to change society into a brotherhood.

**Education aims also at the progressive reconstruction of
society.** Adjustment of a child to society just as it is does not
satisfy the educational conscience, or even the conscience of
society in general. Our social conservatives themselves would
condemn an educational system that sought to preserve our
social organization unchanged. No; education selects some
parts for preservation, while it condemns other parts, and
toward still others is silent lest children should find out how
bad we are. What a confession society makes in every school
that it supports! It says, in substance: "Here are a few things
of permanent worth that we have already achieved; here, in
addition, are our many unfulfilled aspirations, our unsolved
problems. Try to be wiser and better than we have been."
Thus, education is not only society's supreme act of self-
preservation; it is also society's most sincere judgment upon
its own defects, and its supreme effort at self-improvement.

These statements do indeed outrun most of our educational
practice. Our dealings with the young, especially our institutional dealings, have no immunity from the inertia of tradition
or from the anæsthesia of self-interest; and our thinking, as
was indicated at the beginning of Chapter I, grows within
practice, not in a different world. Actual education is a mixture of points of view. Nevertheless, the idealization of life,
which implicitly if not explicitly condemns our actual life, is of
the essence of educational practice. At the present moment,
far more than yesterday, this idealizing takes on the social hue
of almost all intense ethical reflection in our day. If, then, I
have myself idealized the social aim of education, I have merely
used with respect to education its own method of viewing life.

The basal process in education is social interaction. To
bring society and the individual child together is the aim.
This means that what we have to teach the child is humane and
just living in the various relationships, and also active, well
directed labor that contributes to the common life of the present and likewise to the improvement of it. It might seem

superfluous, but the history of schools proves that it is not, to point out that, in the last analysis, social experience is the only thing that can thus socialize any one. The first concern of education is not a text-book or anything that printer's ink can convey, but the persons with whom the pupil is in contact, and the sort of social interactions in which he has a part. On the face of the matter, how could any one become adjusted to society in the absence of society, or become socially efficient without social practice?

Some applications of this principle appear as soon as we begin to reflect upon it, but others are less obvious and more at variance with tradition. In respect to the more obvious personal relations between pupil and teacher, and between pupil and pupil, the principle is already in operation in progressive schools. Thus:

(1) *The conduct and the personality of the teacher are generally recognized as of prime importance.* It must be admitted, nevertheless, that present methods for training teachers do not luminously suggest any theory as to how the desired personal qualities can be developed. Moreover, neither the economic status of teachers, nor methods of appointment and dismissal, nor provisions for growth and for social practice after entering the service, can be quite reconciled, as they stand to-day, with the universal emphasis upon personality.

(2) *In the organization and management of a school, and of each schoolroom, every enlightened teacher sees an opportunity to train children in co-operation and self-government.* The term "self-government" should not be restricted to experiments in which pupils have been organized in imitation of the State, with its legislative, judicial, and executive officers. Self-government is more than social⁻ mechanism of any pattern. It is first of all socialization of the teacher's attitude toward pupils, that is, recognition of the present value of the pupil's personality. From this recognition will flow encouragement to free action, to free reflection, and to specific methods for the organization of freedom, with its inevitable social pleasures and pains. It is not the elaborateness of these methods that

counts, nor yet the absence of influence from the teacher. There can be, and in some experiments in pupil-government there appears to have been, an artificial sociality—artificial because created merely *ad hoc* and isolated from the larger society. What is needed is the development of freedom, initiative, and co-operation within the existing relations not only between pupil and pupil, but also between pupils on the one hand and their teachers, the local community, and the State, on the other. Self-government in this sense is the sure touchstone of school discipline.

(3) *In the modern school, the play of pupils, which is made up almost altogether of social interactions, comes under supervision.* The least reason for supervision is the prevention of abuses; the primary function is the promotion of social and socializing play. Hence, the supervisor of the playground teaches the children games adapted to their respective social capacities, and assists in the management of contests, all with a view to the discipline of social joys through the enrichment of them.

(4) *Studying and reciting also are a field for social experience.* Instead of trying to isolate each pupil with his book, and then instead of stimulating each one in the recitation to selfish emulation, or to purely self-regarding avoidance of discomfort, the teacher treats the subject-matter as a social possession, and as a sphere for a co-operative enterprise in learning, so that each pupil "contributes to the recitation."

(5) *The school of to-day introduces the pupil to community life, and gives him real functions in it.* Around elections, holidays, civic anniversaries and festivals, much instruction in the ideals and the ways of society is made to centre. Historical incidents are dramatized, and community pageants are produced. The pupils are made acquainted at first hand with the machinery of the local government. They meet the policeman face to face, and learn from his lips how they can co-operate with him in the maintenance of laws and ordinances. Children are organized to keep streets and alleys clean, and to combat disease. A few hours before these words were written, there passed under my window a squad of children ("squad" is the name that they

used for the group) all equipped with paraphernalia for removing cocoons of the tussock moth from the shade-trees of a city. It is significant of the educational organization of this campaign that the squad was under the command of an elder pupil.

(6) It now becomes evident that *if the basal process in education is social interaction, the ancient isolation of school experience from other experience must be overcome all along the line.* This, I take it, is the fundamental idea of a new type of boarding-school that has appeared in the German and Swiss *Landerzieh-ungsheim,* and in the Bedales School in England. Children, both boys and girls, ranging in age from the primary to the mid-high-school grades, are placed in a country home under conditions that reproduce as far as may be the life of a family that supports itself upon the land. Here, in connection with the traditional "studies," the pupils sow and reap, manage domestic animals, construct and repair buildings, and make apparatus for their games and plays, all in the continuous society of their teachers. These groups are necessarily small, but the same principle appears in the large public schools of Gary, where pupils repair the furniture, keep the accounts, and even pay the teachers.

The same principle is determinative of the subject-matter, the order, and the use of the curriculum. The procedures that have just been described have general approval because they provide for social training through social experience. But they are almost altogether outside the pupil's experience of the contents of the curriculum as something to be learned. Can the curriculum, too, be brought under the head of social experience, or must it, in the nature of things, remain, as it is in most schools, a thing that contrasts with practice, a preliminary to social experience rather than a part of it? The answer has been given by Professor Dewey. Organized and stated in my own way, it is this:

(1) *The claim of any sort of knowledge or of skill to a place in the curriculum must meet the test of social fruitfulness.* It must be something that enriches the common life. The content of instruction is to be drawn primarily from the area of social

experience in the strict sense, that is, experience that· men
have of one another, and specifically from experiences that
society has an interest in reproducing and developing. Subject-matter that is not thus directly social, as parts of mathe-
matics and of the physical sciences, is to be treated as social
in the sense of being a common interest of society.

(2) *The "knowledges" and "skills" thus selected are to be
taught in an order that is determined by the pupil's own growing
social needs and functions.* In his relations within the family,
the play group, the school, the city, a child has from the beginning problems of social adjustment, social efficiency, and
social reconstruction of his own. Grading the subject-matter
of instruction consists primarily in introducing him, in each of
these social situations, to the material that he can use and
enjoy. This genetic-social order cuts across and to some
extent supplants the old logical classification or linear arrangement of studies (reading, arithmetic, history, etc.). What has
to be mastered at each turn is a function or enterprise—a term
that applies equally to learning a trade, learning the duties of
a voter, and mastering the processes involved in playing at
storekeeping or with dolls. In the strict sense, the curriculum
is a succession of these enterprises, not a succession of "subjects
of instruction." These subjects will now come along in order
and amount as they are needed, and they will draw their vitality
as instruments of education from the fact that need for them
has arisen.

(3) *Each piece of subject-matter is to be approached through a
motive that is, in this very act, in process of social growth.* The
ideal is that no pupil should ever have a purely individualistic
attitude toward any item or toward the labor that is required
to master it. To develop self-centred individuality first, as
traditional methods tend to do, with the intention of subsequently transferring its strength to social enterprises, is a double
blunder. On the one hand, it tends to defeat its ultimate social
purpose by forming individualistic habits that are hard to break;
on the other hand, it makes no provision, or inadequate provision, for the *growth* of social purpose, but assumes that it can

spring into being fully formed. The social approach to subject-matter that is only indirectly social may be conveniently illustrated by one of the present approved methods of teaching certain numerical processes. Instead of merely drilling the pupil upon printed tables and imaginary problems, the play of storekeeping is introduced, with its demand for measuring and weighing, making change, and keeping accounts.

(4) *All this means that the old separation between living and preparing to live is to be done away with even in studies.* The separation is to disappear from the mind of both the pupil and the society that educates him. Just as play, which is so large a part of real life from the pupil's point of view, is being incorporated also into the adult's interests, so, on the other hand, the occupations of adults, and their civic ideals and enterprises, instead of being withheld from the pupil until he shall in some mysterious way pass from education into life, now become material of education, a sphere in which the child and his seniors live an unbroken community life. In short, in their entire life in the public schools, pupils are to be thought of as simply fulfilling their functions as members of the State.

An important corollary, or more properly part, of this movement to identify education with life, is the transformation that is taking place in our notions of what constitutes a school. We are beginning to see that a school is not a thing to be graduated from and left behind. Within a mile or two of the desk at which I write these words there are school buildings and grounds at which the people provide for themselves the following facilities for their common life: Evening classes in woodworking and cookery; classes in citizenship for immigrants, and a reception to new citizens upon their naturalization; free baths for young and old; match games of baseball for the young men; dancing-classes and dancing-parties under wholesome supervision; a forum for political discussion; art exhibitions; entertainments of various kinds, as on the evening of election day, when the returns are received by a special wire.

A brief formulation of this theory of school organization, methods, and curriculum is as follows: Social character and efficiency are to be achieved through social experience; social experience is to be had primarily through the performance of social functions, but it may be extended through imagination in the use of well-selected and well-graded subject-matter that represents the social experience of the race; school experience is most effective educationally when the pupil experiences the least break between it and the life of the larger society.

CHAPTER III

THE PHILOSOPHICAL SETTING OF THE NEW SOCIAL IDEALS IN EDUCATION

The general relation of education to philosophy. The tendencies to which the last chapter called attention may be summed up as the social idea in education. Because of its depth or comprehensiveness, this idea may be called philosophical, and as far as it controls educational practice we may say that education is applied social philosophy. We do not stumble any longer at the notion that life and philosophy may be one. To the old saying that "Philosophy bakes no bread," the reply is, What but philosophy can bake bread? Wheat does not make itself into loaves; fire and oven are breadless without the baker, and he is a baker because of the ideas that guide his hands. These ideas, because they concern the ends and means of living, represent, as far as they go, a philosophical interest. To philosophize is to open one's eyes and gaze all around the horizon so as to see whence and whither one's steps are tending. Neither by its subject-matter, nor by its methods of analysis, nor by any aloofness of aim is philosophical thinking set off from any other. It is distinguished as philosophical by its comprehensiveness, thoroughness, and persistence.

A glance at the setting of the movement for socializing education will show that we are dealing with no split-off part of thought or of social life, but with the whole moving social mass, and with its growing awareness of the meaning of its own movement.

The educational ideals that this generation inherited. If the question "What is the ideal of modern education?" had been asked thirty years ago, the most probable answer would have been somewhat as follows: "The mark of moder-

25

nity is recognition of education as falling within mental growth, which proceeds from within outward by unfolding, not by accretion. This implies that the freedom of the child is respected, and that the great function of teaching is to assist him to adequate free self-expression." If one had asked to see a distinctly modern school, a kindergarten would have been pointed out, and the progressiveness of other schools would have been measured chiefly by their responsiveness to the great message of the movement that bore the name of Froebel.

In the ideal of freely unfolding individuality two closely related influences are discernible, that of philosophical idealism and that of the movement for popular government. On the philosophical side the greatest single impulse came from Kant. In his *Kritik der reinen Vernunft* (1781) he maintained that mind does not come upon its world as something ready made, but builds it forth out of mere raw materials of the senses. We have a coherent world at all, it was said, only because we impose upon these materials certain forms and categories that are of the nature of our mind. Otherwise stated, the structure of our mind is the organizing principle of any world that we could possibly know. In a sense, then, the meaning of all experience is preformed in us. Kant's great idealist successors, Fichte, Schelling, and Hegel, labored to show, each in his own way, what this meaning is and how we become aware of it.

The educational corollary of this idealistic movement is that we should not impose ready-made ideas or rules upon the child mind, but rather provide conditions favorable for spontaneous mental growth whereby what the child already implicitly is will become explicit both as world-outlook and as ethical self-guidance. Thus it was, in part, that teacher-wisdom took on forms like these: Adjust your procedure to the child mind, not the child mind to some preconceived method (hence the necessity of child study and of child psychology); to teach is not to impart ideas, but to develop the ideas that the pupil already has; no impression without expression; we are not to mould the child, but to provide material for him to mould; we learn by doing; utilize, do not repress, the child's curiosity, his imagination, and his impulses to play and to construction; the end of the whole is not information or skill, but a free personality at home in its world; the ideal teacher is not a taskmaster, much less a mechanic, but a friend, a revealer, a protecting divinity.

We cannot stop to inquire what specific part Pestalozzi, Froebel, and Herbart had respectively in making such educational ideas convincing, or in devising methods for applying them. Nor is there space to show how far these ideas ever prevailed in the schools. But the essentially religious presuppositions that are here involved should be noted. Mind has the primacy in the universe; experience has meaning that we can discover, and even be a part of; duty is the voice of God. Hence, if teaching becomes a prophetic office, none the less the child himself becomes a "prophet of the soul." To the reverence for their elders that had been demanded of children, the nineteenth century added reverence of adults for childhood itself. Every birth was a fresh incarnation of the ultimate meaning that pervades things. To invade the personality of a child was more heinous than to rob a householder of his goods.

The second great factor in this educational ideal is the aspiration for political freedom that came to partial expression in the French Revolution and in the early stages of the American experiment in popular government. Consider the extraordinary value attributed to the individual by the Declaration of Independence: Freedom is the natural right, the inalienable inheritance of every man; all just government derives its powers from the consent of the governed. These conceptions belong in the same thought-sphere as idealism, and they reinforce its educational corollaries. Into the phases of this reinforcement, from Rousseau's demand for education that shall protect the child from social conventions to Horace Mann's labor in behalf of schools for all the people controlled by all the people, we are not permitted, in this discussion, to enter. What characterizes the whole is insistence upon opportunity for the individual, and emancipation for him. As far as the schools were interested in good citizenship, it meant, predominantly, individual competency, particularly intellectual competency, for the use of the ballot.

Why religious education has been slow to assimilate the educational doctrines of the nineteenth century. At the beginning of the present century we behold in religious circles an awakening of educational consciousness that takes the form, to a large extent, of self-criticism for the formalism of religious teaching, and for its failure to appreciate growth and free self-expression. Here was educational twilight after a whole century of essentially religious ideals in educational thinking. The explanation lies partly in the slowness of schools and colleges generally to respond to the newer ideals. The practical problems with which the present generation of educationists had to start were still those of a curriculum imposed upon growing minds rather than expressive of their growth, and of formalism in method rather than free self-expression. But the main reason for the backwardness of religious education lies elsewhere, namely, in the control of ecclesiastical machinery by belief that the meaning of life was fully and authoritatively revealed in ancient times, so that the central function of religious teaching is to pass on a completed, unchanging deposit of faith. It is true that in the latter half of the nineteenth century some attention was given to methods in the Sunday school. Efforts to train teachers were by no means altogether lacking. It is true, also, that in large ecclesiastical areas the conscious aim of the Sunday schools was religious life, not merely orthodox belief. Yet religious living was prescribed, imposed, added to the child; under the ruling assumptions, spiritual life could not be treated as a free forthliving on his part. In Protestantism, then, as well as in Catholicism, our century inherited a hiatus between appreciation of free individuality and the content and the methods of religious teaching.

How the ideals of the scientific movement modify the notion of education. Regulated observation and experiment; the resultant discovery of laws; new control of natural forces as an end result—these are the marks of the scientific movement.

Its progress during the nineteenth century constitutes perhaps the most momentous, as it certainly does the most rapid, change that has ever taken place in the method and the content of thought. The already accomplished increase in man's control of nature is astonishing; the possibilities that it suggests are fascinating. But the scientific movement has bearings upon the relations of man to man that are solemnizing, in some cases terrifying, as when we contemplate the present industrial conflict and the clash of nations.

The most obvious educational effects of the movement are the introduction of various sciences into the curriculum, and increase in the number and the thoroughness of technical courses and of technical schools that have as their aim fitness for an occupation. A cultivated individual, valued for what he is in and of himself, is less and less the standard of educational success. The purpose is shifting toward increase of human efficiency.

The notion of efficiency or scientific control is modifying our approach to educational processes as well as our ideals of culture. Psychology, having become an experimental science, is bringing back into educational theory the concept of definite control of pupil by teacher—not control in the old school-masterish sense of command and compulsion, yet something different from the "protecting divinity" attitude, which assumes that the proper control for the child is already implicitly within him, and in need of nothing but adequate encouragement to self-expression. What psychology offers to-day is such insight into details of the teaching process as teachers never before possessed or dreamed of as possible. Just as agriculture is moving from control by the traditional wisdom of generations of farmers to "scientific farming," with its analysis of soils, its tests of seeds, and its plant pathology, so the generalized, largely incalculable, and partly intractable "human nature" of school traditions is being replaced by measured relations of antecedence and sequence.

We are beginning to control certain factors of inheritance also. The upspringing of eugenics brings within sight a time when congenitally defective individuals, who produce the least educable of children, will be estopped from reproduction, and the better-endowed strains will deliberately control the choice of mates, the number of offspring, the conditions of birth, and the care of children, all in the interest of an improved human stock. Thus education and eugenics, working together, will place in somebody's hands unprecedented power over our social destinies. A humanly guided development of racial quality, and a humanly guided application of human energy in the mass—foresight of these things must be included in any comprehensive philosophy of education.[1]

Scientific education requires a political philosophy. Scientific control of nature, which is now an end in education, is not separable from scientific control of men and of society. It is true that when we arrange the parts of the universe in the order of their significance or value, as when we rank them under the category of means and end, we contrast man with nature. But when we think of the world as an orderly process, as when we ask under what conditions this or that change occurs, we include man within nature and its laws just as we include the winds and the clouds. Consequently, the sciences of man, revealing the specific conditions of specific human acts, become a means for controlling men, and scientific education puts this control into the hands of specific members of society. Mental hygiene and therapeutics, the psychology of advertising and of salesmanship, analysis of vocational aptitudes, the movement for "scientific management," and various parts of sociology—all are recent advances in this direction.

We are confronted, then, even as educationists, with the question: In what part of society is control to be lodged? And to what ends shall control be guided? By educational procedures we can make an aristocratic or a democratic attitude

[1] Control that approximates this already exists in Germany. Reproduction is consciously guided, as respects the size of families, by a national ideal, and the same ideal permeates education from top to bottom. Back of the amazing efficiency that the German nation has displayed in the present war is something more than military training and scientific organization of material resources; there is also a mobilization of feeling and thought that was made possible by previous regimentation of the mind by educational processes.

toward one's fellows habitual. We can produce submissiveness or self-assertion. We can fix the assumptions of our pupils' social thinking. The paramount question, therefore, is this: What social likes and dislikes—that is, habits of feeling with respect to the regulation of human life by human beings—shall we cultivate? For what kinds of authority shall we secure respect? We should flatter our day and generation unduly if we assumed that educational philosophy has kept pace with the multiplying needs for reconstruction of our social controls. Yet, all in all, the political philosophy that has the greatest influence with American educationists looks forward to democratic rather than aristocratic control of the resources of both nature and man. That is, the trend is toward industrial democracy.

The educational significance of the doctrine of evolution. The evolutionary view of nature, man included, has not only provided fresh matter of instruction, it has also placed the whole educational enterprise in a new perspective.

(1) *A genetic view of the human mind has been achieved.* When Kant lectured upon the categories of the understanding, or upon the pure practical reason, he referred to mind as he thought he found it in himself, an adult human being. Such was to him "the" human mind. He felt no necessity for asking how it had acquired the traits that he attributed to it. The moral imperative—to take the point in his thinking that is of greatest social importance—could be understood, he thought, by mere introspection, without reference to the moral growth of the child, or to the moral development of the race. But present thought is convinced that exactly the contrary is the truth. We cannot understand the fact of a moral imperative without examining the genesis and growth of the sense of duty. Mental faculties, or better, processes, of whatever kind have a history that connects the adult mind with the child, and the human mind with animal minds of all grades. Therefore mental beginnings and growth processes in both the human and the subhuman realm become significant determiners of economical educative processes.

(2) *The instincts acquire a fundamental place in educational psychology.* The older treatments of the learning or the teaching process were occupied with perception, ideation, and reasoning; to-day we include as fundamental a mass of unlearned tendencies to action, and also the constant influence of pleasures and pains. A teacher must now be ready to answer the following question concerning each part of his dealing with children: Upon what habits already formed, and upon what original or instinctive tendencies do you rely for securing the reaction that you desire the pupil to make? This question applies in the same sense to the learning of arithmetic and the learning of courtesy and upright conduct.

(3) *The doctrine of evolution,* which contemplates the individual in his relations to a species, *leads us to think of education in terms of racial processes and of racial betterment.* Individualistic notions tend to be crowded out of our minds even by our attempts to follow nature. For the inclusion of education within the notion of natural history looks both forward and backward—backward from the human toward the brute, forward from the brute toward the human, and from the human that is toward that which may be. The idea of progress, it is true, has no place in the definition of evolution as a mode of change. Yet the actual history of life cannot be contemplated in its entirety without seeing that progress does occur under natural law. Each stage of this history has for us a forelook that gives it poetic coloring. Says Emerson:

> "And the poor worm shall plot and plan
> What it will do when it is man."

Thus in its own way evolutionism reinforces idealism. If from the natural-history point of view children belong to nature, from the same point of view nature belongs to them. In their education nature takes possession of herself and reaches consciously toward goals that are only dimly foreshadowed in prehuman species. Whether or not acquired characters can be inherited, Davidson is right in regarding education as conscious evolution.[1] For, in the first place, eugenic control of the stock through education concerning reproduction and racial interests is already in sight, and in the second place, education organizes and directs the actual use of the instincts, which are so large a part of our mental inheritance.[2]

The influence of industrial conditions upon educational philosophy. Machine manufacture, the factory system, great cities, steam and electric transportation, electric communication, the massing of capital, and mass movements of laborers— these, joined with popular suffrage, have produced not only our characteristic social strains, but also a type of social thinking that is comprehensive enough to be called philosophical. Those who say that our problem is to determine the place of the human factor in industry do not go deep enough. We are really working at the problem of the place of industries in human life. Here the question that underlies all others is this: Shall there be a permanent servile class?

The outlook with respect to social stratification has immediate and far-reaching educational bearings. The so-called laboring classes have cherished the public schools largely as a means of lifting their children above the necessity of manual labor, or if possible out of the class of employees into that of employers. On the other hand, industrial training in the schools, with its correlate of vocational guidance, constitutes in effect the actual predetermination of masses of children to manual pursuits and the rank of employee. Labor leaders have been apprehensive lest capital should secure control of industrial training, and make it not only a means of supplying skilled labor, but also of strengthening capitalistic control of the terms and conditions of labor.

That the wage-workers carry an undue proportion of the social burdens has become clear. The wage system itself is competition in getting the most out of men for the least return. Those who receive the least wage are the ones who bear the heaviest burden of unemployment, industrial accidents and dis-

---

[1] Thomas Davidson, *History of Education* (New York, 1901).
[2] I shall deal more at large with this point in Chapter X.

eases, and the support of children and of the aged; and this condition coexists with unprecedented fortunes amassed by applying the labor of these very men to the freely given resources of the earth. This situation is producing a demand that the entire maintenance of the laborer and his family in health and disease throughout life be included in the cost of production, so that it shall be paid for by those who consume the product. But the sense of justice, having gone thus far, does not stop. Once take the point of view of a life in its wholeness, especially a life in which father, mother, and child count as one, a life therefore that entails itself upon the future without known limit—once take this point of view, and you will go on to ask why the human factor in industries should not be the controlling factor; why the conditions under which human energy whether of hand or of brain is expended should not be determined by those most immediately concerned; whether all the producers should not determine the distribution of all the product of their joint expenditure; further, in view of the inextricable intermeshing of the industries with commerce, finance, and politics, whether the whole economic mechanism must not be taken over by organized society as an instrument of the common life.

When we commit ourselves to a genuine popular franchise and to humanitarianism, we commit ourselves against social stratification. Education, under such presuppositions, is bound to undermine whatever makes for the permanence of a servile class on the one hand, and a leisure class on the other. However long the road that leads to industrial democracy, popular education has entered upon it and cannot turn back.

Educational bearings of the pragmatic movement in philosophy. I shall assume that the reader has some familiarity with the fresh philosophical doctrines called pragmatism. It is a river into which four streams that are of immediate interest to us have poured themselves. *First*, psychology, moving away from intellectualism toward voluntarism, away from mind as contemplation of a world to mind assisting in the struggle for existence, provoked the question: Why, then, look for the constitution of reality in intellectual structure? Why not look for it in the direction of will and action? *Second*, theology, largely because of the results of historical study, found a shift of position necessary. The shift was partly toward mysticism, but far more toward an ethical grounding for faith. To this the Ritschlian movement, which gave the first position to value judgments, had already made a large contribution before pragmatism as an inclusive philosophy appeared. *Third*, the scientific movement, emphasizing active experimentation as the supreme method of discovery, and leading on to the notion of indefinite extension of the control of nature in the interest of human welfare, secures a completely generalized expression in the pragmatic doctrine that the very notion of truth is to be assimilated to that of active experimentation and its results. *Fourth*, the fascination that an age of machinery experiences in its unprecedented enterprises and in its immense efficiency crystallizes into the thought that life as a whole is enterprise within a universe that contains nothing eternally finished and final, but rather invites us to be part creators of its flowing destiny.

Metaphysical idealism had bequeathed to educational philosophy the notion of a predetermined human nature moving toward an eternally predetermined goal, which is the same for all individuals. Pragmatism reverses all this as far as possible. It undertakes to carry out the notion of cosmic becoming, plasticity, potentiality. The glory of human life, it teaches, lies not in the faithful repetition of any prescribed program, but in fresh impulses that have the vigor to test themselves in action.

Some specific educational tendencies of this mode of thought may be formulated as follows: (1) Dissolution of the traditional generalized ideal of the cultivated man. Each man is now defined by his purposes and what comes of them. (2) Consequently a drastic criticism of traditional curricula and methods of teaching on the ground that they are removed from the world's work, that they lack definiteness of purpose, and that they are unable to develop the spirit of enterprise or to test the results of it when it is present. (3) Demand for definite standards and tests of school efficiency. Measurements in education are stimulated—measurements of the ingo at every point in terms of space, time, dollars, and persons, and of the outcome in terms of health, amount and accuracy of work done, rate of improvement, extension of interests, and persons equipped for specific functions in society. This insistence that we shall know how costly and how efficient each factor is tends to displace the notion that faithful teaching is patient persistence in prescribed methods. (4) The unification of the school with the enterprises of the community, among which making one's living is frankly included. In a farming population the old break between the school and the farm will be done away with by bringing agriculture into the school. A shoe-manufacturing community will be recognizable as such from its schools. This principle has many applications, some of which, especially those that involve conflict between social ideals, are far from being easy.

The pragmatic movement takes as reality that which works, or has positive results, satisfactory or otherwise. It invites us to measure the world and men in these terms, and to steer our further enterprises accordingly. But in view of the multiplicity of satisfactions, the various levels of desire from instinct upward, and the conflicts between undertakings that are equally natural, some principle of discrimination is necessary. It does not appear that we guide ourselves altogether by the satisfactions that we have found achievable in the greatest amount and with the greatest certainty. Some enterprises that achieve just what they go after, and are therefore successful from their own point of view, are nevertheless regarded as in reality dismal failures. What pragmatism might conceivably do with this "in reality" I shall not stop to inquire. The query is raised merely for the sake of indicating the chief difficulty in the pragmatic control of education, namely, how to avoid a shallow pragmatism of immediate ends. Pragmatists are in general convinced that social enterprises and social satisfactions have validity that individualistic ones do not. Thus far pragmatism reinforces the social philosophy that we have seen forming itself within the theory of education. Moreover, the forward look of pragmatism, its expectation of the unprecedented, its readiness to press onward into the unknown, relate it closely to religious faith and to the practical influence of idealism itself.

These various lines of thought converge toward social **idealism as a philosophy** of life. The metaphysical idealism that underlay the educational aspirations of the last century offered an inspiring view of human nature. Enfolded in the personality, or coming to consciousness in human experience, was infinite reason, absolute moral law, the ultimate good. Men shared in the very life of God. From such convictions there could but grow concern for common welfare, as when, under the stimulus of Thomas Hill Green's teaching, Arnold Toynbee started the social-settlement movement.

What happens to this reverential regard for man when empirical science proclaims that there is continuity between him and the brute; when philosophy denies the existence of finished and eternal principles in his mental structure; when man as he is, not as he ought to be, has the franchise; when teeth and stomach take seats at council tables where heretofore intellect and conscience only had conferred together in solemn dignity; and when education takes into its hands the grimy tools of industry? What has already happened is an unprecedented convergence of conviction that experience finds meaning, and aspiration finds scope, in social welfare and social progress. This is not the place for raising the question whether this conviction can be reached from so diverse starting-points by rigorously logical processes. For our purpose it is enough to note that attention, in so many types of reflection, does as a matter of fact focus upon man as of supreme significance, and upon social good as the one adequate sphere of man's endeavor. Social idealism is the philosophy of life that prevails among reflective persons, and it constitutes the corner-stone of progressive educational theory.

CHAPTER IV

THE PLACE OF THE INDIVIDUAL IN A SOCIALIZED EDUCATION

Ambiguity of the terms "social" and "individual."
Shall we assume, even in our use of terms, that life can become "individual" without reference to society, or that "society" implies of itself nothing as to individuality? Are the two merely antithetical, or may they be complementary phases of the same experience? The term social is sometimes applied to mass action simply as such. In this sense of the term, social action might be the blindest sort of conduct, and it might have no regard for other human masses, or even for the individuals who constitute the acting mass. On the other hand, the term individual is sometimes used in a way that suggests, if it does not assume, that individuality can be construed without reference to any human interrelatedness. Yet action might conceivably be most highly individualized precisely where it is most highly social, and because it is so. Individual welfare might be individual just because it is shared. For separatistic self-regard we already have a special term, "individualistic," but we have no corresponding term for mass action that disregards either individuals or other masses.[1]

The crowd versus the deliberative group. When we speak of the movement to socialize education we should understand, not increase of mass action merely as such, but increase of effective regard for one another—regard of individual for individual, reciprocal regard of the individual for his group and of his group for him, and regard of one group for another.

[1] "Nationalism," however, is coming to mean something of the sort.

Now, social living in this sense involves as a basic function in education the disengaging of the individual from the mass, both in the consciousness of the teacher and in that of the pupil. *Social education as such individualizes men.*

It is sometimes assumed that if we only induce children to act together in groups we shall thereby socialize them. To forget oneself, and gladly to expend one's energy upon something that brings no private profit has, in the statement of it, an ethical sound. And the sound is not altogether misleading. When a small child is allured beyond the solitary plays of infancy into even the planless romping of an unorganized group of children he unquestionably makes a social gain. It comes by the way of simple mental contagion or imitation. But soon his play, if it is to continue to be educational, will require some planning, and especially "rules of the game" and keeping the score, all of which must develop in the players a sharper and sharper realization of one another as individuals. Again, adults as well as children find it wholesome to relax now and then by "letting themselves go" for a while with some crowd that is bent upon innocent enjoyment. But the complementary truth is that in the background even of "letting go" there can and should be some "choosing of our crowd," and some trained tastes with respect to what constitutes fun.

Within mass action we must therefore discriminate two main types, that of the crowd and that of the deliberative group. A crowd is made up of persons who in the process of forgetting self forget others also. What so heedless of individual welfare as a mass that is consolidated by forgetting or failing to take notice? What so incapable of appreciating other groups, and therefore so ready for partisanship? We observe this not only in primitive society, but also close at home, as in the senseless, lawless, sometimes cruel conduct of student crowds and school-boy gangs. It is a trite remark of social psychology that without any compunctions of conscience the members of a crowd often conduct themselves as nothing would induce them to do when they act singly.

In a deliberative group, on the other hand, mass action—

so far is it from the crowd type—stimulates rather than suppresses reflectiveness and regard for others.   In fact, we have
here mass action that arises and maintains itself precisely by
promoting individuality.   This is seen most distinctly, perhaps,
in groups that have formal rules of order.   Here, preliminary to
each common act, the entire mass "pauses, the chairman saying: 'Are there any remarks?'   Then, as if challenging each
individual to full self-expression, he asks: 'Are you ready for
the motion?'   This procedure has been devised so as to prevent action under suggestion.   Individual inhibitions are not
avoided or suppressed, but invited, spread out for inspection,
often acted upon separately by dividing the question or by
voting upon proposed amendments."[1]   The same social principle appears in many groups of a less formal character.   Thus,
a kindergartner offers to retell the story that is best liked,
whereupon one child says: "I like this one best," and another
child: "I like that one."   "How many like this one best?"
says the kindergartner, "And how many that one?   Why do
you think it the best?" and then she acts according to the
deliberate preference of the majority.   Similarly a recitation
can often take the form of a mass opinion of the deliberative
sort on what "we should do next."   In this way classes are
led, in actual practice, to assign their own lessons and to agree
upon one another's proper grade.
   Let it be noted, now, that children of school age act in crowds
without any assistance or training from their elders, but
that without such assistance the deliberative type of sociality
lags.   The needs of the situation are not met by merely guiding
crowd action toward worthy ends—the group's *mode* of action
must be transformed into co-operative deliberation.   There is
no security for worthy ends short of the habit of considering
others' points of view.   Without such consideration party
government becomes tyrannical.   Therefore, education for
society must consist in no small measure in replacing crowd
action, and susceptibility to crowd influences, by deliberative

[1] I have discussed these distinctions more at length in chap. VIII of *The
Psychology of Religion* (Chicago, 1916).

groupings and by habitual readiness for reflective co-operation.

Motive, as well as knowledge and skill, must become a conscious possession of the pupil. A socialized education will have four immediate aims: (1) That the pupil shall acquire control of the tools and methods of social intercourse, such as language, number, and various social forms and conventions. (2) That he shall be favorably introduced to society through happy acquaintance with the sciences, literature, and the arts, and through participation in the present social life. (3) That he shall be trained for an occupation. (4) That the motives of his conduct, that is, his own individually appreciated and chosen ends, shall be intelligently socialized.

All four of these aims are included in the educational aspirations of the day, but the putting of aspiration into articulated theory and practice has not proceeded equally in the four directions. The problem of scales of values, of inmost loyalties, of life purposes—of this germinating centre of every growing character—this is the educational problem that teachers are taught least about, and it is the one with respect to which their plans and methods are least definite and consistent. Along with constant proclamation of the ethical or social purpose of the schools there goes disagreement, as well as much haziness, as to the particular ends and processes of moral education. In practice there are corresponding hesitation, delay, fragmentariness, and opposition of methods. Some phases of the problem of "direct or indirect" methods in moral education must be postponed to a later chapter. But we cannot complete our present sketch of the social conception of education without a preliminary statement upon the point.

The social aim in education includes the purpose to produce individual self-guidance toward the social good. Now, such self-guidance implies both knowledge of social causes and effects, and preference for certain effects as against others. Preference for social good implies resistance to natural, instinctive selfishness. How, then, can we train children to open-eyed social conduct unless we train them in social motives or preferences; and how can there be discrimination of social ends unless one thinks about one's own relation to the social whole and recognizes one's own tendencies to selfishness? Self-conquest is an inevitable phase of social education.

This point of view implies, of course, that the ethically good has some reference to the consequences of conduct. Ethical theories that deny this, holding that duty and the good will are something in themselves regardless of satisfactions of any sort, or that the goodness of an act is measurable by some quality of the impulse whence it springs—a quality that can be defined without any reference to the foreseen results of the act—are largely responsible for the confusion that prevails in educational thinking and practice with respect to moral growth. Though these types of ethical philosophy are generally giving way before others that define the good, and duty, and the good will in terms of social satisfactions and social progress, the educational significance of the change has not fully dawned upon the schools. We may sum up the matter by saying that the pupil must be led to form conscious life purposes, not by comparing himself with some abstract ideal of duty or of perfection, but by considering the consequences of conduct, especially in the welfare or illfare of others.

The educational use of rules and of authority. What has just been said gives us a clew to the proper and the improper use of rules and of authority in the school. At least four theories of the matter exist in various mixtures: (1) Rules are necessary because a school cannot do its work without them. True; but how did the teacher become competent to prescribe rules, and how shall these children in their turn be worthy to control the system of education? Parental authority, it is often said, should be so exercised as to make itself unnecessary in the life of the child as early as possible. Does not the same principle apply to schools? (2) We know what is good for children better than they can know; therefore we prescribe for them. No doubt we do know better; but wouldn't it be worth while to bring them up so that they will ultimately know even better than we do what is good for children? If so, what about simply imposing our present ideas? (3) Human experience has settled some things, and to these the children simply must conform. Let us have no ifs or ands here, especially a child's. Yes, we have learned some things by experience. But does it seem likely that a child can learn them by the utterly different sort of experience that the mere enforcement of rules brings him? How are you to make him see and know that the foundations of existing social customs and institutions are sound? And if he does not see, but instead is confronted with what seems to him to be mere power, what is likely to happen? (4) Some things are eternally right, and they simply must be. But is the eternally right actually realized in anything short of the free loyalty of the heart? Moreover, who determines what is eternally right? Do you maintain that capacity for apprehending it has disappeared from the earth never to return? Do you hold that this capacity belongs to one class or set of individuals exclusively?

Unless we intend to have a permanent cleft in society between those who command and those who obey, we must, it is now evident, so employ rules and authority that they shall be continuously passing into something else as the child grows. The primary function of some rules, as those that concern firearms and explosives, may be simply protection of life. But the educational use of any rule lies essentially in furnishing the conditions that are most favorable for deliberative group action. What is required in one case may be postponement of action until reflection can set in, or until other individuals can be heard from. In other cases rules and authority may so dispose satisfactions and dissatisfactions that difficult social conduct is made easier and unsocial conduct less easy. This is not an approval of either anarchy or the sugar-coating of duty so as to conceal its real nature. What is here insisted upon is that pupils shall be able as individuals to find present social meaning and value in their contacts with society in the person of the teacher. Whatever confronts the child at first as a sheer necessity (the occasions for which are far less frequent than we ordinarily suppose) must, even as he faces it, melt into stimulus to the use of his own judgment in ways that are social and pleasurable.[1]

A social interpretation of the sacredness of personality. Something fine, and in its way social, is represented in the phrase, "the sacredness of personality." It means at least this, that we are to place some checks upon our conduct simply because other persons are affected by it. But the "sacred" or "set apart" may be more or less closely related to taboo. Does an exalted view of the rights of persons imply that there is in each individual something that belongs to him in such an exclusive sense that it ought to be kept to himself, forever unshared? Shall we not hold, rather, that personality is sacred precisely because in free individuality, and in it alone, can society fully realize itself? Personality is sacred, not from society, but to society. Therefore nothing over which the individual has control is to remain unshared. There is to be no purely private affair.[2] Society, if it is wise, will, indeed, encourage individual initiative, and also the reticence that keeps the common good in the foreground, and not-yet-socialized impulse in the background. Moreover, intimacies that only a few can share, as in the family, will be encouraged, but only as far as their own happy realization makes also for the wider social good. The right of private property will be understood, not as a natural right with which one's fellows must not interfere, but as an instrument of society for the nourishment and education of its members, particularly in families.

The educational applications of this conception of personality are direct and vital. First, it tends to take officialism

---

[1] On the playground of a certain elementary school the penalty for foul playing and for lying is a week's exclusion from the plays. But the whole management of the playground is such that even this drastic rule expresses the social consciousness of the players. Result: Remarkable objectivity of judgment concerning both one's own play and that of others, gentlemanly acceptance of one another's word, correct scoring, and relative absence of disputes. I have witnessed true sportsmanship, and unclouded happiness in it, among boys of eight and nine years who were thus privileged.

[2] The evils of self-involution have been made strikingly evident by various branches of the psychotherapeutic movement. Merely to open one's whole mind to another, whether physician or priest, often brings relief, inner emancipation, and fresh social capacities.

out of the pupil-teacher relation, as it does also out of parental government. Only a part of the teacher's business can be put into a schedule of specific tasks to be performed, such as subjects to be taught with this or that degree of efficiency. No interest of a pupil or phase of his life is foreign to the true teacher, for everything in every child—everything—is sacred to society. On the other hand, everything in the teacher also is sacred, and therefore to be shared in due season. The teacher and the man are not two. The teacher-pupil relation is that of reciprocal self-realization by the sharing of experience. Happy the teachers—there are many of them—who through their occupation have obtained not only a living but also life!

Education, being an agency of justice, looks beyond social averages. In the juvenile court, as we saw, justice to the offending child takes the form of education. Why should this be considered exceptional? Is not education as a whole the bringing home to each child of what is his due in view of the upbinding of his life with that of his fellows? Therefore the exceptional child, whether a backward pupil or an unusually gifted one, is entitled to exceptional teaching. In the end this will mean, of course, adaptation to every individual, and therefore important modifications of class teaching. We shall thus discover that talent exists in certain "classes" of the population in greater measure, and in other "classes" in smaller measure, than has been supposed. Education will discover favorable variations, and bring them to social fruitage. Enormous social waste exists at present because individual talent goes undiscovered through childhood, and then is smothered by too early entrance into the industries. And there is ground for more than a suspicion that the students who attend our institutions of higher education, where the expenditure per pupil is highest, are not being selected for this post out of the whole people by rigorous demonstration either of superior talent or of superior social spirit in the use of talents.[1]

---

[1] Emancipation of the schools from the fallacy of social averages would help to rid us of it in other directions. What is the social significance of such statements as that the average wealth of the United States is so or so much per person? Or that the average wage in a given industry or industrial estab-

Shall the individual exist for the state? The concept of national efficiency, which the present war has brought to our attention with unprecedented force, is a challenge to educational 'theory and practice in every land that boasts the freedom of its citizens. Can efficiency of the mass be achieved by education that disengages the individual consciousness, and puts it into the attitude of mutual deliberation? Must not national policies be settled long before the people can arrive at a deliberate social judgment? Must not minorities be ignored and even repressed lest they draft off energy from the main purpose? Must not even majorities be circumvented at times because they are clumsy and not overwise? In short, does not national efficiency ultimately depend upon applying human energy approximately after the manner of a machine? Will not the advantage always be on the side of a mechanized group as against any group in which the members have ideas of their own and a will of their own with respect to the work that they do?

Thoughts like these, which are now in the air, put in jeopardy what is most vital to our educational progress. If national and international groupings are not to be of the deliberative type; if society is to consist, even for a part of the time, of masses of men regimented in body and mind, the result will be that in times of excitement, when deliberation is most necessary, the group will become a mere crowd with its impetuous and ruthless mode of action. This view of national efficiency implies, of course, corresponding regimentation within the industries. Signs are not lacking that this implication is at least partly understood by some of the "captains of industry." They

lishment is so or so much per piece, per hour, or per day? Or that the general level of wages has risen a certain amount in a given period? An industrial commission recently listened to an argument for seven-day labor in a certain steel-mill on the ground that the average time off is, or will be, as much as one day in seven anyway. Shall we base a minimum wage for men upon the average family, or for women upon the average cost of decent living for a woman upon whom no one is dependent? There is no room for doubt that we are concealing social truth from ourselves by thinking of mankind as made up of masses, classes, and averages. The average man, or pupil, or welfare, is a mental construct of statisticians. To govern education or the conditions of social welfare by mere averages is to render our dealings with actual men and actual pupils more or less fictitious and unjust.

should reflect that regimentation of labor means ultimately crowd action by laborers.

It is possible to cling to the semblance of freedom when the soul of it has departed. Not all submission is irksome. The members of any crowd feel emancipated when unreflective contagion is at its height; at the moment when a designing leader makes tools of them, they imagine that he leads by virtue of their free choice. This is the pseudofreedom of irresponsibility. It may easily seem preferable to the birth-pangs of real liberty. Let us not be blind to the possibility that, under the influence of some nation-wide emotion, our public schools, instead of going steadily forward toward democracy, which must be deliberative, may be made instruments for fastening upon the people one or another class control concealed under such specious concepts as efficiency, patriotism, and self-sacrifice.[1]

The cost of a socialized education. We have reached the conclusion that socialized education, precisely because it is social, must be individualized. The alternatives that have to be considered are not "social *vs.* individual," but "social *vs.* individualistic," and "society *vs.* a class within itself." In-

---

[1] Do we realize the import, as respects our liberties, of the recent merciless hazing of militiamen to compel them to enter the military service of the United States, the hazers and the hazed both being under military command at the time? In the free land to the north of us a newspaper was suspended by military order because of an editorial opinion that Canada had already furnished her proper quota of soldiers for the European war, and that enlistments should cease. In the same land a recruiting officer may accost a citizen upon the streets, and tease him any number of times, but if a citizen replies disrespectfully he subjects himself to legal penalties. It is a fair question whether war can be engaged in by any free people without sacrifice of liberty within its own borders. For, must not military control extend not only to industries and to consumption, but also to communication between men, which is a fundamental process in any popular government? Is it not of the essence of war to repress criticism of military acts and policies? Repression begins by egging on those who are willing to hurl disrespectful epithets at their fellow citizens. This of itself interferes with conditions that are necessary to the life of a deliberative group. But this informal censorship, which is of the crowd type, is crowned by a legalized censorship which, whatever its conscious purpose, has the effect of party government maintaining its policies and perpetuating its control by force. The inference to be drawn from this is that government by the people has a vital interest in discovering some way to end war forever. There will be no security for democracy until peace is assured. This truth has educational consequences the full consideration of which must be postponed to another chapter.

dividualistic education need not be costly, but individualized education must be. For, *first*, it will require educational diagnosis, and educational adaptation, with respect to each pupil, and therefore a larger budget; *second*, it will undertake the hardest of educational tasks, which is the production of self-sacrifice, and therefore will call for the highest training of teachers; *third*, it will make the new generation discontented with the social-economic order. Let us consider for a moment the third of these items, and in a subsequent paragraph return to the second.

To make children deliberately social implies in the first place that impulsive good-heartedness must be transformed into steady, reflective good-will. It implies, further, that mere rules of conduct toward others, as giving money or goods to the unfortunate, are to be supplemented by a habit of reflection upon the situation of others as individuals, that is, a habit of putting oneself in their place. This will lead straight to the question, Why should their situation be what it is? Why need there be poverty? Why is there so much sickness? Is there sufficient knowledge, and are there anywhere sufficient resources to remove in any large measure the causes of poverty and of disease? If so, why are not knowledge and resources applied to these primary human necessities? What is it that stands in the way of the widest distribution of human welfare?

When we teach the young to think socially they will not regard social classes and economic class conditions as naturally predetermined and static, but rather as a sphere for the deliberate justice that values human life supremely, and that values things and even rights only as they actually minister to life. Moreover, such teaching, with its tendency to produce deliberative group action, will lead the inheritors and the disinherited to sit together in calm judgment upon the justice of their respective situations, and upon the possibility of a more just, that is to say humane, distribution of opportunities for adequate living.

The result is bound to be discontent with the existing social order. It is futile to think that any effective teaching of democracy, or of the supreme value of human life, will leave un-challenged the present control which a few exercise over the conditions of life—mental and moral as well as bodily life—of the many. The outcome must be, not alone increased doing for others, but also surrender into their own hands of the means to do for themselves. Not less than this will be the cost of a really socialized education.

Consequences with respect to the theory of interest. The doctrine of interest in education, stated most generally, runs to the effect that the material of instruction must be chosen and graded, and methods of teaching devised, so that the activities of the pupil in the learning process will produce spontaneous pleasure, and therefore be performed from free internal impulsion rather than from external pressure emanating from the teacher. The pupil is not to be driven, but led; and he is not to be led by any and everything but by the inherent value of the material or of the enterprise from his own point of view. At first sight this may seem to imply "soft pedagogy," which follows the whims of the child, letting him do what he likes instead of seeing that he does what is good for him. This would be the consequence if children were shut up by nature to a single interest at each period of time. But as a matter of fact diversity and mobility of interest are prime characteristics of childhood. The educator always has several possible interests between which to choose, and therefore it is possible to feed one repeatedly while allowing another to atrophy from lack of exercise. This is not the same as following a child's whims, nor is it equivalent to indulging him in doing what is easy and avoiding what is hard. On the contrary, the theory of interest requires us to put before the pupil what is inherently so attractive that he will work hard with a feeling that the enterprise belongs to him as a part of himself. This individualizing of what one is doing as one's very own is essentially what we mean by interest.

In point of technic the first requirement for social education is socialization of the habitual interests of the pupil with respect to his school work. This implies, first of all, choosing material of instruction and arranging the conditions of school life so that instinctive social satisfactions shall be the basal ones. But this is not all. The pupil must be helped to advance beyond the unreflective level of instinct. He must be led up to the point of self-denial. He must be initiated into the great paradox of personality, which is, ability, after facing an easier and a harder alternative, to choose the harder as one's very own, and thus determine where one's satisfactions shall lie. The social way is not that of smug self-security through canny control of others, but of self-sacrifice for them. We shall never stabilize human relations by playing off one selfish interest against another, but only by freely sacrificing selfish interest, only by taking into one's individual will the very thing that opposes it.

Here is where the teacher's view of interest in education will meet its severest test. Shall the last appeal to the pupil be addressed to selfish interest, or to unselfish? Can the teacher reveal in his own conduct, and demonstrate to the pupils by their own guided experiments in living, that to live we must lose our individualistic life?

PART II

THE SOCIAL INTERPRETATION
OF CHRISTIANITY REQUIRES SOCIAL
RECONSTRUCTION IN RELIGIOUS
EDUCATION

CHAPTER V

THE AIMS OF CHRISTIAN EDUCATION

Traditions as to the aim of Christian education. The aim has been conceived in all of the following ways:

(1) That the purpose is to *instruct* the child in the things that a Christian ought to know. Back of this purpose lies an assumption that our religion consists primarily of a completed, authoritative revelation concerning God and duty that needs merely to be handed down from generation to generation.

(2) That the purpose is to prepare the child for full *membership in the church*. This definition rests upon such assumptions as that the church is the authoritative expositor and administrator of the fixed revelation just referred to, or that the will of God is to be done on earth by drawing men into a particular society of the saved.

(3) That the purpose is to *save the child's soul* here and hereafter. Behind this lie the dogmas of depravity, guilt, and redemption out of the world as distinguished from redemption of the world.

(4) That the purpose is *unfoldment* of religious capacities, or of a germinal divine life, already within the individual. Here we witness the influence of idealism, with its doctrine of the eternal within the temporal, the infinite in the finite, and with its maxims regarding free self-expression.

(5) That the purpose is the production of Christian *character*. This may mean any one of several different things according to the view that is taken of "Christian character." In the statement as it stands there is, for example, no discrimination between the notion of a merely individual goodness or merely individual relation to God, on the one hand, and the

53

contradictory view that genuine goodness can never be merely individual and that the Christian God permits no merely individual reconciliation with him.

Without denying that in each of these aims there is something that is worthy of permanence, we may assert that they do not, either singly or collectively, do justice to the social idealism that characterizes the most vigorous Christian thought of the day.

The ideal of a democracy of God as the determinant of ultimate ends. I use the term "democracy of God" in place of "kingdom of God," not because I desire to substitute a new social principle for that which Jesus taught, but because the idea of democracy is essential to full appreciation of his teaching. After making all needful allowances for the influence of contemporary political and religious conditions upon his modes of speech and the content of his thought—allowances that are to be determined by New Testament criticism—the fact remains that his desire for a brotherhood of men leads on with the inevitableness of fate to the ideal of a democratic organization of human society, and that his fusion of divine with human love presents us with a divine-human democracy as a final social ideal.

Without doubt this view of the Christian life has been hastened by our experiments in popular government, and by our experience of social strains connected with the new economic order. These modern factors have contributed to Christian thought partly by challenging social conditions and assumptions that had been accepted by Christian teaching as the very sphere in which the Christian life is to be lived. Instead of being a Christian within these limitations, we are asked why we should not remove the limitations. The virtue of feeding the hungry, for example, loses something of its impressiveness unless it is combined with determination to find and remove the causes of poverty. A re-examination of prophetism, the teachings of Jesus included, has made it clear that thinking upon ethical problems, and upon the will of God, in terms of social causes and effects belongs within Christian teaching; it is not merely a modern accretion or fashion. On the other hand, modern conditions have helped to reveal the mind of Christ by displaying more significant outlets for the ancient sentiment of brotherly love. When the business relations of most men were limited to a small circle of neighbors, good will seemed, naturally enough, to find its circumference in the misfortunes that fell under one's own eye. But the enlargement of our social horizon by the enormous increase of human intercourse, together with the realization that a man's ballot counts simply because he is a man, reflects itself in a vast enlargement of meaning in the command that we love our neighbors as ourselves.

Therefore such questions as the following are becoming a prime concern of Christian thought: If one human life outweighs a world, as Jesus taught, what should we do with a social order that stunts multitudes of human lives for the sake of money, and does it, not by disobedience to the laws of the state, but under the protection of laws and of courts? How can we really believe in human brotherhood if we are willing to acquiesce in a stratification of society into the servers and the served, the rulers and the ruled? Moreover, if brotherly love is, as our religion has always taught, the carrying out of the Father's loving will in human relations, how can the Father himself be willing to be an autocrat, an aristocrat, or a plutocrat? Must not Christians think of God as being within human society in the democratic manner of working, helping, sacrificing, persuading, co-operating, achieving? "My Father worketh even until now, and I work." Divine love, it appears, cannot realize itself anywhere but in a genuine industrial democracy.

Granted this social idealism as the interpretation of the life that now is, the aim of Christian education becomes this: *Growth of the young toward and into mature and efficient devotion to the democracy of God, and happy self-realization therein.*

The aim is growth because there is now no separation between human society and divine, and because the rudimentary conditions of human society are already provided for in our social instincts.

The aim is devotion to a cause, not the attainment of a status. Whoever thinks that Christian education has achieved its main end with any pupil when it has led him to cross a line that' separates the saved from the unsaved—whoever thinks this misses the meaning of love. Love is active, outgoing. The lover accepts no security that does not include his loved ones.

Moreover, because the aim is active devotion, Christian education does not consist primarily in the transference of a set of ideas from one generation to another, but rather in the cultivation of intelligent will. When our will is in accord with the loving purpose of God, we have the good heart, the life that is from above.

Though the goodness of such a will must be measured by its intent rather than by its power, the only test for the Christian education of the will lies in increase of the social efficiency of our pupils. There can be no successful Christian education that does not increase the amount of effective, not merely sentimental, brotherhood in the world.

Efficiency in achieving these ends must be measured by concrete evidence such as health, food, laws, ballot-boxes, homes, streets, schools, happy children, and happy husbands and wives. Patience or any other virtue on a pedestal is unconvincing.

In and through his growing participation in the creation of an ideal society the pupil will realize his fellowship with the Father. Not by release from toil or from the turmoil of social endeavor, not by any retirement within himself as an individual, will the growing child achieve a mature Christian experience, but only by doing God's social will even to the point of suffering with him.[1]

In this losing of his individualism the pupil will gain life. He will gain it, not in the ascetic sense of despising satisfactions,

---

[1] This does not deny all value to times of retirement. When they are not a method of evading or forgetting the issue, but of gathering up one's powers to meet it, they are as Christian as hours of active labor. Moreover, aesthetic contemplation of nature or of art is a fitting thing for a child of God whenever it does not separate itself from the purpose of putting all of God's children into possession of their proper aesthetic heritage.

not in the mystical sense of denying value to the individual, but in the social sense of individual satisfactions that are heightened because they are shared. Everything that is worth while, from health to good music, from play to scientific learning, from food to friendship, will be most worth while when the distribution of it is most wide. Here will be found Christian peace because feverish calculation of benefits to one's little self has ceased. Here will grow Christian joy in a fellowship of endeavor so profound that it can rejoice even in tribulation. Here hope lifts up its head unabashed by the vastness of time and the tragic frailty of life. This is the life of faith, which is the identification of one's very self with ideal good.

Social issues of the present as determiners of the end. When we ask a Sunday-school teacher what he is trying to accomplish with his class, the reply that we commonly receive is that he is endeavoring to make his pupils Christians. But if we examine the text-book that is in use, or listen to the conversation between teacher and pupil during the class session, or observe the general exercises of the school, how much consciousness do we find of the concrete situations wherein lie the issues of to-day between the love of the Father and the love of the world? In most cases we behold an effort to make pupils Christians in a general, unfocalized sense, which is almost certain to encourage a private, ineffective sort of goodness. The expression of this goodness in palliative benevolence may even beget self-deception as to the Christian quality of one's character. Softening the inhumane results of an unjust social order can partially, but not adequately, represent the Christian purpose. Let us teach pupils to respond heartily to the call of distress, but let us not lull them into spiritual slumber by representing charitableness as the luxury of the good.

We must reveal the terrible meaning of love. Suppose that parental love should suddenly acquire power to deal as it likes with everything that blasts or stunts the life of offspring; suppose that wives and husbands could deal as love would dictate with every human condition that tends to break up the happiness of families; suppose that a neighbor could do as a neigh-

bor would like to do with everything that injures one's neighbor; suppose that welfare workers could control the causes of
illfare; suppose that every business and business method, every
law, all civil and criminal administration were to be halted
until it could prove that it is an expression of human good
will; suppose that love in all these relations should suddenly
insist upon having its way—what wreckage of our social assumptions and standards should we witness! Religious education must bring to the light, discredit, undermine, attack, these
assumptions and standards. It must be clear in its own mind
that the vocation of the Christian is not to be as benevolent
as an unbenevolent occupation permits, but also to re-create
the social system that tends to restrict the sphere of good will
in his daily occupation. The social issues of the present, then,
must be taken as the call of God to our pupils, and as the sphere
of entire consecration to the will of God.

These issues may be conveniently classified under three heads:
(1) *Social welfare*, which has to do with the control of the
non-human environment in the interest of human life. Here
belong relief work of every kind; the fight against disease,
especially at the present moment against tuberculosis, syphilis,
and gonorrhea; the fight against the saloon; the struggle for
proper housing; for adequate wages; for good conditions of
labor; for short hours of labor; for provision against accidents,
illness, unemployment, and old age, and for facilities for culture and for recreation.

(2) *Social justice*, which has to do with each man as a factor
in the life of some other man. Justice to the child means the
abolition of child labor, provision for the best education, provision for play, and protection from unwholesome influences.
Justice as respects family relations implies a life-and-death
fight against the disintegrating influences that are all too evident. Justice to the citizen requires that he be enfranchised
in fact and not merely in form, and that partisanship and civic
corruption, both of which circumvent and depress the franchise,
be overcome. Justice with respect to the criminal requires
that society shall requite his evil with good—the good of oppor-

tunity for a better life and help toward it—and that the making of criminals by social forces shall stop. Justice to each man as a man commands that we find ways to rebuild our industrial and economic system, which at present invites each man to grab what he can of the free gifts of nature, and then to grab what he can of the products of other men's toil. A brotherly economic order will be vastly different from regulated grabbing, mere selfishness made respectable by rules of moderation; it will be nothing less than love employing law' as a means for securing the maximum benefit of every person in the industrial commonwealth.

(3) *A world society,* or the regulation of the conduct of each social group with respect to other groups in such a way as to promote the integration of all mankind into a single, democratically governed brotherhood. What justice requires from each individual in his relations with his neighbor is required also from each nation in its relations with other nations. The idea of the sovereignty, that is to say the irresponsibility, of the state may possibly represent a stage in the social integration of men, and therefore not a fall from brotherhood but progress toward it. But the same is true of tribal morals. Like tribal society, nationalism is at best nothing more than a step in a stairway; to pause here as though we had reached finality is as unjust as to rest in prenational achievements. Patriotism must melt into a larger regard for men. Is it not monstrous to find twentieth-century Christians less cosmopolitan than the ancient non-Christian maxim: "Nothing human is foreign to me"? Religious education must take up as one of its specific tasks the production in its pupils of a world-consciousness controlled by a sense of justice.

Amelioration of the horrors of war, important as it is, is not enough. War does not merely happen to us, like earthquakes and tidal waves; it is rather a climactic expression of the selfishness, that is to say the injustice, that is organized in our legal systems and our national sovereignties. It is a part of the same economic grab that erects seizure of natural resources into a right to them, and then makes laborers into hirelings.

The inner reality of war, of armaments, of national sovereignty, and of national policies that seem to render armaments necessary must all be revealed to our pupils so that they shall enlist —heart, conscience, intelligence—in a lifelong, never-relaxing crusade against the legalized injustice that underlies them all, and for positive measures for organizing good will on a world-wide scale. Nothing less than this can be the will of God, who is love.

Are the social issues of the present the affair of adults **only, or of children also?** It seems to be taken for granted that if the specific social issues of the present are to be introduced into the Sunday-school curriculum at all, the proper place for them is in the adult class or at most in the later years of adolescence. Up to this point the instruction and training are directed to the formation of such good habits as obedience, truthfulness, and fair play; induction into such exercises as private prayer and public worship, and into such enterprises as missions; and a meagre introduction to social welfare in the form of relief of the poor, the sick, and other sufferers, and in some instances in the form of the fight against the saloon. Not a word is ordinarily said to children and young people with respect to the enormous extent of poverty and the reasons therefor, nor as to the reasons why preventable sickness is so prevalent, nor as to the interest of fundamental justice in such current events as labor disputes and international friction. There is, probably, a sincere belief that tender minds should be shielded from the luridness of the contrast between Fifth Avenue and First Avenue, and between the multimillionaire and his employees. These are felt to be the hard problems of maturity, not at all subject-matter for the instruction of children.

But let us not deceive ourselves. While we thus sleep the enemy sows tares. From infancy the pupil is in contact with the social order as it is; through this contact he is forming habits, and not only habits, but also the presuppositions of his thinking with respect to men and society. He meets the industrial system in many cases in the family "servant," and in all cases in the various purveyors of the goods that the family consumes. He forms very early in life his notions of buying, selling, bargaining, and employing. The current ideas as to what constitutes success he takes as his own just as a sponge soaks up water. The unrighteous standards all about him constantly whisper: "This is real life; this is what human nature is; this is what everybody does; grab your share!" He gets acquainted with newspapers and with newspaper morality long before the Sunday school even mentions problems of social righteousness. He is aware of the general run of current events, and he interprets them incautiously under the influence of whatever social standard happens to get his ear. If, then, education postpones mentioning these great issues until the near approach of maturity, it has to correct social presuppositions and purposes already formed. Shall we forever go on making the foolish assumption that the will of the child remains neutral for years and years with regard to the contest between justice and injustice? Shall we go on postponing in education what is not and cannot be postponed in the child's social experience?

Some consequences of not focussing the pupil's attention upon concrete social issues. Ethical reality is found in social relations, and nowhere else. Here and here only are the issues of conscience and of character. Hence it is that, when the ideals that religious education seeks to inculcate lack social insight and breadth, results like these follow:

(1) *The pupil is led to struggle* against *faults conceived as simply his own instead of* for *co-operative objects that will supersede his faults and help some one else at the same time.* Whenever we lead a child to think that he alone is blameworthy for his faults, we err as to the facts. A faulty will, as distinguished from mere inexperience, always involves a conjoint fault in which adults have some share. The child has taken on the selfish ways of adults, and then been blamed for doing so; or adults have indulged or neglected childish impulses that require training; or adults have misunderstood and mistrained him. The cure for these conjoint faults is not introversion of the

child mind, but enlargement of social outlook and purpose, particularly in co-operation with adults.

(2) *The pupil is led into unwholesome, sometimes paralyzing introspection* of the ups and downs of his inner life, or into fruitless reflection upon his status in the eyes of God. That is, religious education that ought to fix the pupil's attention upon the things that express the outgoing, self-forgetting character of the Father, does exactly the contrary. Consequently pupils form petty and distorted notions of the divine. God is taken to be a taskmaster, or spy, or aristocrat instead of a worker with whom all workers can have fellowship, and from whom all can get help.

(3) *The machinery of the church, and exercises that go on within church buildings acquire undue prominence* as compared with the influence that the church has upon the world that surrounds it. Ecclesiasticism, it is true, readily associates itself with remedial charity even to the point of noble self-sacrifice. But this is not the same as devotion to justice in the broadly human sense, which is also the broadly divine and democratic sense. On this broad basis churchmanship, and all ecclesiastical zeal and loyalty, have to be judged, like the love of one's country, by their tendency to pass or not to pass through all narrower societies into world society.

(4) *The pupil is led to separate his daily occupation, the sphere in which he makes a living or accumulates property, from his Christian vocation.* Instead of trying to Christianize his business, he endeavors to be a Christian in business. Consequently he imagines that he fulfils the law of love when he gives away, by his own arbitrary act, some part of a product that is due to the joint labor of many besides himself. If wealth be his, he is taught to think of himself as a divinely appointed steward, even though traces of God's love are not obvious in the process whereby the wealth was accumulated. The point of this is not that one should blame oneself or be blamed by others for doing business in the only ways that are possible at the present time. Accumulation of property does not necessarily imply accumulation of individual sinfulness, for the fault

is a conjoint one. In every business that is conducted under our present system of competition in profit taking, the owner has associated with him all the social forces that make and administer our laws, all those that create rigid business customs, yes, earlier generations that have bequeathed to us their own ideas and ways. What is to be expected of the Christian business man is that he will not only be generous as generosity is measured under our capitalistic presuppositions, but that he will also be just by doing everything within his power to curb and ultimately make impossible the exploitation of human life for the sake of profits. The real function of every business must be held to be, not the greatest possible concentration in the control of goods, which are conditions of welfare, but the greatest possible increase and the widest possible distribution of welfare itself. To hold business to this function is one of the fundamental phases of any real Christianization of the world. In the daylight of a purpose like this, what a shadowy thing is the private goodness upon which the attention of our pupils has been traditionally fixed!

CHAPTER VI

THE FIRST ESSENTIALS OF AN EDUCATIONAL PLAN

We have seen that the social idealism of Christianity prescribes for religious education as an ultimate goal the transformation of a social order that is largely unjust into one that shall be wholly just, and that, consequently, religious education must enter directly, not merely by distant implication, into the social struggles of the present. Let us now see how this large purpose can become a guiding principle for determining the main essentials of an educational plan. It is hardly necessary to argue again that to socialize the group we must individualize the pupils, that is, lead each one to adopt justice as his very own desire, purpose, and practice. This involves four aspects of religious growth, and provision therefor.

I. Provision for growth in knowledge of the Christian ideal, and of the means and methods whereby it is gradually securing control of social forces. The function of the curriculum maker is to select and systematize such knowledge; the function of the text-book maker is to prepare it in some detail with reference to the established principles of the learning process; the function of the teacher is to effect the assimilation of this material by particular pupils with their individual capacities and needs. The whole may be called instruction.

(1) *The aim of instruction is not to impose truth but to promote growth.* The whole teaching enterprise is to be brought under the notion of growth—of vital, not mechanical processes. Hence the term "instruction" must be emptied of its traditional implication of telling pupils what to believe. To impose our beliefs upon a child, even though the beliefs be

utterly true, is not to promote the growth of a free personality—
it may even be an invasion of personality; it may subject one
individual to another instead of emancipating each and every
one into full membership in a self-governing society, the democracy of God.

To argue that we already possess the truth, since it has been
revealed, and that therefore we ought to impose beliefs upon
children, betrays an interesting confusion. The elements
with which the argument deals are three: The truth, the pupil,
and the teacher who is supposed to bring these two together.
What, now, if the teacher is unable to eliminate *himself* from the
finished product? What if the teacher comes between the
pupil's mind and the truth, and stays there? This, in fact,
does happen when the attempt to impose beliefs is most successful. When pupils are tractable, what is the authority to which
they submit—what is it, that is, from their own point of view?
It is the Sunday-school teacher, the pastor, the text-book, or
tradition in the form of hearsay. Even if we train the pupil
to say sincerely that it is the Pope, the church, or the Bible to
which he submits, this say-so of his is our own handiwork;
we have interposed ourselves between the pupil and reality,
and we have no guarantee that the truth becomes his own
possession.

The whole notion of transferring ready-made thoughts to the
mind of another is psychologically fallacious. When a pupil
trustingly repeats our formulæ after us, and even when he
sincerely believes that he grasps and holds as his own the truth
that the formulæ represent, what really happens is that he is
moved by social forces to conform to the group that surrounds
him and to separate himself by pseudoknowledge from other
men. What we have here is neither knowledge nor belief in
any vital sense, but partisanship. This kind of instruction in
childhood produces not only in Catholicism but also in Protestantism an easily recognized adult type, the man who settles
historical and scientific questions without historical or scientific
study, and by the results judges whether his neighbors are sheep
or goats.

(2) *What is gradation of material?* The essence of instruction is promotion of genuine thinking. Consequently the content of instruction should change with the pupil's growing capacity for thought. Here is the foundation for gradation of material as an unescapable necessity of good teaching. The principle goes deeper than is realized even by many who insist upon it. From the history of religious instruction a ladder like the following might be constructed: First, a fixed and formulated body of doctrine or of ritualistic forms is drilled into the pupil's memory. Second, in order to secure some adaptation to the pupil, the language is simplified, or the formula is abbreviated. Third, still further to help the pupil to understand this material, stories, pictures, and analogies are introduced from outside. Fourth, when the fallacy of the attempt to transfer a whole system of doctrine to child minds becomes unbearably clear, the next move is to select from this system, or from the Scripture, or from ecclesiastical history, traditions, and usages, the parts that seem likely to have the greatest inherent interest for children of each grade, so that a part of the system may be transferred at one age, a part at another, and in due time the whole. Fifth, when the religious growth of the pupil as distinguished from the transfer of a system comes to be accepted as the proper aim of instruction, a curriculum is constructed by picking out from the same presupposed body of doctrine, history, sacred story, and church usages the parts best adapted to help pupils live religiously on their own level at the different periods of growth.

Many teachers have believed that here at last the principle of gradation is completely in control. But is not the ancient fallacy still here in the limitation of the sources when the material of instruction is drawn? When we have made clear to ourselves what sort of world the Father and we as his children desire, must not our next concern be that the young also should *desire* it? What boots it if they know all Scripture, all doctrine, all church history, and church usages, if they have not both the forward look and the sort of desire that can reconstruct a world? What the pupil needs to adjust himself to is not anything as it has been, but something as it ought to be. Let the curriculum be drawn from any sort of material— Scripture, history, church life and enterprise, the world of the pupil's present experience and of his imagination—anything that will most surely and rapidly make him share in the Father's desire and labor for society. At each point in the child's growing experience, the essential question is: What in all the world is most likely, if we turn his attention to it, to increase his active, intelligent devotion to the Christian purpose?

(3) *The sources of material for Christian instruction.* Two sorts of knowledge are central in Christian instruction, knowledge of what the Christian purpose is, and of means and methods for making it prevail. The Scriptures are to be used as a means to this end, not as an end in themselves, and we must not assume in advance that they contain everything that is needful for this vital sort of graded instruction. As a matter of fact, they do not. We might guess as much from the simple consideration that nearly all parts of the Bible were written with adults and their problems in mind. But the limitation goes deeper than this. Every biblical writing reflects, to a greater or less extent, the social presuppositions of its own age, presuppositions that have to be examined, criticised, and revised. Elements of our own social problems we do find there, indeed, and they are highly instructive, as the land problem, for example. But if we would master the fresh perplexities that have come with the advent of popular government and machine manufacture, and if we would press toward a democracy of God, we must turn the attention of pupils to many matters that are this side of the biblical horizon.

The notion that the Bible contains everything that is needed in Christian instruction is sometimes supported by the assertion that if we loved our neighbors as the Bible tells us to do, our whole social problem would be solved. This statement is either a paralytic truism or else it is false. If it means that love, intelligently exercised by all persons concerned, would find a way to cure the ills in question, it is a truism, and it is almost as ineffective as the insight that if we could keep all the cells of everybody's lungs functioning properly we could rid the world of pulmonary tuberculosis. On the other hand, if it means that our social ills arise altogether from the fact that men who have faced the issue of justice take the side of injustice, it is false. One of the fundamental reasons why we do not love one another more generally and more intelligently is that the conditions under which children grow up constitute a training in selfishness and in partisanship. We are prevented from seeing the real issues, and from getting sufficiently acquainted with our neighbors to know how capable they and we are of disinterested neighborliness.

What we need is not merely to be advised to love men more regardless of conditions, but also to see clearly that we are supporting social customs and even laws that actually reward selfishness with power and honor. We who would like to love our neighbors as ourselves are maintaining systems of social control that actually prevent us from doing it. What ails us is not merely that we have grown up in ignorance of the Scriptures, nor that our hearts are unresponsive to the call of Jesus. How many men and women who are well versed in the Scriptures, and whose loyalty to the Master is unquestioned, nevertheless do not see that Scriptural principles, and particularly the mind of the Master, are vitally concerned in the present struggle for social justice. A glowing inner life of good will and tenderness and aspiration, a life that feeds daily upon the manna of religious history, is of itself no guarantee of the kind of intelligence that is necessary for the reconstruction of the world. To produce such intelligence, Christian instruction must turn the attention of pupils directly upon economic, political, and any other social conditions that contradict the spirit of brotherhood, upon successful experiments in social living, and upon outreaching ideals and reforms.

This conception of Christian instruction refuses to separate knowledge and belief from the enterprise of living. It assumes that intelligence and active desire should be awakened as a single experience. Yet this is far from implying any narrow-gauge practicality or spiritual fussiness. A social conception of life has room, as perhaps no other has, for high valuation of art, nature, literature, philosophy, and historical forms of doctrine. The worth of them all grows from being shared, and because the generations are knit together. Everything that can be democratically enjoyed without consequences that are undemocratic belongs within the Christian conception of the life that is appropriate to sons of the Highest. "All things are yours."

II. Practice in using the tools of the Christian enterprise. Just as a child's social thinking is influenced from infancy by his contacts with society, so his actual practices with respect to others tend from the beginning to become fixed as a permanent mode of life. Because this practice is constant, there is no neutral period during which specific training in social enterprises must wait. Planned or unplanned training goes on anyhow; the hand is being shaped to some sort of social tools. Habits formed now go deep in respect both to what they include and to what they exclude. For it is by doing something in a given situation that particular elements of it come to our attention. Thus it is that we form habits of noticing or of not noticing the feelings and interests of others. A habit of not noticing is also a habit of not sympathizing. Many an amiable man is callous toward one or another class of his fellows, and impermeable to important humanitarian appeals, because in his plastic years he did not acquire the technic of seeing and feeling and acting in such matters.

Nothing in Christian education can be more fundamental, therefore, than participation of pupils with one another and with their elders in Christian enterprises, that is, enterprises that aim at social welfare, social justice, and a world society. Reserving for succeeding chapters various problems of method and of organization that are related to this training in the use of social tools, let us now guard against possible misconceptions of its place in a total view of educational ends. Caution is particularly necessary lest "tools" and "practice" be thought of as something apart from normal social living, as mere preparation for such living. On the contrary, the point is that children obtain the best social training by being a real part of the working force of the world. They mature their control of tools not by merely handling them or by brandishing them in the air, but by doing some part of the world's work. We as educators are not to place the child in any invented scheme of spiritual gymnastics—things done wholly for the sake of the future—but rather, recognizing the vast variety and scope of social need, we are to admit even little children to partnership with us in the enterprise of meeting it. This is the way for them to acquire not only the mechanics of social work, but also the intelligence and the trained and sympathetic perceptions of a mature Christian. What a practical absurdity it is that so many church members should make their first real acquaintance with philanthropies, social reforms, and missions, in mature life, and what wonder is it that intimate acquaintance under these conditions is so rare?

III. **Preparation for a particular place in society, first in the family, and second in an occupation.** The inclusion of domestic and vocational training within religious education is necessitated by the fact, already pointed out, that the love that is justice demands the whole of a man's social allegiance. To help, in his own sphere, to rebuild society is the life-work of every Christian. It is to be foreseen, studied, planned for in the true professional spirit, and with the same regard for technical proficiency that one looks for in a lawyer, a physician, or a mining engineer.

This is the spirit that should control marriage, family life, and the procreation and rearing of children. Domestic life is to be governed and tested, not by its contribution to the comfort of the individual members as such, but by its actualization of the democracy of God within itself, and then by its outgoing influence upon the wider society. Marriage is to be specifically prepared for as a calling of God, and the domestic habits of both husband and wife are to be lifted above mere conventionality, inclination, and happen-so into the sphere of defined social service and efficiency. The household labor of women, and the bearing and care of children, are to be treated as a professional, skilled occupation—a sphere for ambition, study, and social recognition. That women who devote themselves to these duties have at present so scanty recognition as producers, being regarded as dependents upon their husbands, or as being supported by the industry of another, is a partial indication of the reconstructive work that has to be done by education.

.It is no new thing to think of all legitimate occupations as so many spheres for the service of God. But one does not serve God in one's occupation any further than one serves human society. God does not require to be fed and clothed; the only thing that we can do for him that he cannot do for himself is to be brothers one to another. Every occupation is to be transformed into a specialized method of an effective brotherhood, and to this end a proper part of every occupation is to help in improving the social standards, including the laws, that apply to it. Our religion dissents profoundly from the world's generally accepted standards. If we were half awake to the radical character of this dissent, we should not accept the current assumption that vocational studies concern simply the methods of getting certain things done; instead, we should insist that analysis of the human relations involved in any occupation is the fundamental vocational study. Until such analysis is included in our systems of general and vocational education, the churches should themselves provide it for the children and young people who are committed to their care. In and through such analysis we can hope to develop a Christian vocational purpose, the purpose to use one's particular position in the social and economic complex as a fulcrum for moving this complex itself toward the level of brotherhood.

IV. **Growth in social motives.** Our discussion of knowledge, practice, and vocational preparation has already included the notion that all along the line of advance there should be a growing socialization of the inner life of desire. Growth in motives is now set down as a fourth phase of growth, not because it·is separate or separable from these three, but because it requires special attention. It requires attention in the first place because existing religious education does to a considerable extent assume a separation between motive on the one hand, and on the other hand knowledge and practical activities. What is the ordinary meaning of loving God, or of accepting Christ,· or of entire consecration? Are they not presented as if they could take place in a social vacuum, and as if the character of God, of Christ, and of oneself required no reference to concrete brotherhood? Is it not true that children and young people are being taught to "get right with God" first, and be social-minded afterward?

The result of such efforts to produce an inner life, or Christian motive, as something *per se* we behold in a multitude of church members who mean well but do not know what "well" means; who intend to be loyal to Christ but do not realize to what he is loyal; who sincerely desire the triumph of right but leave social technic to those who have individualistic interests to serve by it. We shall overcome these things, which are a reproach to us, only when, accepting in simple literalness our ancient doctrine that the supreme revelation of God is one with the supreme revelation of man, we teach the young that to know God we must be socially intelligent, that to make his will our own is a matter of social practice, and that entire consecration is a strictly vocational concept.

Another reason why motives require specific attention is that *growth* in motives is a relatively neglected notion. We must make clear both that change is normal and in what a normal change consists. Here again we are dealing with the forward, not the backward, look. What distinguishes a motive from a merely instinctive impulse is just looking ahead. A motive is anything in a contemplated, not yet actualized, situation that renders it attractive and thus stimulates us to make it actual. The good heart is nothing esoteric, nothing merely inner; it can always be defined objectively in terms of that upon which we are actually expending our energy and our resources. Growth in Christian motives means, therefore, changes in the pupil's outlook toward future social good. It means finer discrimination between relative values, and between ends and means, and corresponding change in fineness and breadth of appreciation, which is the beginning of fine and broad social conduct.[1]

This is the inner life that is to be cultivated; this is "growth in the grace and knowledge of our Lord and Saviour Jesus Christ." To this end is Christian self-discipline. To this end also is culture of the devotional life, whether in public worship or in private meditation and prayer. That we may be conformed to the social will of God, and enjoy being conformed to it—this is the purpose and meaning of devotional exercises of all sorts. This does not mean substituting human society for fellowship with God, but rather finding God where he himself is pleased to dwell. Where shall the child find the Father? Wherever the child's desire goes out after the things that the Father loves, that is, the persons who are the supreme objects of divine solicitude. There can be no purely private relation to God, for our very selfhood is conjunct. We are made selves by a give-and-take with others—and we are made in his image.

[1] This brief statement must suffice until we reach Chapter XIV.

CHAPTER VII

THE EDUCATIVE PROCESS IS RELIGIOUS EXPERIENCE

Why do some persons deny that religion can be taught? In some types of Protestantism the following remarkable anomaly is to be found: Insistence upon religious teaching for the young, but denial that religion can be taught. The argument for religious teaching runs to the effect that the impressionable, plastic years of childhood and youth are of crucial importance for adult character. The argument against the possibility of teaching religion bases itself upon the assertion that real religion, at least in the fully Christian sense, is an inner, intimately personal, and therefore incommunicable experience. The attempt to teach religion simmers down, according to this view, to teaching *about* religion.

That the two elements of this view have not been reconciled in practice will appear from the next section. How, indeed, can one produce an educational system when in the same breath one asserts and yet denies the efficacy of teaching? Let us ask, then, how any Christian thought could manœuvre itself into this corner. The answer is twofold:

(1) *Because they endeavor to hold at the same time to a vital or experiential view of the Christian life, and a dogmatic-intellectualistic view of the Christian revelation.* If the Christian revelation consists in certain dogmas, then the Christian life should consist in the intellectual act of learning and holding the dogmas. In this case Christian education would be identical with intellectualistic instruction. But if, on the contrary, the Christian revelation is "made flesh," if it is a concrete life that inspires and renews our life, then to be a Christian would be

something far more vital, and Christian education, instead of being instruction about dogmas, would be an initiation into actual living upon the plane of the Christian purpose.

But what will be one's view of Christian education if one holds at the same time to an intellectualistic view of revelation and an experiential view of the Christian life? What has actually happened in this case is this: Education has been viewed as essentially a means of transmitting dogmas; but, since even the devils can believe and still be devils (as we are often assured), it has been insistently claimed that religion cannot be taught. And indeed vital religion does not and cannot get into education through dogmatic-intellectualistic assumptions as to God's approach to man. The language that is attributed to God is not that which the child's heart speaks; the problems that are raised are those of the theologian, not of the child, and, besides, the whole is finished, fixed, rigid, while the child is all movement, all becoming.

Yet many who hold to a dogmatic view of revelation insist upon an experiential or vital view of the Christian life. They cannot be blind, of course, to the significance of childhood plasticity for such a life. But, having committed themselves to a dogmatic type of religious education, they deny that religion can be taught, and then they flounder in search of some method for religiously influencing children. All the inconsistency and all the floundering could be avoided by a wholehearted acceptance of the idea that God's revelation of himself is always in the form of flesh; that it is in Jesus, and in every human will that follows him. One could then look upon a child's gradual achieving of the full Christian purpose as itself a growing communion with God, a gradual self-impartation of God to his beloved child. The educational process would then fuse with Christian experience.

(2) A second reason for this educational anomaly is that *this type of thought, though it holds that religious living includes both relations to God and relations to men, does not fuse the two as Jesus did.* If we can hold that the love that is toward God and the love that is toward men are not two, but one, and that

this one is communion with the Father, then the social unfolding of a child can be luminous with divine meaning. There is then no antithesis between the socializing of the will and Christian experience. God speaks to the child, and the child to God in a language that both understand. But if we hold that one's primary relation to God is purely private, that it has to do with subjective mysteries, and that only through a preliminary grasp of these mysteries is one prepared for truly Christian social relations, then indeed religion cannot be taught.

Consequences of the doctrine that "religion is caught, not taught." The attempt to teach religion at the same time that the possibility of teaching it is denied leads quite naturally to dualism in practice.

(1) *Unsteadiness of aim prevails, and consequent failure to set up definite standards.* If we ask what the purpose of a Sunday school is, we are told that the purpose is to teach the Bible. But if we point out that those who avow this as their purpose do not teach the Bible with any thoroughness at all, the ground is shifted. We are now told that the purpose is to mould the character of the pupil by placing him directly under Christian influences for an hour and a half every Sunday. If we go on to ask why these influences have not been systematized, and why recognizable standards and tests of their efficiency have not been set up, we are reminded that religion is caught, not taught!

The virtue of this epigram is missed by some who are fond of using it. It is, or should be, a drive at intellectualism, or at the identification of instruction with education. When it is used to discredit system, and standards, and tests, in the Christward guidance of the child's social experience, it becomes an arrow shot at the goose that lays the golden eggs. It is true that many a teacher untrained in methods, and making many a blunder in methods, has nevertheless had a profoundly educative influence upon his pupils. Shall we not assume that his success is due to the fact that he really conformed, though without realizing it, to fundamental laws of religious growth? Surely the life of the spirit is a realm of order, not a chaos of forces. . Why, then, do we not analyze the ways of teachers who succeed, whether with or without training, to the end that we may systematize the principles of their success, and thus show others how to succeed? In other words, the laws that underlie effective religious education are identical with the laws of spiritual growth. Therefore a wabbly scheme of religious education justifies a query as to the views of religion that underlie it.

(2) *Interruptions of the educative process are tolerated, and even regarded as normal.* Any one who will take the trouble to analyze the experience of a pupil minute by minute through one session of an ordinary Sunday school can know for himself how constantly non-educative procedures mix with education. The opening exercises are a jumble of worship, business, and drill. If we ask why these exercises should be held at all, we may be told that the children should learn to worship. But if we examine the program and method, we find only a feeble grasp, or none at all, of the idea of education in and through worship. The aims of the worship are indefinite, and both content and method are unsystematized, unadapted, and untested. Besides, the setting of worship—the way it is elbowed by business, speechmaking (sometimes from visitors who can only guess what the situation demands), and crude disciplinary measures (banging of bells, calls for order, shouting above the din, scolding)—this setting is not strongly suggestive of a growing sense of the presence of God. And this sort of thing in the opening and the closing exercises occupies the major part of the meagre time at the disposal of the school. The lesson period, during which educative procedures are supposed to be entirely in control, is pared down to a minimum. Not only so; even this minimum is reduced through interruptions by secretaries, through encroachments of prolonged opening exercises, and through the demands of anniversaries and "special occasions."

Nor do interruptions of educational procedures end even here. Irruptions of child evangelism occur in various forms, from exhortations by preachers or teachers, through high-pressure "decision days" that are not integrated into the general educational work of .he school, to mass-meetings of children conducted by itinerant evangelists over whom the educational authorities of the school have no control. All this gives one an impression that "getting religion" is independent of religious education, and it leads one to wonder what, then, religious education is supposed to be and to do.

The roots of these incongruities are doubtless manifold. We must of course give religious education time to grow up, and we must not make its immaturity an occasion for belaboring the faithful men and women, mostly laymen without opportunity for technical training, who are giving the best that they have to the children. All honor to the workers in our Sunday schools! Here is massed together such an amount of Christian consecration, such an amount of unrequited labor for others, as was never before seen in the history of our religion. Our present question concerns the effective organization of this enormous energy. We need to know whether it is being scattered, or misdirected, or thwarted by inconsistency of plan and method. If so, we must know why. The conclusion that we have reached is that there is vast leakage of energy, enormous waste of consecrated labor, because so many persons, believing that "religion is caught, not taught," counteract their own efforts to teach religion.

(3) *A third consequence of the doctrine that "religion is caught, not taught" is unfairness to teachers.* If religion is to be spread among the young solely by a process of infection, it follows, of course, that the one thing needful is to bring the pupil within the area of a teacher's personal influence. That a profound educational conception lies hidden in the notion of spiritual life as communicated from person to person by fellowship will appear from our next section. But dim vision of a great truth may give it the effect of a half-truth, and half-truths have remarkable power to hurt as well as to heal. The current emphasis upon the teacher's personality is a case in point. How often do we hear that the success of a given teacher is due to a "natural gift for teaching," or to an attractive personality, or to intense consecration. If we should take this at its face

value, what ugly implications it would carry with respect to the rank and file of earnest teachers who do not have success of the shining sort that brings out such remarks. Because certain persons have stumbled upon methods that succeed, we praise their personalities; because the stumbling of others has not turned out quite as happily, we put them in an inferior class. Yet within this class we shall find, if we look for it, the capacity to succeed if only the requirements of the work in hand can be pointed out clearly. Here are Christian character, zeal, faithfulness, intelligence; what right have we to discount them? Granted the presence of these qualities, with no positively counteracting twist, we ought to be able to say: "We will show you how to succeed, and we will provide the remaining conditions of success."

(4) *A fourth consequence is inertia in the matter of teacher-training.* There are several reasons why the training of Sunday-school teachers has been so halting an affair. We shall have occasion after a time to analyze the complications that are involved. But, running through the whole, at least in certain quarters, is the silent, counteracting, anæsthetizing vapor of an educational scepticism that supposes itself to be religious faith. If such scepticism were not abroad, and deep seated, how could so many pastors give religious education only a secondary place, or worse, in their plans for pastoral administration, and how could they abandon teacher-training to the chance that somebody else will see its importance and do something about it? To correct this educational scepticism we must proclaim not only laws of psychology, but also laws of Christian life and experience. We must think of Christian living neither in terms of a dogmatic system nor in terms of an esoteric and incommunicable salvation, but in terms of objective social relations that produce and are produced by the individually realized attitude and purpose called love. From this point of view we shall be able to see that Christian education falls under the head of promoting a life of deliberate purpose, a life that fulfils itself by methods that it itself can objectively view, analyze, and systematically control. How readily the elements

of the educative process fall into place, and form a unified whole, under this conception we shall now see.

The. central fact of the educative process is a growing Christian experience in and through the pupil's social interactions. If we really believe that "where love is, God is," and if by love we understand, as Jesus did, not a mere sentiment or impulse, but a purpose, a policy for self-guidance, a thing that does not evaporate as soon as one turns deliberate attention to it, then we can have a religious education that moves entirely within religion. It will consist fundamentally in providing for children conditions in which love is experienced, practised, wrought into steady and deliberate living by the help of both intellectual analysis and habit formation, and developed into a faith that illumines the crises and the mysteries of life. To speak more in detail, such education will include the following part processes:

(1) *Making the pupil acquainted with persons who really love him and others also.* The first thing in Christian education is not an idea, but a personal fellowship. Here is the truth that is confusedly contained in the current emphasis upon the personality of the teacher. The confusion lies in the substitution of personal attachment between pupil and teacher for attachment of the pupil to society through the teacher. The importance of the acquaintance depends upon the degree to which the pupil realizes that the love that the teacher has for him is not a merely individual attachment, and that the joy of it is all the richer because others have a share in it. We merely express this in another way if we say that the first and fundamental element in the Christian educative process is the introduction of the pupil to the specific happiness of being a member of a society. Here lies the measureless potentiality of the family as an agency of Christian education. Here, as we shall see, is the base-line for a theory of the church as educator. In the detailed work of religious teaching, the principle is already beginning to appear in such practices as these: The teacher of a new class of beginners undertakes as her first task to make the little children happily acquainted both with her and with

one another; the principle of the organized Sunday-school class is moving downward from the adult and senior divisions through the whole school, effort being made to cause each class to feel itself as a little society, even though there be no formal constitution or by-laws; and effort is being made, by many enrichments of social joy, to obliterate the break between the social grouping on Sunday and that of week-days.

(2) As far as any pupil finds satisfaction or what seems to him to be real life in such sharing, he experiences what is fundamental in the divine purpose—he has, to this extent, a Christian experience. But Christian education undertakes to develop this experience from such rudimentary beginnings into the full and large purpose of the democracy of God. Therefore, the next part process may be stated as *causing the pupil's social attachments to expand from narrower to wider groups.* Family loyalties must be merged into humane interests of the widest scope. The social consciousness of a Sunday-school class must enlarge into a school consciousness, and this into a church consciousness; and the whole must flow outward toward the whole needy world.

(3) This outgoing purpose can be fulfilled only by *an expanding series of social activities.* One's social status, in the Christian sense of "social status," becomes a firmly accomplished fact only by repeated social acts that become social habits. Social character means nothing less than arriving at a point where social conduct occurs as a matter of course. Likewise, the exodus from a lesser to a greater group consciousness is effected not merely by fresh sympathies but also by fresh acts out of which habits can grow. Enlargement of social consciousness does not have to precede, but to be developed in and through, enlarging co-operation in serious social undertakings. It would be a happy circumstance if the term "curriculum" could be understood to mean not merely an orderly succession of ideas or knowledges appropriate to the pupil's expanding experience, but also an orderly succession of enterprises in and through which social appreciation, social habits, and social loyalties may grow into the full stature of the Christian's faith.

Religious education moved a step in this direction when occasional, unsystematized talks about missions, and appeals for missionary contributions, gave way to definite missionary, enterprises and specific contacts with particular missionaries and missionary fields by a school or by a class. The movement is now proceeding much further by including works of mercy and help within the regular program of each class. Here and there an older class has adopted a program of investigation and of labor for community betterment. These are signs of mighty import for the future of religious education. They are the rosy fingers of dawn opening the portals of day.

(4) *Within this practice in loving we find the basis for a most vital theory of Christian instruction.* For now, instead of attempting to transfer to the child mind certain truths that we hope will enter into his experience in a vital manner at some indefinite future time, we help him to define, understand, and improve something that he is already doing and enjoying. There is no longer the deadly separation of knowing from doing, or of Christian doctrine from Christian experience. The function of instruction now becomes this: To assist the child to analyze the situations, purposes, and activities with which he has to do, so that impulsive goodness shall grow into a deliberate good will; so that the sphere of the good will shall be better and better understood; so that co-operation in social causes shall be organized on a wider and wider scale and with ever-increasing efficiency, and so that all the resources of a cultivated spirit may be known and made available for all.

This is not a narrower or less intellectual conception of Christian instruction than the one that takes its starting-point from the dogmatic-intellectualistic notion of divine revelation. Stimulus for intellectual activity is here, and the interest to which appeal is made is as broad as the Christian ideal itself. Anything in history, literature, or doctrine that actually illuminates the path of active love, any kind of knowledge that can be turned into power for social living, anything that imagination or discursive reason can contribute to thoroughly socialized satisfactions—all this belongs within Christian instruction under the social presuppositions that we have adopted. We extrude intellectualism, but not intellect. A mere pitter-patter of imposed activities would not meet this standard any better than a pitter-patter of imposed dogmatic formulæ or of memorized fragments of Scripture. In short, the Christian law of active, world-wide love is the foundation of Christian instruction as well as of Christian conduct, the foundation not only for selecting material, but also for grading it, the foundation likewise of the pupil's interest in it.

(5) Finally, *this education in the art of brotherhood contains within itself the most vital of all possible methods of evoking faith in a fatherly God and in a human destiny that outreaches all the accidents of our frailty.* Let it be freely granted that less social methods of education can induce children, and men also, to confess without a shadow of insincerity a belief in God and in the life everlasting, and even that beliefs thus acquired may grow, and deepen, and enter creatively into conduct. To say that there is a still more vital way is not the same as saying that all ways except one are bad. Our practical concern, however, is not merely to produce sincere belief in God and immortality, but to make our pupils yearn for God and for the complete triumph of his social desire. In our capacity for loving, which is the same as our capacity to desire complete justice, lies the possibility of a faith that is not merely an intellectual antechamber of the divine presence, but a faith that is one with divine fellowship itself. In the spirit of the writer of the First Epistle of John, which is the spirit of Jesus also, we may frankly question whether it is important to cultivate in the young any belief in God that can coexist in the same person with deafness to the human cry. Is not any such belief actually dangerous to society? History shows that belief in God may be used to sanctify and strengthen unjust social ordinances and authorities, and that from this possibility even belief that sincerely regards itself as Christian is by no means exempt.

If it be possible thus to fuse love and faith, so that even in childhood the voice of God and the voice of human need shall be one voice, this is the path that religious education should by all means choose. It is possible. As Mrs. Mumford's experiments show,[1] the small child's first prayer can be a genuinely social reaction, and he can be led directly forward in the identification of his fellowship with God with his fellowship with men. In a considerable number of Sunday schools the social approach to God already begins to control the teaching about him. A child compared two Sunday schools as follows: "In that one they teach you all about God; in this one they teach you to help God." We are still in the beginnings of such instruction, of course, and much experimentation, with many blunders, is still before us. But the way ought by this time to be known. It is the way of love, which is the whole law, not only of the deeds that are worth doing, but also of the beliefs that are worth holding. In religious education as elsewhere love never faileth, and in the triunity of faith, hope, and love, it is supreme.

[1] E. E. R. Mumford, *The Dawn of Religion in the Mind of the Child* (London, 1915).

CHAPTER VIII

THE CHURCH AS EDUCATOR

The religious dependence of the individual. In all our common human interests that which the individual achieves and that which society contributes to him are inextricably intertwined. They are more than intertwined; the relation is like that of a leaf to the trunk of the tree that bears it. We see this clearly in the political attitudes of a free citizen; however free may be his thinking, his convictions are a result of historical processes and of association with some existing group. This is not less true of religion, which is historically an affair of groups—tribes, nations, churches, and parties—and of drifts within and without the churches. Our religious progressives, mugwumps, indifferentists, and even secularists, as well as the conservatives and reactionaries, are incarnations of group sentiments. Even the self-made man obtains material and design to a large extent from the social medium in which he moves.

No church is made up of men and women who belong to it simply because of their individually reasoned-out convictions. No; a church makes its members more than the members make the church. This fact—the infusion of social sap in what we nevertheless rightly call individual—is the net remainder of the mediæval realistic notion that the church is the *prius* of its members, or the eternal "form" of which they are the "matter." Here is authority in its inevitable actuality; reasoned or unreasoned, intended or unintended, it is here by virtue of the fact that men move in groups. But, as we shall see, this does not imply that one part of a group must be passively moulded by another part.

85

The church considered as an instance of "social heredity." The term "social heredity" has been invented to designate the fact that acquired characters of a mental sort are passed on from generation to generation without any necessary dependence upon our prevision or planning.[1] They are not transmitted in the procreative process, of course, but by nondeliberative mental processes of which suggestion is the type. Thus it is that numberless modes of action, feeling, and thought that have the appearance of being instinctive, or self-evident, are in reality matters of habit. Our sense of propriety as to this or that, our conscientious feelings as to this or that conduct, a mass of preferences that seem to be almost as inevitable as gravitation, a large proportion of the things that we regard either as self-evident or as absurd, might have been otherwise; they *are* otherwise in other times and among other peoples. However they got started, they continue from generation to generation by reason of continuous pressure from the set ways of older persons upon the plastic minds of the young.[2]

Our social inheritance includes a vast number of man-ways, from the merest trifles to the most momentous concerns of peoples and of humanity itself. Satire has found its happy hunting-ground in our subservience to conventions. Who but a very inferior, or else a very exalted, person, male or female, dares to dress as comfort and common sense dictate? The starched collars that plague my neck are a yoke of servitude; I would put them away if I were strong enough. And I would emancipate myself from stiff head-gear, and from coats during the torrid days of summer, and instead of limiting myself to the sombre colors of conventional male attire, I would learn color schemes from leaves and blossoms, from sea, sky, and cloud, from sunrises and rainbows—if I dared!

[1] J. M. Baldwin, *Social and Ethical Interpretations* (1906), chap. II, and Appendix A. There are disadvantages in the use of "heredity" in any but a strictly physiological sense, but I permit myself the liberty because a specific term is needed, and no better one has been suggested.

[2] The manner in which things-as-they-are tend to become presuppositions of our thought as to how they ought to be is well illustrated by this incident: A gentleman who resides in a state that has recently granted the franchise to women remarked: "Now that we have actually seen women voting, it seems natural enough, and the wonder is that we ever thought otherwise!"

Our religious convictions, whether they are true or not, and even our passionate aspirations, arise within us and become fixed as the meaning of life for us very largely because there are churches. A church is an educational institution primarily because of this kind of fact, because, in short, by its very presence, it produces so largely the presuppositions of social thinking, and maintains a great body of standards that are taken for granted.

The interplay of social purpose with social suggestion in the churches. The fact that "what is" thus easily and spontaneously transforms itself in our minds into "what ought to be," or at least into "what is natural," gives rise to the need for some provision for an ever-recurring re-examination of standards, with resultant revision and freshening of life's enterprise. Convention, institutionalism, and vested interests are always ready, in religion as elsewhere, to suffocate the spirit as well as to serve it. The church of the spirit must therefore provide means and measures for continual spiritual renewal at the sources of spiritual life. To education in the non-technical sense of transmission of standards by suggestion, must be added education in the technical sense of deliberate choice of what shall be transmitted, and systematic procedures for securing effective transmission. But this involves, as a phase of the church's educational vocation, ever-repeated re-examination of her own conduct.

It is easy to deceive ourselves as to what the church is doing with the young. Because we put edifying words into a textbook or into the mouths of teachers, we imagine that we are putting the whole weight of the church upon the side of ideal goodness. Not so! What the church is—to paraphrase Emerson's epigram—speaks so loudly that the young do not hear what the church says. Social assumptions that are unexpressed in words but lived out in conduct modify and interpret every ethical formula. When we who pray to God as Father, and call humanity a family, and exalt the idea of service, nevertheless take unprotesting comfort in the antidomestic, unbrotherly, caste-like inequalities of opportunity that prevail in the world, then, however unconscious we may be of compromising our religion, we actually become teachers of an anti-Christian ethic. A teacher of a Sunday-school class of self-supporting young women said: "Many of my working girls do not grasp the ideal of the Consumers League, for they have never consciously known persons who sacrificed their own comfort in commercial transactions that persons less fortunate with whom they were unacquainted might be benefited."

Therefore the church's conscious selection of what is to be presented to the young ought to extend beyond and below all lesson material, all school activities, and all devotional exercises, even to the social setting of the whole in our present life. If the social setting of Sunday-school experience produces in the pupil no sense of a social contrast between the church and the world, no awareness that there is going on within the church the self-criticism through which alone it can emancipate itself from its limited sociality, no realization that church life means *per se* agonizing for a better social order, then the church itself becomes an agency for perpetuating the unbrotherliness that its words condemn. There is even a possibility—a certainty, rather—that individuals, if not whole ecclesiastical groups, will attach a divine sanctity to civil laws and social incrustations that actually hinder the love that is justice.

The church as a fellowship of old and young. We may now go as far as to assert that the church, considered as educator, is primarily a fellowship of older and younger persons, and that if this fellowship be rich and aspiring it will be educationally effective, whatever be the material and the method of instruction. Our purpose should be, of course, to make the fellowship and the instruction one consistent whole, one movement toward the same point; but it is well to remind ourselves that fellowship on the plane of the social principles of Jesus, even if it be joined with defective instruction, has far more power to develop actual Christian living in the young than the best of instruction can have if it be separated from the living word, which is human love in actual operation.

Thus it comes to pass that church education at its best is an initiation into a living fellowship, being in this respect a true successor of ancient tribal initiations. But wherein does a truly educational fellowship on the Christian plane consist? This deserves careful study, for good will can miss its way by misunderstanding itself.

(1) *Christian fellowship is, in the first place, "good-fellowship," or having pleasures in common, and heightening them by the very fact that they are enjoyed together.* Pleasurable experiences are a fundamentally necessary part of the child's acquaintance with the church. They are necessary because, since satisfaction in any act tends toward the repetition of it, they help toward habit formation. Training is most effective when it takes place in a pervasive atmosphere of cheer, amiability, and happy expectancy. Training in Christian living is most effective when its activities include the present *sharing* of pleasures, that is, present Christian living. The happiest experiences of the young should be found first of all in the family, but next in the church.

(2) *Good fellowship in the church is itself a process of Christian education; it is not to be used as mere bait* wherewith to induce the young to submit to an education that is not to their taste. The church has a direct interest, not merely a derived one, in play and frolic, in the interplay of the sexes that leads up to courtship and marriage, and in the cultivation of acquaintance just because persons as such are worth knowing. There are few developments of religious life in modern times as significant as the little-heralded introduction of play into the churches. What, a church at play? What would our spiritual fathers say to it? Here are Sunday-school baseball-teams, with references thereto from the sacred desk on Sunday! Here are cooking-stoves and kitchens in the churches, and club-rooms, and gymnasiums, and swimming-tanks! Well, whatever the fathers might say, the voice of love declares that wherever and however we enrich human fellowship on the simple, democratic plane of regard for men as such, we do the will of the Father, we bring nearer the world-wide realization of the democracy of God.

(3) *Christian fellowship, though it start on the plane of a child's fondness for play, must continuously grow into community of purposeful labor—community not merely between children, or between children and their respective teachers,· but between all the members of the church group, both old and young.* "Come, let us live with our children," said Froebel. We are accustomed to apply this to parents and teachers, but it is applicable also to any social institution that brings children and adults into contact with each other. To live religiously and ecclesiastically with the young means to play with them, but it means also to let them work with us. It implies that we lay responsibilities upon them—real, not imitation responsibilities—that we train them in initiative by giving them initiative, and that we develop their judgment by letting them into the inside of church affairs. In many churches there exists a social stratification based upon age that works directly against effective training in church activities.

(4) At the risk of repetition let it be said that *fellowship with the young does not consist in giving gifts, or in providing privileges, or in promoting the social happiness of the young as a class by itself, or even in promoting good works on the part of such a class.* These ought we to do, but not to leave the other undone. The elder must give *themselves* to the younger. "I want not yours, but you!" is the appeal of young life to maturity. The appeal is partly responded to when maturity plays with children and youth, but the response is not complete until the experience of the child in the church, from the kindergarten age onward, includes continuous and growing participation in the most serious purposes, labors, and deliberations of the mature members and leaders.

(5) *All this implies, without doubt, some reversal of traditions.* In some Protestant quarters children have been expected to remain outside the fellowship until some indefinite future. Even the formal doctrine that they are within the fellowship has not always produced real community life, but rather participation in the symbols of it, or even less than this. Somewhat generally the church has made itself a schoolmasterish

setter of formal lessons, or a judge and rebuker of faults, or a regulator of amusements, rather than a coworker. Not seldom the young look upon the church as an administrator of mysteries that are solemnly remote from social joys. Every one of these traditions is anti-educational. To overcome them will require one measure in one communion, another in another, according to varying ecclesiastical constitutions, laws, and customs.

(6) *Finally, when fellowship of old and young in social joys, in purpose, and in labor becomes the basal thing in the educational policy of the churches, we shall lay the indispensable corner-stone of Christian unity.* The disunion within our religion goes far deeper than multiplicity of independent administrations, diversity of doctrinal standards, and contrasting modes of worship. Nothing less is involved than the fundamental impulses and attitudes upon which society itself depends, and specifically those upon which alone a democracy of God could possibly be built. Do we not lack in all the churches a social purpose so profound that young as well as old can appreciate it? For in truth that which can produce genuine Christian unity between youth and maturity is the fundamentals, such as active desire that everybody should have enough to eat, that everybody should be protected from disease, that all the sick should be cared for, that everybody should have friends, that everybody should have opportunity for education and for enjoyment of the finest products of the human mind, that children and youth should everywhere be protected from vicious influences, that war should cease, and that the Father should be able at last to look upon human society and say: "Behold, it is very good!"[1]

It is because we are not ready to unite with children in such fundamental, socially reconstructive purposes that we ransack history for a basis for Christian-union. It is the future, the unfulfilled task, the unreserving love of men, the yearning

[1] The capacity of children to appreciate the simple justice that is profound has been remarked again and again. A very small boy who was eating the inside of his slice of bread, but rejecting the crusts, was told: "There are lots of little children who would be glad to get as much as a crust of bread. They sometimes pick over the refuse in garbage cans in order to obtain food." The young thinker, with a worried expression, replied: "Why doesn't the Heavenly Father give them enough to eat?"

desire of the Father that all men should be one family; it is common objective purpose and labor, that must heal our divisions. When we have raised a generation or two of church-members united with one another in their various denominations upon this basis, we shall find the barriers between denominations very, very thin.

The church as a worshipping society. If what has just been said leads to the question wherein, then, the church differs from any other organization of the good will, and why a child needs any social training beyond participation in ordinary philanthropies and reforms, the answer is that, in spite of shortcomings, the churches, and they only of all our social institutions, undertake to accept the radical consequences of Jesus' social idealism. They have adopted—let us say it frankly—a point of view that leads to consequences that they did not at first foresee, consequences the portent of which even now we feel more than we can define. We Christians have a sad smile to-day for the simple-mindedness that could believe that the missionary task would be essentially completed when everybody on earth had been told something. We are beginning to face the appalling duty of building a world civilization based squarely, uncompromisingly, upon the proposition that all men are brothers; and we are beginning to see that our fellowship with the Father—the whole problem of worship—is tied up with our relations to this enterprise. We have, then, two aspects of the church as a worshipping society that are of the first importance for religious education.

(1) *The peculiar significance of the church as educator is found, in the first place, in the comprehensiveness and the radicalness of the principle of human fellowship that it professes.* Go over in your mind all other groups and group activities that aim at the betterment of mankind, including the state, the state schools, the most social-minded political party that you know, the reform organizations, philanthropic agencies of all kinds, institutions for research and for teaching, and for æsthetic and social enjoyment. What a magnificent array it is! What a tonic for our faith in man! No enlightened Christian but thanks

God for these forces that are all helping to bring us onward toward a real brotherhood. The function of religious education with respect to them is to raise up intelligent supporters for every effective humanitarian and socializing agency. Yet the fact remains that each of these group activities—wisely enough, no doubt—declines to contemplate man as man in his total need; no one insists upon complete justice, but only upon justice in some restricted sphere; every one puts off upon somebody else the declaring of what brotherhood in its uncompromising wholeness means; no one proposes the radical dealing with human nature, the reconstruction of motive, that is involved in effective brotherhood; no one goes with men into and through the deepest valleys of sorrow and the poignant issues of destiny.

But the churches mean to undertake this. They are, of course, beset with human frailty and error, but we criticise their defects precisely from the standpoint of their own avowed principles. They have in fact taken into their hands a sword that pierces their own bosom, and it is their hold upon this sword that gives them a peculiar function in social education. The Christ-spirit within us urges us to believe in man to the utmost, holding that any human life outweighs all possible private profits; to believe in loving to the utmost, and that only by losing our lives as merely individual can we have fulness of life; to believe in the possibility of purifying the motives of men until selfishness is really eradicated; to believe that a divinely good social order is possible on earth; to believe that the apparent defeat of love by death can be swallowed up in a greater victory of love, and to be unabashed by the tragedy and the mystery before which so many social forces shrink; and in all this to remember that we are not going to war at our own charges—the charges of our imperfect wisdom, and of the poverty of our resources—but that the eternal God is herein uttering in us a love that will not be denied. The churches are called by their own avowed principles to carry this social radicalism into life. They are to be quick to provide for any unfilled social need, but they are also to work within all constructive social agencies, and to inspire them to believe in brotherhood to the utmost, that is, to be as radically social as their respective limitations permit. This spirit of loving to the uttermost, which is likewise the spirit of self-criticism to the uttermost, is the first thing that specifically Christian education adds to the other agencies of social progress.

(2) *The peculiar significance of the church as educator is found, in the second place, in its maintenance of worship of the Father,* the source and the present inspirer of the love that, because it will brook no limits, is so terrifyingly just. There is no break, or partition, or point of transition, between the Christian's friendship with men and his friendship with God. Hence the significance of *common* worship. Communion of man with man reaches its climax only when the human is felt to contain the divine. Emerson called this the experience of "the Oversoul." The continuity of love with worship manifests itself variously. Parental and conjugal affection in their purest and most elevated self-consciousness feel something of awe, of reverence, of fulfilling a mission. Though our formulated faiths grow weak, duty goes on speaking to us as "Stern daughter of the voice of God." When our sympathy enters most unreservedly—that is, with the eyes of justice—into the woes of the world, then in the very depths of the dark valley there descend upon us elevation of spirit, illumination of the world darkness, a realization of an encompassing One as rejoicing within us.

The common worship of Christians is ideally, and to some extent actually, the fostering of this communion, which is at once human and divine—most human because it is divine, most divine because it is incarnate. When we worship together we remind ourselves of this God—*our* God; we reflect upon his goodness, so outgoing, self-giving, all-encompassing, and upon the ways in which it has unfolded itself to us, particularly upon Jesus; in the light of the goodness of God our pettiness and self-centredness are held before us until we repent and set about removing the inner obstacles that obstruct the utterance of divine love through us to our fellows; here, pausing from the multiplicity of affairs to seek a central, organizing principle for them all, and lifting our eyes from the particular stitches that we have been taking in the flowing garment of divinity in order that we may contemplate the garment itself, we find meaning, rationality, in our existence; rationality, however, not as something static, not as something to be merely gazed at and admired, but rationality as direction for our forces, as effort that is satisfied to be effort, as labor that asks for no idleness as its reward, as suffering with and for others that does not count itself as loss, as purpose that is large enough.

Christian worship is thus realization of the democracy of God—realization by imagination, by fresh insights, by rectification of purposes, by the coincident consciousness of God and our fellows—nay, the interfused consciousness of them, the consciousness of God as here and now incarnating himself in us as a society. When worship is fully Christian it is fellowship through and through, fellowship freeing itself from all restraints, and therefore continuous with everything in the world that makes for brotherhood.

Such worship has tremendous educational possibilities. They are to be realized partly by suggestion in words reinforced by music, by architectural beauty, and especially by the presence of a whole congregation that is attending to the same things and performing outward acts in unison. But both method and content of such suggestion need careful scrutiny in order that the congregation may be led away from the crowd type of consciousness into that of the deliberative group. How is this to be done? By ever fresh applications of the ancient Christian doctrine that God is made manifest in human life. To see life objectively, discriminatingly, and to reflect upon what we, with God, want it to be—this is of the essence of Christian worship. When we resort to the church to escape from the problems and the perplexities of human society, we do not follow the Christ who ever takes upon himself the form of man, ever becomes the servant of man. Worship as escape from this degenerates into non-Christian crowd æstheticism or else into non-Christian clubdom.

Again, when worship has its centre in priestly manipulation
of supernatural mysteries, it uses suggestion as an instrument
for keeping the many obedient to the few, and for repeating
the past instead of using the past as material wherewith to
build fairer structures of the spirit of brotherhood. The
methods of suggestion can be used either to hold children at the
crowd level, or to produce the sort of pause that leads to reflection, and to bring to attention objective material upon which
a deliberate social will can be formed. In short, true to the
meaning of incarnation, worship can develop communion with
God in and through growing social intelligence and growing
social purpose, as these, conversely, can be developed through
communion with God.

CHAPTER IX

A NEW THEORY OF THE CURRICULUM

The elements of the problem. At one point and another our discussion has already touched upon the curriculum, either explicitly, or by way of implication. But not until now have all the elements of the problem been before us. Broadly considered, the problem to which our discussion has led us is this: How to plan a progressive order for the pupil's social reactions— progressive in the sense of moving toward and into the full, intelligent, active sociality of Christian maturity. Such a plan would constitute a curriculum.

This social and functional conception of a "course of study" is fundamentally at variance with our traditions. Until very recently "curriculum" has implied that we formulate a body of ideas that we wish to impose upon the pupil, arrange an order in which they are to be learned, and plan ways for inducing him to attend to them. This, which may be called the "imposition theory" of the curriculum, grew out of and expressed the individualistic view of salvation, which was at the same time an intellectualistic view of the faith that saves. Not that any consistency was achieved in practice. Quite the contrary. After telling the things that must surely be believed unto salvation, the teacher still felt and knew that the task of Christianizing the heart remained over. Hence the assiduity with which "applications" were appended to every piece of curriculum material. Hence also the overemphasis upon the personality of the teacher, and the resort to beguilements, persuasions, and emotional pressure to induce pupils to be religious, all of which testifies to a cleft between curriculum and life.

The point of view that we have now reached in the present discussion bases the very notion of curriculum upon the vital

97

reactions that the older scheme merely appended to the course of study. The new theory unreservedly accepts the truth that out of the heart are the issues of life, and that consequently a curriculum is not primarily a systematic set of ideas, but a progressive order of motives actually at work, actually fruiting here and now. The elements that have to be considered may be stated in a chain as follows:

(a) To help the pupil to experience growing communion with God.

(b) In and through growing human fellowships in the family, the church, and elsewhere.

(c) Fellowship in the act of worship, with the help of music and the other arts.

(d) And in constructive and remedial social activities.

(e) Which include the missionary enterprise, but expand it.

(f) All of which requires constant and growing discrimination, foresight, and deliberation.

(g) And for this reason calls for illumination from Scripture, history, doctrines, science, current events, and the creations of imagination.

Under the concept of curriculum we are to think of the pupil as moving thus through social experiences; of these experiences as arising in active dealings with real situations of the present; as including the rise of intelligent social purposes; as coming in a prearranged order that is governed by the growth of the pupil's social capacities, and as including human and divine fellowship in a single whole. Fundamentally, then, the curriculum is a course of living, not a course in supposed preliminaries to real life.

The pre-social view of the curriculum. Before going on to further exposition of the implications of such a socialized curriculum, let us pause to realize just where the defects lay in the conception that prevailed in the church's educational yesterday. Here is a wee book entitled *Our Daily Guide*, or *Wise Words for Young Disciples*,[1] which consists of a text of Scripture

---

[1] Published by T. Nelson and Sons. It has been in circulation recently, I believe, and very possibly is still on the market.

and a meditation for each day of the year. "Enter not into the path of the wicked," reads one of the Scripture selections, and the meditation attached to it runs thus:

"Why should I join with those in play
In whom I've no delight;
Who curse and swear, but never pray,
Who call ill names and fight?"

Associated with the command, "Remember the Sabbath day, to keep it holy," is this resolution:

"I'll leave my sport to read and pray,
And so prepare for heaven;
Oh, may I love this blessed day,
The best of all the seven."

A third specimen is this: "The dead were judged out of those things which were written in the books, according to their works."

"Then let me always watch my lips,
Lest I be struck to death and hell;
Since God a book of reckoning keeps
For every lie that children tell."

We are accustomed to dismiss documents like this with a comment upon their dreadful theology. But something more is revealed, even the affinity of individualistic religion, with its worship of an incompletely socialized god, for an educational method that consists in telling and commanding, but not in the growth of motives. The method, as well as the content, isolates the pupil from his fellows and from divine fellowship. The last thing thought of here is that a child might appreciate love or justice or real fellowship of any kind.

How ingrained the individualistic notion of teaching was, how mechanical were the methods to which it led, and how remote it was from the pupil's real life, may be seen from the following questions and "applications," which are quoted from nineteenth-century question-books for use in the Sunday school.

·Date, 1832. Lesson material: Paul and Silas at Thessalonica and Berea (Acts xvii, 1–16). "*It was Paul's habit to attend public worship,* ver. 2;—learn, That wherever we are, it is our duty to do the same, nothing can excuse it, but sickness, or some unavoidable calamity." . . . "*Paul reasoned with the Jews, out of the Scriptures,* ver. 2;—learn, That the Scriptures are the only sources from which we can draw correct and weighty arguments." . . . "*Some of them who heard Paul believed,* ver. 4;—learn, That truth affects different persons differently." . . . It is pleasant to record that this dreariness is not altogether unrelieved by references to matters that really concern children. Thus, when the text-book reaches the story of the shipwreck, we read: "*Many were saved by swimming,* ver. 43;—learn, That it is useful to learn to swim; our own lives, under God, may sometimes be indebted to it; and, besides this, if we know how to swim, we may assist others." [1]

Date, 1845. A whole lesson is given to the two verses, Matthew xiii, 51 and 52. A few of the questions are as follows:

"12· How should children treat their religious teachers? Heb. xiii, 7, 17; I Thes. v, 13.

13. What danger is there in refusing to receive instruction? Mat. x, 14, 15; Pr. v, 23.

.　　.　　.　　.　　.　　.　　.　　.

15. Why should you desire to be taught in the truths of the Gospel? II Tim. iii, 15.

16. What is your duty in the Sabbath school?"

In a lesson on "The Barren Fig Tree," questions like this are asked: "What divine attribute is exhibited in granting to all persons a sufficient reason, and all necessary means of grace?" and the parable of the Prodigal Son is pointed with, "To what great end should all the blessings of providence and grace be devoted?" [2]

[1] *A Help to the Acts of the Apostles* (Philadelphia: American Sunday School Union, 1832).
[2] J. A. Albro, *Scripture Questions, vol. VII, On the Parables of the New Testament. Part I: For the Younger Scholars* (Massachusetts Sabbath School Society, Boston, 1845).

Date, 1862. Here are fifty lessons on the books of Joshua and Judges alone. One lesson is given to Caleb's inheritance, another to Judah's inheritance, and so on. The lesson on the inheritance of the Levites occasions these "Practical Questions": "Where in this lesson do we learn, that: The living of the ministry is not often so great as to tempt men into it for the sake of the compensation? It is the will of God that the ministry be comfortably supported? I Cor. ix, 13, 14. This support cannot be withheld without displeasing God? . . . It is for the convenience of the ministry and the good of the people that they live near the sanctuary in which they minister?" [1]

Date, 1884. "What have I learned?" is asked in connection with a lesson on The Thessalonians and Bereans (Acts xvii, 1–14), and the answer is given as follows:

"1. That the Scriptures tell us what we are to believe and what we are to do.

2. That it is ignoble to reject and oppose the Scriptures.

3. That it is noble to receive and study the Scriptures.

4. That we should search the Scriptures with earnest desire to find out just what they teach.

5. That if we thus study the Scriptures we will be led into the truth." [2]

Date, 1894. "Practical Lessons Learned" from the story of Cain and Abel are as follows:

"1. We should bring our best gifts to God.

2. We should offer them in faith in Christ.

3. We should beware of envy, jealousy, and anger.

4. Passion in heart leads to sin in life.

5. We should seek pardon through Christ, the only Savior." [3]

What a valley of dry bones is this! How *unreligious* it is! The reform of the curriculum that set in early in the present century was fundamentally a religious reform. It was an attempt to remove paraphernalia, mistakenly supposed to be educational, that had been interposed between the child and religion. The spirit of the new movement is dominated by faith in the possibility of child religion and of growth in

[1] John Todd, *A Question Book embracing Books of Joshua and Judges for Sabbath Schools and Bible Classes* (Massachusetts Sabbath School Society, Boston, 1862).

[2] *Westminster Question Book*, 1884.

[3] *Westminster Question Book for Teachers and Older Scholars*, 1894.

religion.   Let us have religion itself, it says, not these deadening reiterations about it; let us help children to be Christian now, each in his personal world, however narrow it may be, and let us understand that herein the teaching of religion consists.   This is the direction in which the reform of religious education is going.   Many steps will have to be taken before our courses of talk about religion are wholly transformed into courses in religious living, we may be sure.   Therefore let us go a little farther into the theory of the matter.

The primary "content of the curriculum" is to be found **in present relations and interactions between persons.**   The curriculum, we have agreed, is to be a scheme of growth in social motives that are actually in operation as the pupil goes along.   The essence of teaching, then, will lie in leading the pupil to make experiments in social living whereby he shall know for himself, not merely by the hearing of the ear, the meaning and the validity of the ancient law of love which is also the law of justice.   With children as with adults the doing of God's will is the true way to insight.   How, then, can the pupil be led to make experiments in the organization of his little social world upon the principle of good will and justice? Not by the old method of telling and commanding, but primarily through the attraction that he finds in persons who already live socially in his own environment.   It is "living epistles," known and read in family, church, or Sunday school that first make Christian fellowship a reality to him.   This initial, pleasurable experience is what produces the momentum for carrying the principle of fellowship into other groups.   In order to lift this process above mere imitation, mere good-natured drift, which lacks aggressiveness and power of achievement in difficult situations, the pupil's attention must be turned to these situations so that he shall discriminate differences, recognize problems, and see causal relations.   That is, to study "the way" is primarily to notice the differences that exist here and now between social relations that are governed by active love and those that are not thus governed.

This proposition does not ignore or minimize the significance of historical material, but points, rather, to the vital, experiential way of using it. How, indeed, can the past be anything to us but a "dead past" until we discover by our own experiments that there is continuity between the living and the dead? As a matter of fact, the Bible, even parts of it that quiver with imperishable human interest, are to-day dead and inert things to multitudes because their approach was that of the old-fashioned curriculum. The very attempt to exalt the Bible devitalized it, concealed it, by making it a thing *per se*, to be first known apart from experience and only afterward applied in experience. The sparkle of its high lights, and the gloom of its shadows were missed alike, because it was all there merely to be learned, all on a dead level. Similar waste of precious power for living will always occur when "curriculum" means facing the pupil toward the far-away, the inexperienced, instead of toward present demonstrations of the meaning and the power of love. The word that gives life is always that which is made flesh, and dwells among men. "I in them, and thou in me, that they may be perfected into one; that the world may know that thou didst send me, and lovedst them, even as thou lovedst me."

When we thus transform the curriculum into a graded series of experiments in social living, making the present relations and interactions between persons the primary objects of study, not only shall we vitalize the parts of history that are of real religious importance, we shall also have a corrective for the present abstractness of much of our teaching. A notion is abroad that almost identifies the teaching of morals and religion with inducing pupils to analyze qualities of character or to discriminate the virtues one from another. "What sort of man was Abraham?" asks the teacher, and the pupil replies: "He was a man of faith," or "He was generous." Sometimes the questions run: "What do we call a man who conducts himself in this way? Yes, we call him generous," etc., etc. Extended plans have been made for moving on from one such quality or virtue to another until a whole galaxy of virtues has been telescopically viewed and mapped.

We need not deny all value to such study. The pupil's imaginative contact with good men is not likely to be altogether useless, and the acquisition of an ethical vocabulary is certainly desirable. Yet the fact remains that the really important thing about Abraham is his contribution to a certain social-religious movement. The American boy who moves in imagination with Abraham should move with him toward defined social objectives, should be made to realize the difference that the life of the patriarch made for other persons. Studying virtues is not the same as studying men in their social relations. We may glorify a virtue at the very moment that we forget men.

Dissecting virtues, moreover, does not necessarily make them attractive, even in their abstractness. Some inkling of further need is revealed in questions like these: "What do you admire in Abraham?" and "Which is your favorite character among all those that we have studied this quarter, and why?" Even if a virtue is made attractive, toward what, in terms of concrete living, is the pupil drawn? Suppose that we have produced admiration for generosity; there remains the question: In what way have we modified the pupil's purposes? Have we merely caused him to desire a share in the praise that is due to the generous? The desire to be "good" may be a subtle form of self-seeking. The desires and purposes that are worth awakening are those that consciously connect others with oneself in some scheme of objective good, such as welfare, justice, or a broader fellowship.

As long as one keeps one's attention upon inner and private qualities, instead of keeping it upon the effects of this or that conduct upon specific human beings, one can escape the sense of responsibility for the social order of which one is a member. Who does not know that fine personal qualities may be widespread in a socially lethargic community or church? When has "good man" had the connotation of caring for even rudimentary justice? A community in which, in spite of an abundant food-supply, many children lack sufficient nourishment to enable them to do their school work may contain any number of kindly, comfortable citizens to whom such a glaring injustice never comes home as having anything to do with their character. They are "good" men, they have "virtues" many and genuine, they are not hypocrites; yet something fundamental is lacking. This lack will not be made good by adding another "virtue" to their private stock. The whole method of their ethical thinking must be reconstructed. They must approach duty by a different route. The question of conscience should be: What persons are affected by my acts, or by my failures to act, and how are they affected? I am a part of a system of ethical nerves that reaches every member of the community, and binds all into an interdependent whole.

It requires no great acuity of vision, but only pausing and looking, to see that economic interdependence is at the same time ethical relatedness. In every bargain that I make, in every article that I use or consume, I traffic in human energies as well as in things, I relate myself to the health and happiness of men and women whom I have never seen, I take part in making their children what they become. To assume full responsibility for these acts of mine, to form a habit of seeing society as it is, and of tracing social causes and effects, and to think my very own moral life in community terms—these are the rudiments of an awakened, mature Christian conscience. The road toward such maturity is, obviously, training in analysis and in appreciation of human life in its present interrelatedness, and practice in making human relations those of a genuine fellowship.[1]

The changing social situations incident to the pupil's growth, with their inevitable problems of social adjustment, furnish a basis for the order and the use of the material. The social life of a child begins in a narrow circle, widens into larger and larger circles, and becomes a complex of interpenetrating circles. What but this movement of social enlargement and complication could determine the order of the material in a really socialized curriculum? Family life, play life, school life, civic life, occupation, marriage—here is a progressive

[1] The psychological phase of this matter will be discussed more at length in Chapter XIV.

order that is also a natural social order. A brief analysis of the educational problems presented by one or two of these situations will serve to make clear the principle of arrangement and of use.

Under normal conditions a child begins his social experience in a family. Here parental love, starting in instinct, but going on to reflective devotion, becomes the first revelation of the law of love. It does so by the utterly concrete method of attaching the child, by means of his pleasures, to his parents and to the other members of the household. Here is presented the first material for systematic religious education. The objects for study are father and mother, the other children, the domestic helpers, and the purveyors to the family's needs, in their respective activities as these affect the mutual happiness. The inclusion of the divine Father in this group comes naturally as expressing a fellowship of obedience in which the older and the younger share. In a group in which the full enfranchisement of some of the members is not yet possible, there is danger of undemocratic rule and undemocratic subjection. The common Fatherhood here serves as a democratizing principle. It is to be referred to and wrought into the child's daily consciousness, not as an importation from outside the daily family life, not as an individual possession of the child, or as an imposition upon his will, but as adding rich meaning to "our" in "our family."

The child's life in the family extends outward into play groups of members of various families. In a short time the play group buds off and becomes an almost autonomous social life of children with children. Games and plays are handed down from one such group to another for centuries without plan, or record, or adult participation. With the games go codes of conduct. Rather, the rules of each game do of themselves prescribe one or another sort of self-controlled act in the interest of co-operation, and not seldom penalties for non-co-operation.

Moreover, children erect standards, sometimes but not always unreflectively, for the conduct that is due from themselves to various classes of persons. There are standards with respect to competitors in games as compared with team-mates;[1] strange children as contrasted with acquaintances; children of a different economic "class"; older children and younger ones; the school-teacher;[2] the janitor; the street-car conductor;[3] the policeman; persons of other nationalities;[4] and persons occupying different positions in the industrial scale, as domestic "servants," "common" laborers, and capitalists. We adults often fail to realize that in the child world a child public opinion sustains and even enforces these standards. Here a child finds social reality. Compared with it the advice of an adult is likely to seem cold, unreal, unappreciative.

We cannot deal adequately with this child society by merely proclaiming better standards, or by appending prohibitions and penalties to the proclamation. Rather, through our fellowship with children we must help child society to find its own possibilities of greater happiness. Children's codes will not be the same as those of Christian maturity, in any case, for the range of human relations that can be attended to, and the range of

---

[1] Ask boys who are competing in running races what they think of starting ahead of the pistol. You are likely to find, as I have done, approval of such evasion of rules provided only that one can succeed in it.

[2] I know of a secondary school in which at one time the maxim, "A lie to the faculty is not a lie," expressed a common attitude of the boys, even of the more serious minded ones. Even in a well managed elementary school grade steps have been necessary to prevent pupils from altering report-cards sent to parents—"raising" them as a forger raises a check. The point of these instances is not the badness of children, but only their constant tendency to form standards and a public opinion of their own upon the basis of their own too narrow experience. What the teacher has to do is to enlarge the basis for the children's judgment upon social relations.

[3] Using one's wits to get something for nothing has the attraction of adventure, of contest, and of conquest. Boys, at least, trade and bargain with one another with a fierceness of cupidity, and sometimes with a trickiness, that represent in miniature some features of their elders' system of competitive profit getting. It is not always easy to make a child realize that cheating an impersonal entity like a street-railroad corporation is on the level of plain stealing.

[4] Race prejudices on the part of adults find a fruitful soil in the child mind, which is struck by differences in costume, speech, and manner, rather than by the less obvious, underlying identities of human nature. One of the fine, and likewise pressing tasks of Christian teachers in many of our centres of population is to help children who already look down upon "sheenies" and "dagoes" (the latest term, I believe, is "guineas") to discover the fine human qualities that these races are contributing to our American life.

possible adjustment acts, change with growing years. Nevertheless, within the range of childish capacities, immense differences of code are possible, most important shifts in social pleasures. Here, precisely, is where religious education has its opportunity and its call. Its central function will be to stimulate social experiments of certain kinds within the children's own world—experiments in which situations will be analyzed as they would not be without adult help, in which acquaintance of children with one another will be deepened, and in which thereby the joys of co-operation, helpfulness, fair play, and justice will be multiplied.[1]

These two examples, the family group and the play group, are sufficient to make clear how the grades or other divisions of a socialized curriculum can grow directly out of the pupil's expanding social experience. It is not necessary to continue this analysis into the child's school life, with its fresh problems of work, of systematized co-operation, and of authority; nor into his growing contacts with the political, industrial, commercial, philanthropic, and cultural institutions of the community; nor into his relations to a life-occupation, nor into his preparation for marriage. It is, however, important to notice that a progressive course in social living takes the form, as far as instruction is concerned, of a series of problems to be solved —problems, let it be noted, not imported into the child's world by the teacher, but already in the enterprises and the joys and sorrows of childhood. Let it be noted, finally, that under this conception of education the teacher does not give the pupils solutions for their problems, but induces the pupils to analyze and experiment so that they reach convictions of their very own.

How the "social situation" order of the curriculum differs from others. The significance of this new theory of the curriculum may be pointed still further by a brief résumé of other principles, either practised or proposed, for the arrangement of material.

---

[1] Compare what was said in Chapter IV concerning the necessity of helping children out of the crowd type of association into the deliberative type.

(1) *The part-and-whole arrangement,* whereby the Bible or the catechism is simply cut up into a number of parts to correspond with certain periods of time, or an abbreviated and simplified form (as of the commandments or of the catechism) precedes the complete one.

(2) *The historical arrangement,* whereby the pupil first thinks about earlier times, then about later ones, and at last arrives—if, indeed, he ever does arrive—at his own times.

(3) *The supposedly psychological arrangement,* whereby spontaneous interests that are believed to arise in a serial order are to have each its own kind of food in its season. In a later chapter we shall have to touch upon the most extreme form of this theory, which bases the order of the material upon the recapitulation doctrine of mental growth.[1] Here we may point out that in whatever form the supposedly psychological arrangement appears it misses or underrates an important factor in children's interests. The fact that some instincts ripen later than others does bring it to pass, indeed, that spontaneous attention shifts in certain matters by reason of a purely internal impulsion. It is true, too, that the mere presence of powers not yet fully employed is a determining factor.

On the other hand, however, children's characteristic interests are not, on the whole, spontaneous demands for this or that object or for this or that result, but rather for participation in processes of certain types. One of the simplest examples is the interest that is supposed to underlie the voracious hearing and reading of blood-and-thunder tales. Superficial observation may make it appear that suffering and cruelty as such are attractive, or that strength applied to immoral ends is what the child most likes to contemplate, whereas the thing that he is really after is imaginative participation in action that involves rapid changes, stirring contrasts, and simple motives, with the sense of *living* that such action brings. The action may be cruel or heroic, and the motive and outcome may be noble or base; the interest is there in either case.

Moreover, the particular material that attracts the child's

[1] See Chapter XII.

attention, the particular application of his impulses toward participation, is determined in each case in large measure by what the habitual environment offers, and by the kinds of active, overt participation that are open to him. Here, for example, is an only child who has had little contact with other children. When he is brought to the kindergarten he shrinks at first from the very objects and occupations that fascinate the other children. Again, keep a child amused by toys that perform in his presence while he remains little more than a spectator, and you create demands, interests, of a particular kind; pursue the opposite policy from the beginning, providing him with material for self-expression, construction, and initiative, and you create an opposite set of interests. The truth is that there is no serial order of underived interests upon which a curriculum could be organized. We must conform, rather, to the serial order of situations that develop with growth, striving always to *develop interests*, not merely to feed those that happen to be present already.

(4) *The ecclesiastical arrangement*, whereby religious education is made to consist in a gradual initiation into the worship, the activities, and the beliefs of the church, and into full conformity to its authority. This is like the part-and-whole principle of arrangement except that active participation in institutional life is added to "learning about." It is like the "social situation" principle in that it causes the pupil to attend to persons and what they do, and to take for himself a part in the doing. It is unlike it in two respects: It induces the child to conform rather than to experiment, and it introduces him to ready-made solutions instead of introducing him to problems. There is likewise a difference, of emphasis at least, with respect to the relation of the pupil's fellowship in the church to his fellowships in other groups. This point is of so great import that we must pause to consider it for a moment.

The place of the church in a curriculum of social living. If the content of the curriculum is to consist of the relations between persons in a series of social situations—family, play group, school, etc.—where, it may be asked, does the church

group come in? Where does the curriculum introduce the child
to the sacred fellowship and the common worship of the avowed
disciples of Jesus Christ?

The main alternatives that need to be considered may be
indicated by these questions: Shall the child's ecclesiastical
experience be treated as a particular social sphere co-ordinate
with others, as the family and the state, but having a different
principle of fellowship or a different set of problems to work
out; or, shall the child experience the church fellowship as a
specially earnest, co-operative effort to work out the very problems that arise in the family and in the other social situations
that have been named? Again, shall the child experience the
"sacred" or "set apart" as something inhering in the church
group as such but not in others; or, shall he experience all love,
all justice, binding men together anywhere, as the sacred?
Shall his initiation into common worship take him out of the
social consciousness of the work day and of the play day into
a new and separate communion; or, shall the fellowship of
prayer be continuous with all good fellowships, even a confirming of them and an inspiration within them? Where shall the
child be taught to look for God?

Underneath all these chapters on the new religious education
is a particular assumption. It has been vividly phrased by
the writer of the First Epistle of John: "This is the message
that ye heard from the beginning, that we should love one
another. . . . Love is of God; and every one that loveth is
begotten of God, and knoweth God. . . . But whoso hath
the world's goods, and beholdeth his brother in need, and
shutteth up his compassion from him, how doth the love of
God abide in him?"

If the Christian ideal were a divine autocracy, or a divine-
human aristocracy, then indeed it could promote itself by making attractive to children a common worship that by its solemn, .
majestic, and overawing mysteries should seem to tower above
and apart from the associations of the common day. If the
fellowship of the avowed disciples of Jesus were a *particular
species* of love, and not just plain, unreserved good will, then

the child's introduction to the church would be, indeed, an initiation into a society of the peculiarly good, the favorites of heaven. But if we grant that the fellowship of Christians is rooted in a kind of divine love that desires to enfranchise every man into democratic society, a love so divine that it knows no favored class on the one hand, and no undivine goodness on the other, then we shall induct children into common worship and the communion within the church as a heightened consciousness of what we are about in our every-day social relations. The presence of God will be made manifest in united prayer, not as something done in a church building, not because it is uttered by a privileged person or group, or according to any formula, but because the content of it brings to a focus the social problems of the common day, and gathers together the children's powers of aspiration after the good will that is the solution. Where is God? Wherever a mature man or a little child faces the problem of the mutual adjustment of two or more human lives to each other, there he meets God.

Love that is so divine as to be utterly democratic makes a church aspire to be, not so much a superior sort of society, as an exponent of society in the large as the very dwelling place of God. Ecclesiastical ambition now runs, not toward centralization of power in the ecclesiastical organization, but toward diffusion of the light of love through the whole social complex. The church itself now becomes a living exegesis of the great paradox that only by losing our life do we gain life. Such a church will be quick to minister to any human need that is not otherwise provided for—any need, from food to fun, and from athletics to art—but it will stimulate the family, the school, community institutions, and the state to take upon themselves every social function that they are adapted to perform.

The church of the spirit of love seeks thus to infuse itself into the whole social body, not to maintain eternal separateness therefrom. It does not find a competitor in any philanthropic institution that efficiently organizes good will. It does not depreciate as merely secular the social enthusiasm of any one who loves men as men, for God so loves them. It does not grow apprehensive lest the social movement should substitute the sacredness of humanity for the sacredness of worship. It is apprehensive, rather, lest men may not hold life sacred enough, may not love deeply enough to satisfy divine justice, may not make the happy discovery of themselves as work-fellows of the great Lover who is in all love, may never know that love itself is worship.

The position of the church in a socialized curriculum is that of a present fellowship that runs through all the developing fellowships, inspiring them to fulfil themselves, and urging them on toward the deep love of men that is also the conscious worship of God.

The place of the Bible in the curriculum. I have said, in substance, that the theory of the curriculum is to be based squarely upon the idea of incarnation—that God makes himself known to us in concrete human life; that we obey him and commune with him in any and every brotherly attitude that we take toward any of his children, and that this experience of God does not occur merely once or twice in history, but continuously. The realization of God on the part of the prophets and of Jesus is transmitted to us primarily in the human lives that have already come under its influence. We are linked with God in ancient history by nothing less than God himself within the intervening generations. Life is continuous. The generations are not separated from one another like the banks of a stream over which a bridge must be built. No non-living thing could communicate the divine life to us, but only this life itself. The consequence for religious education is that it consists primarily in the awakening of religious experience in children through their contacts with persons who already have such experience. The Bible then takes its place as a means that mightily assists in promoting, illuminating, and confirming these contacts, and in extending the Christian fellowship backward to Jesus and the prophets, and forward toward the fulfilling of the prophetic ideals.

From of old it has been a custom among Christians to go

to the Bible for specific help for specific needs. Does the shadow of death menace us? We turn to the Twenty-third Psalm or to the fifteenth chapter of First Corinthians. Do the uncertainties of life's struggle tempt us to compromise with evil? The sixth of Matthew comes to our aid. Does our prayer life require refreshing? We restudy the Lord's Prayer. Do we desire to think straight on the social question? We ponder the profoundly simple words of Jesus and of the prophets concerning justice and brotherly love. In short, we take our start from needs involved in our present situation, and we then select from the multitudinous wealth of the Scriptures the part that gives us the greatest help.

We shall discover the true place of the Bible in the curriculum by applying to childhood the same principle of using the Scriptures in the interest of present living. If the curriculum is fundamentally a course in Christian living, the Bible will be used at each turn of the child's experience in such a way as to help him with the particular problem that is then uppermost. We as teachers shall then select for the child just as we select for ourselves, leaving unconsidered for the time anything in the Bible that does not feed the pupil's present need. The result will be that the progressive social experience of the child will be reflected in the successive passages that are chosen, and if need be repeated from time to time. That is, we shall have a truly graded scheme of biblical lessons. It will begin with stories topically arranged, but as the pupil's outlook grows, it will deal with whole periods, whole books, and finally the whole movement of the religious consciousness that the Bible reflects.

On precisely the same principle so-called extra-biblical material will be used as it is needed. When I as an adult Christian meet the problem of how large my missionary contribution shall be, I seek information concerning the missions of to-day. When I want to know what my duty is with respect to the liquor traffic, I study its baleful effects and also the methods of fighting it. When the preacher asks me to support a proposed child-labor law, I want him to give me the facts with regard to children in industry and with regard to the laws on the subject. If loyalty to the church is in question, I must know something of the history of the church, something of its actual position in present society, and something concerning the more effective forms of church life. This is the way that we adults study to be Christian. The way for children is not different in principle but only in the application. Extra-biblical material for study is just as necessary for them as for us because their problems, like our own, have to do with enterprises and adjustments concerning which the Bible gives no whit of information —missions in lands unknown in ancient times; philanthropic enterprises under conditions and by methods not so much as conceived of by any biblical writer; social adjustments in the home, on the playground, at school, in the choice of an occupation, in the conduct of one's occupation, in the use of the ballot, which must be studied directly if they are to be understood at all.

Such extra-biblical factors in the problems of Christian living are bound to have a large place in the socialized curriculum. But they will not supplant the Bible, or derogate from its uniqueness as an instrument for social education. For the Bible contains a body of social literature of unique power for the stimulation and criticism of social motives and ideals. It is in and through the use of the Bible that we come into fellowship with the greatest of our social leaders, meeting God in them. No mystical introduction to the Christ who dwells in the heart of every believer can be substituted for fellowship with the historical Jesus and with the great Old Testament characters who influenced his own social education. The fellowship of a common social purpose is, indeed, the foundation of Christian education, and this foundation is laid in the pupil's present acquaintance with persons in whom God's presence shines out as love. But this fellowship, this social experience, can be extended by imagination. It is thus extended through memory, for how often does one become better acquainted with the real character of a loved one by separation from him. Similarly, imagination extends our fellowship to persons whom we have never seen, whether they are separated from us by oceans or by centuries. "Whom, not having seen, we love."

The educative power of such imaginative association depends partly upon the law of suggestion. Merely associating with persons of positive goodness tends to habituate us to the expectation of goodness in ourselves. Likewise emotional reactions against imagined badness can have a part in forming habitual attitudes. But this is only atmosphere or background for something far more specific, namely, the use of imagined persons, events, and situations in the analysis of present issues and of universal laws of living. The uniqueness of the Bible as a source of material for social education lies, in large measure, in the sharpness with which it presents issues without abstracting them from persons and events. Here is the truth of life presented in the form of life, a form so characteristically drawn that he who runs perceives the ethical meaning. There are many biblical tales that one can hardly read or listen to in a naïve manner without, in the very act, criticising one's own conduct. There are aphorisms and formulæ without number that become tools for mastering our own experience.

Nevertheless, the history of religious education shows that even this magnificent body of concrete truth can be so taught as to seem far away and unrelated to us. We must therefore assume, on this ground also, the necessity of the living teacher, and of art in teaching. Thus the literary material of the curriculum finally becomes, not something *per se*, but ideas actually performing their function. Material and method become indissolubly one.

PART III

THE PSYCHOLOGICAL BACKGROUND OF A
SOCIALIZED RELIGIOUS EDUCATION

CHAPTER X

THE SOCIAL NATURE OF MAN

The problem of Part III. We come now to the nature of the human material that religious education undertakes to modify. What, for the purpose of the present discussion, is a child? That is, what is there in children that justifies any expectation that they will make a favorable response to the social principles of the Christian religion? Does child nature include any obstacle to such response? What is child religion as compared with the religion of adults? Are there any laws of growth that condition a child's religious experience? What sorts of situation, controllable by the educator, are most conducive to religious growth? And what is the process whereby a social purpose grows mature?

These questions are different from the ones that text-books for Sunday-school teachers ordinarily undertake to answer. Child study for teachers of religion abounds in discussions of children's imitativeness, their imagination, their memory, their activity and changeability, their play, their constructiveness; all of which is important, but little of which touches upon the religious capacities of childhood. It fails to touch upon these capacities because it concerns the general form of children's reactions rather than interests and motives. As a consequence, a teacher who understands all these formal characteristics of children, and guides the teaching process in the light of them, may nevertheless appeal to either social or individualistic motives, and therefore may start the child either well or ill. Therefore, with our eyes upon the content of the Christian purpose, the democracy of God, we must go on to ask what capacities children have for being interested in any such thing, or for responding to any part of such an ideal.

Some of these questions have already been touched upon in our sketch of the new religious education, particularly in Chapters VII, VIII, and IX. The general conception of a child's religious progress there presented is that of the continuous achievement of intelligent good will in his growing social relationships, and the enlargement of these relationships themselves in the church and in its worship. We assumed that children respond to social incentives, and that worship of a Father who loves us can be a vital experience in childhood as truly, though not necessarily in the same degree or form, as in adulthood.

These assumptions are not violent ones. Perhaps they do not need defense, but they do need further analysis in the interest of specific control of particular sorts of reaction. Relatively simple as a child's interests and motives are, they are nevertheless sufficiently complicated to make the understanding of children, and skill in teaching (as distinguished from knack) something of an achievement. We shall presently see some evidence of the ease with which we misinterpret children, and it will grow increasingly clear that the misplacing of a motive in teaching is a most serious matter.

What is meant by "the psychological background of a socialized religious education," then, is this: The social and the anti-social impulses of a child, and particularly how social instincts can grow into social purposes of ideal scope. This is background only. If middle ground and foreground also were to be presented, practically the whole of educational psychology would have to be reviewed. For the teaching of religion, as of anything else, involves such matters as sense-perception, imagination, memory, habit, attention and interest, judgment and inference, the laws of transfer and the laws of fatigue. For topics like these the reader is referred to the general works on educational psychology.

Instinct-factors in the conduct of one human being toward another. By instinct is meant, in this discussion, any readiness to act in a specific way in a particular sort of situation without having learned to do so, or (as it is often put) the first time that a situation of the sort is presented. This definition, it will be noted, refers to specific kinds of action rather than to broad tendencies in either the race or the individual. There are such broad tendencies. The evolution of the race exhibits movement toward refinement in various directions, and toward the organization of conduct into social institutions of increasing scope. Similarly, growth of an individual mind consists, in large measure, in the achievement of organized self-consciousness and self-control. These tendencies are of course to be included in the concept of man's social nature. They will have our attention in subsequent sections. But first it is important, for the purpose of effective control through teaching, to see that human nature is not merely a few general tendencies that are to be promoted or resisted by appealing to general motives, but also a vast complex of readinesses to act in this or that specific way under specific conditions. What the teacher has to do is to secure particular social reactions and to prevent particular antisocial ones, to the end that social habits and social thinking may grow with the pupil's increasing contacts with his fellows. The effectively good will is more than a benevolent sentiment toward mankind in general; it is also a will trained to meet particular human situations.

In the following summary of instinct factors in social and anti-social conduct I shall follow chiefly Thorndike, who has carried the analysis of the instincts farther than any other psychologist, but I shall subsequently make use also of certain analyses by McDougall. The list summarizes factors only, treating each one in its simplicity and in isolation, and without reference at this point to the integral life of individual self-control or of social organization. We are to notice, as it were, certain bones of the human skeleton, rather than the living body performing its functions.[1]

---

[1] Even if limitations of space permitted me to describe in detail the situation that evokes each sort of response, and the muscular and physiological features of each response, I could do little more than reproduce the substance of Thorndike's descriptions. The reader is advised by all means to read them for himself. See E. L. Thorndike, *The Original Nature of Man* (which is vol. I of his three-volume *Educational Psychology*). New York, 1913, pp. 52 *f.*; 68–122.

(1) *Simple gregariousness,* or pleasure in the mere presence of other members of the species, and discomfort in their absence.

(2) *Special interest in what is being done by human beings,* as distinguished from all other objects in the environment.

(3) *Wanting to be noticed by other human beings.*

(4) *Craving for approval from other human beings, and discomfort from their disapproval,* whether the grounds of it be ethical or not.

(5) *Approval or admiration not only for those who are useful to us, but also for those who exhibit strength, daring, or beauty; and disapproval, scorn, or disgust for persons of the opposite sorts, even though they have not injured us.* This instinct is primarily directed toward qualities that are important for savage society, but the sphere of its application grows with the growing standards of society. Thus it is that moral strength (what is "moral" being determined by the then existing standard) is an object of instinctive admiration.

(6) *Effort to master others, particularly weaker animals and human beings, and to subdue them if they resist; but also readiness to submit to the strong or self-assertive individual.* Thorndike classes instinctive display or showing off as a partial manifestation of the instinct of mastery, and shyness as a partial manifestation of the instinct of submission. Both are prominent in courtship, but they play a part also in much other conduct.

(7) *Rivalry* (attempting to get something for oneself rather than let another get it), *greed* (getting for oneself regardless both of the need of others and of oneself), *and jealousy* (annoyance with, and perhaps attack upon, another who receives attention or benefits that one desires for oneself).

(8) *Hunting.* Though primarily related to the securing of food, the hunting instinct does not stop here, but goes on to killing for sport, mastering and tormenting animals, bullying weaker human beings, callous pursuit of persons whom we dislike, and some forms of warfare.

(9) *Anger and pugnacity.* The primary instinctive response to situations like being physically restrained, thwarted, or attacked is (unless submission intervenes) struggling, or screaming, or kicking, or striking back, or counter-attack, commonly with more or less of the emotional commotion called anger. Secondarily, pugnacity applies to any kind of thwarting, as in argument, and it becomes pleasure in combat as such, whether with weapons or in sport, whether with muscles or with wits.

(10) *Sex attraction.* The social significance of the sex instinct far outruns the mere perpetuation of the species. "It is true that sex attraction as such does not seem to include regard for another's interests; nothing can be more ruthless than the sex instinct, in some of its manifestations, at least. Yet it does not generally exist 'in and by itself' in the human species. The fixation of attention upon another, the vivid realization of his presence as this particular individual, which is characteristic of sex attraction, has an important consequence. We individualize another by *Einfühlung*—that is, by imaginative putting of oneself in another's place—so that we reciprocally feel one another's satisfactions and discomforts. Now, sex attraction, as well as parental instinct, strongly individualizes its object. Therefore we may assume that sex makes a direct contribution to the appreciation of benevolence and justice. Something very like the parental attitude also appears between lovers—the attitude of protection, intense response to every sign of pain, cuddling."[1] It is a matter of great social import, moreover, that sex attraction influences conduct toward persons with whom sexual union is out of the question, as in the attitudes of the two sexes toward each other in the family, in social gatherings and diversions, in friendships, and in the many respects in which we treat the two sexes differently. The emotional accompaniments of the adolescent sex awakening affect even the attitudes of males toward males and of females toward females; yes, the fresh æsthetic, idealizing, and companionship-seeking state of mind often modifies one's whole social attitude, and even one's attitude toward nature.

(11) *Parental regard.* It is most obvious and most tender in mothers, being related in origin to sensations connected with suckling and with other close and frequent physical contacts. But it is instinctive in both men and women. Undoubtedly the attachment of the father for the mother has much to do with the attention that he gives to their children, and thus with the activity of paternal affection. Possibly -self-giving maternal affection is the evolutionary link that has united the father with the child, and thus given rise to the permanent monogamous family. Yet the father's regard for his children is, conversely, an added bond between him and their mother. In any case, whatever was first in origin, the spontaneous readiness of both parents to feed, pro-

[1] G. A. Coe, *The Psychology of Religion.* Chicago, 1916, pp. 163 *f.* (note).

tect, and succor their offspring through the extraordinarily long human infancy is a prime psychological foundation of what is finest, and most difficult, in the larger social integrations of men. Its relation to the larger society grows out of two circumstances: *a.* In the family, which rests upon parental instinct, and specifically through the intimate domestic manifestations of this instinct, children receive social training that is in some measure transferred to their life in the larger society. *b.* The parental instinct is not limited to parents, nor are small children the only objects that stimulate it. This matter is so involved and its social bearings are so important that detailed attention will be given to it in a subsequent section.

(12) *The kind of imitativeness that produces crowd action.*

The unique social significance of the parental instinct. Two groups of facts will indicate how broad and deep is the influence of this instinct in the evolution of society, particularly of democratic society.

(1) *Parental attitudes arise spontaneously long before physiological capacity for parenthood arrives; they live on through life, even though one never has children of one's own, and they attach themselves not only to children, but to adults as well.* Nothing less than parental are the relations that small children, boys as well as girls, assume with dolls, animal pets, smaller children, and toys. This is not mere imitation of older persons, for the activities are clearly different from those of adults in many respects, and the emotional fervor and tenacity are too obviously original with the child. There is no escaping the conclusion that this is actual parental instinct. Its instinctive character is proved by: (1) Its universality. (2) The possibility of identifying its primary objects as a class, namely, smaller things thought of as living, especially those that are helpless, lonely, or suffering. (3) The specific nature of its motor discharges, such as taking into one's arms, keeping near one (as at night), providing food (real or imaginary) and other objects to meet particular assumed needs, patting, stroking, laying the cheek against. (4) A surprising confirmation of this theory that has been brought to my attention by one of

my students. The evidence consists of photographs of two half-grown bluebirds, one of which is in the act of feeding a worm to the other. One of the pictures shows the two facing each other, one with the worm, the other with open mouth; the other picture shows the bill of the first bird well down the throat of the other. Here the instinct to swallow whenever a worm is in the mouth is inhibited exactly as it is when a mother bird has her first brood; it is inhibited, obviously, by another instinct.

That this instinct lives on through life, especially if it receives frequent indulgence either in affectionate acts toward one's own offspring or toward other objects, hardly needs argument. The parental petting of animals does not cease with childhood; with the childless it is often a substitute for literal parenthood. A baby, too—anybody's baby, white, yellow, or black—is an object of peculiar interest. I have seen the tired faces of a whole group of men and women in a New York subway car relax and mellow as their eyes all sought the face of a baby playing in its mother's lap. Austere men, hard men, boys who are ready to bully those only a little younger than themselves, all are gentle, all take the attitude of protection toward very small children.[1] The teaching profession, education as a whole, is permeated by a truly parental interest in the young.

When parents reach the weakness of old age, then the children, in their turn, assume the parental attitude toward those who bore them. A gentleman who was showing exquisite tenderness toward an aged parent remarked: "I have had no children of my own, you know." In general, too, does not reverence for gray hairs contain this instinct as one of its constituents? And why is it that everybody is ready to help a blind man find his way upon the street? No doubt the impulses that underlie our relations to our fellows are complex, and to some extent contradictory. Some of them become dominant, others are smothered, or contradictory impulses

---

[1] Without doubt males would be more demonstrative in this direction but for a social tradition of sex inequality, and but for that other baleful tradition, that manliness is demonstrated by fighting rather than by tenderness. These, too, rest back upon instinct, of course.

alternate. But any one who has eyes can see continually coming to the surface, in fragmentary ways at least, spontaneous helpfulness of the parental type.

; (2)· *The parental instinct is the chief source, probably the exclusive source, of tender regard for individuals as such, that is, taking another's happiness or woe as one's very own.* Thorndike is, on the whole, inclined to regard the pitying response to signs of weakness, fright, and pain, as an instance of, or derivative from, "motherly behavior." [1] Whatever be the fact in this matter, pity is only one aspect of mothering, and it is only one aspect of regard for individuals as such. The major manifestation of this regard is demand for justice for all men simply as men, and readiness to suffer actively with them in the struggle to obtain it. There is something in us that makes us individualize our fellows, think of them one by one apart from possessions, apart from their age and social status, apart even from their individual defects, and *believe in them.* The one point at which we can indisputably discern an instinctive tendency to do this is the relation of parents to their children. We follow the line of probability, then, when we look upon the sacrifice of one's own welfare that others may have their rights (welfare, that is, as measured by any less social standard) as being, on the large human scale, the same thing as a parent's insistence that each of his children shall have life, and liberty, and happiness.

Our problem here, it will be perceived, concerns the instinctive basis of the love of mankind that is required by the second of the two Great Commandments. We call it brotherly love, and speak of its goal as the brotherhood of man. But what is brotherly love, even within the limits of the family? Is the bond between brothers and sisters a specific fraternal instinct? The existence of such an instinct is by no means proved by the obvious naturalness of the affection. Consider the closeness of the association between brothers and sisters, then consider the long period through which it lasts, and finally ask what, under these conditions, is to be expected from the instincts numbered

[1] Pp. 102 *f.*

1 to 6 in our list. From these alone, under the laws of habit formation, we should expect a rather close group life which is likely to make a lifelong distinction between one's own brothers and sisters and other persons. What we have to account for in addition is positive outgoing affection, which far transcends the habitual accommodations to one another that grow out of the instincts just referred to. That is, we have to account for affection like that of parent for child. What if fraternal affection, in its most intimate phase, is the exercise of parental instinct? We cannot be mistaken in seeing this instinct in certain attitudes of older children toward brothers and sisters who are much younger. We are not likely to err when we interpret in the same way all the rest of the sympathetic fraternal loyalty that springs up in domestic intimacies. Finally, the parents' own instinctive attitudes act as a constant suggestion to the children to take the same attitudes toward one another. The sum of the matter is that the fraternal relation in the family is a highly complex thing, and that it gets its quality of justice or feelingly taking the brother's interests as one's own, from the factor of parental instinct.

From what quality of original nature comes the affectionate response of a child to a parent's affection? Love begets love, no doubt, but how? If we had to rely upon antecedent probabilities we should guess that there is a filial instinct that answers to the parental. But when we analyze an infant's earliest reactions to maternal care, we discover that they fall chiefly under the first six heads of our list together with the twelfth. What remains to be accounted for is filial affection or love in the strict sense already defined in the last two paragraphs. But this is the same sort of attitude that distinguishes parental affection. What, then, if filial affection, like the corresponding phase of fraternal affection, is an early manifestation of parental instinct? What but this is the attitude of protection and of succor toward a father or a mother who is weary and heavy laden, sick, in sorrow, injured by others, or suffering reverses and disappointments? Family intimacies provide precisely the opportunity, scarcely existent elsewhere, for small children to play the parent to mature persons. Small children pat and stroke a parent's face or hand, and when is a little one as happy as when he can play parent to the whole family? A boy of about four years, when his mother was nursing him through the croup, said: "Show me just what you do for me, mother, so that when I have little boys and girls with croup, I will know what to do for them." About six weeks later, when his mother had a headache, he assumed the attitude of physician and parent to her just as he had done to his own prospective children. Nothing seems to evoke filial affection as surely as being permitted to help father and mother. Doing things for a child does not touch his heart half as much as permitting him to do things for you![1] The conclusion is that our love for our fathers and mothers is of the same instinctive quality as their love for us. We can be good sons and daughters by letting free in ourselves the very thing that makes a good parent.

A side-light upon this question may be discerned in the common chivalric devotion of sons to their mothers, to which nothing in the ordinary relations of sons to fathers corresponds. This devotion probably has one of its roots in some obscure response to sex differences, but another part of the explanation, without doubt, is that the more frequent manifestation of weakness or of distress by the mother has called out, and by habit confirmed, the son's parental instinct.

It is not less true that love for mankind as such, to the extent that it is anywhere realized, is an exercise of parental instinct. We see this clearly in child-welfare movements. The parent mind in us is what yearns over sick babies. This it is that insists, even at great expense to ourselves, upon giving to the next generation, through education, a better and larger life than we have had. It is the same impulse that hastens to the relief of sufferers from famine, flood, and war, and that takes pure joy in seeing others well fed and happy. To this, in the end, must we appeal for the community spirit that puts sanitation, education, civic beauty, and diffused happiness upon the plane of simple humanity, that is above all consid-

[1] *Cf.* Patterson Du Bois, *Beckonings from Little Hands* (1900).

erations of private advantage, either immediate or ultimate. What makes us struggle for democracy, too, is that, putting ourselves imaginatively in the place of the narrowed, thwarted, stunted lives about us, we feel toward them as we would if they were our own children. What we democrats demand, in fact, is that all men everywhere should have opportunity to grow up.

Because all men are potentially parent-minded, the world is capable of being won to democracy. We can make the sacrifices that this will require—sacrifices of our substance, of our labor, and of our aristocratic and plutocratic privileges—for the same reason that we can do it for our natural offspring.

Social education requires that some instincts be suppressed. When the term instinct is used for broad, general qualities of human nature rather than for readiness to act in a specific way in a specific situation, it is possible to claim that no instinct should be suppressed. If, for example, we classify all spontaneous getting under an "acquisitive" instinct, we shall hold that it has some permanent value. But when we come to details we discover that some acquisition is just a grabbing that increases in intensity if another person is seen to get or to be likely to get any part of the desired objects. Grabbing *away from* others goes on, too, until one accumulates more than one can use. In such rivalry and greed one's relation to persons is exactly contrary to parental instinct, which delights in seeing another feed himself. What must be done with rivalry and greed in the interest of society is to suppress them if we can. Similarly, scorn for those who are weak, physically defective, or lacking in good looks, seems to serve no present social ends, but to hinder them only.

Likewise, instinctive mastery and submission seem, though not quite as certainly, to be at least needless, and possibly without exception a hinderance to the growth of society toward democracy. What democracy requires is co-operation. Leadership is of course necessary, but leadership that is itself co-operation, a fulfilling of the will of the led, not mastery of them. Curbing of individual will also is required, but this again is, ideally, not submission to the arbitrary will of another, but one's contribution to a common will from which arbitrariness has been eliminated by making it truly a common will. These remarks apply to sex relations as well as to others. Instinctive mastery by the male, and instinctive submission by the female, are a social evil because of their effect upon the character of both the man and the woman, and because of the support that they lend to social inequalities beyond the conjugal relation. Conjugal affection must be democratized along with the other social relations.

The instincts of hunting, anger, and pugnacity, in many instances, though scarcely in all, have an antisocial tendency. The tormenting of animals, or the killing of them for other purposes than food and protection, the hunting down of men in partisanships, persecutions, and wars, and all the purely destructive forms of anger and pugnacity, are obviously unsocial in fact and in tendency. But most persons suppose that these instincts are sometimes useful socially, not for purposes of destruction, but as constituents of a rationally controlled good will. There can, it seems, be anger and pugnacity toward evil without hating the evil-doer. But how much reflectiveness, how much self-restraint are required to maintain this distinction in practice! We need to be cautious lest the undeniable pleasure of destroying living things that we dislike be indulged under the specious name of "righteous indignation," or "hatred of wrong," or "standing for righteousness." When anger or pugnacity separates me from any human being so that he ceases to have value for me, or so that the value that I theoretically attribute to him does not control my conduct toward him, social ends are not promoted, they are hindered only. If I must fight against something that you fight for, I must herein fight *for you*, for a better and happier you, yes, for a fellowship with you that is yet to be.

The deep depravity of war, just as of enmities between individuals, lies in the implied denial that my enemy is still my brother, and that I am his keeper—all the more his keeper if he has faults that I can help him to overcome. Herein consists the profound difference, the impassable gulf, between war and the exercise of police power. If a policeman discovers me in the act of picking your pocket, he does not dispose of my case by clubbing me. No, he brings me before a court in which, though I have done wrong, I still have rights which society protects, the very society that I have wronged. Here, in the calmness of reason, my relations to the welfare of society are determined, and also, in any enlightened penal system, my relations to my own welfare. What modern penology aims at is not to separate me from my fellows, but by separating me from my evil ways to unite me closer to my fellows. If, now, the policeman undertakes to settle my relations to society with a club, if he assumes that I am nothing as against the offended will of the state, if he is not *my* policeman, acting for me as well as my neighbors, he exemplifies the tooth-and-claw conception that underlies war. War, which endeavors to impose one national will upon another by force, must be supplanted by a system of world-law, world-courts, and a world-police, which will seek the welfare of offender and offended alike, and work always toward the maintenance, and if need be the restoration, of fellowship. This implies educational measures for suppressing our socially destructive instincts, for stopping war at its source in our own minds.[1]

The socially constructive instincts, all of them, require training. Even the best natural impulses, taken by themselves, are uneconomical; they are not sufficiently fine for the work that has to be done. Maternal affection prompts mothers to give to infants coffee and beer as well as milk; and until this

[1] See H. R. Marshall, *War and the Ideal of Peace. A Study of Those Characteristics of Man That Result in War, and of the Means by Which They May Be Controlled.* New York, 1915.

[NOTE.—The above paragraph was written while I still believed that a war between the United States and Germany might be avoided. Before I commit the paragraph to the typesetter I have opportunity to review my words in the light of the actuality of the dreaded conflict. It is clear that the purpose of our war as defined by President Wilson takes the standpoint of what I have called above "the exercise of police power." There is, in fact, a remarkable parallel between my conception of "world-law, world-courts, and world-police," and the requirements of world-decency as he defines them. For he calls upon us to employ force, not to impose our national will upon any nation, but to secure "the rights of nations, great and small, and the privilege of men everywhere to choose their way of life and of obedience." "We have no selfish ends to serve. We desire no conquest, no dominion. We

instinct is trained it reacts in the same way to pure and to im-
pure milk. Thorndike remarks that "the irrational impulse
to get the sick to eat seems to prevail the world over."[1] These
examples would of themselves be convincing. The full proportions of the task of positive social training should, however,
be faced. This can be done by going carefully through our list
of instincts, noting how, from beginning to end, they constitute the basis of possible social conduct, *not at one level only but
at any one of many levels.* This is most often recognized in
respect to sex attraction, which underlies conduct that ranges
all the way from brutality to saintliness. The same sort of
analysis will show that, in the sphere of the gregarious instinct
also we may habituate ourselves to pleasure in one type of
society as against another. We have an instinctive interest in
what other human beings are doing; yes, but we may acquire
a habit of being more interested in important than in unimportant doings. Here is the possibility of growing out of gossip
into conversation! We want to be noticed by others; yes,
but we may learn to take more pleasure in being noticed by one
sort of persons than another. We instinctively like to be
approved, but by training we can make ourselves unresponsive
to praise and blame from certain quarters, and we can concen-
trate our claims to approval upon that in us which we can ourselves approve. We spontaneously admire beauty, but upon
our training it depends whether or not we notice beauty of
spirit. We instinctively go with the crowd, but we can form a
discriminating taste with respect to crowds, so that some of

seek no indemnities for ourselves, no material compensation for the sacrifices
we shall freely make." We are "seeking nothing for ourselves but what we
shall wish to share with all free peoples." We are to work toward "the
ultimate peace of the world." We are to make the world "safe for democracy"
by "setting up amongst the really free and self-governed peoples of the world
such a concert of purpose and of action as will henceforth insure the observance of" . . . "peace and justice in the life of the world as against selfish and
autocratic power." "We are at the beginning of an age in which it will be
insisted that the same standards of conduct and of responsibility for wrong
done shall be observed among nations and their governments that are observed among the individual citizens of civilized states."

The implication of all this is that we have before us the task of establishing
a genuine world-police power.]
[1] P. 193.

them we do not enjoy. In short, there is not a single point at which our instincts are sufficient of themselves to provide for social progress. Blind impulse makes happy hits, of course, as it makes unhappy ones. What we have to do is to raise above chance the proportion of hits and misses. An inevitable part of our ethical calling is to bestow sight upon even the best of our instinctive qualities.

Popular confusion between what is instinctive and what is acquired. How often do we hear it said of one child that he is "naturally" amiable, and of another that he is "naturally" self-willed, the implication of "naturally" being that the quality in question is a matter of original endowment, and therefore unchangeable. No doubt the amiability and the self-will are both natural. But the popular mind does not realize that habit-formation (which is as spontaneous, as "natural" as anything else), intertwining with instinct, fixes some of the early instinctive responses so that they will be repeated thereafter to the exclusion of other responses that are equally possible at the beginning. One's instinctive endowment is not a walled lane that offers no alternatives to one's feet, but an open trail, with many forks and branches, some leading into life's swamps and quagmires, some onto the meadows of conventional goodness, some upward to the bright peaks and the dark valleys of social idealism.

Children's dispositions are complexes of what is native and what is acquired. The acquired part is the habits whereby certain impulses, specialized by experience, are given a permanent and specific direction, while other native impulses, unused or repressed, remain in the background, or decrease toward complete atrophy. Favorable or unfavorable nervous conditions (whether they are determined by health and disease, or by such hygienic matters as proper and improper feeding) are one fundamental factor. When nerves are irritated, and vitality is depressed, the range of possible happiness is limited, and the particular narrow range of satisfactions tends to become permanent in its narrowness. If peevishness, obstinacy, or screaming is what brings the child his satisfactions, of course it becomes a habit. It is then called the child's disposition, and is attributed to the stepmotherliness of nature! On the other hand, granted favorable nervous conditions, *plus* constant and abundant opportunity for mutual pleasures (the child with his parents and with other children), *plus* steady, unrelaxing arrangements whereby individualistic reactions are prevented from bringing pleasure—granted these things, any child will acquire an amiable disposition. Unthinking persons will attribute it to some mystery of original nature, whereas, as settled disposition it is a result of habit formation, a product of social training, whether intended or unintended.

The superinstinctive factors of our social nature. The inventory of man's original social capacities includes, as was noted a little way back, certain general tendencies toward the organization of a self, and toward the increasing integration of men in social institutions. The special instinct-factors that have just occupied our attention are not a mere collection of zoological specimens—odd forms, odd voices, odd ways—each living its own life without regard to others. Our instincts are more like the multiplicity of a city.

When we look from the upper stories of a tall office-building far down into streets thronged with incessantly moving men, our first impression is likely to be that of the utter irrationality of what we behold. It seems to be a meaningless coming and going, like dust particles carried in air currents hither and thither. Yet what we see is not a chaos of impulsive acts, but acts organized into great systems—systems for feeding and clothing the people, for teaching the children, for distributing news, for healing the sick, for protecting the public health, for restraining those who lack self-restraint. Moreover, if we look into each of these moving particles of humanity, we find its own diverse elements at least partly organized, each man being an individual self, not walking at random, but going somewhither that *he* desires and approves. There is not a man in the throng who has not to some extent taken notice of his instinctive impulses; there is not a man who is not holding some of these impulses in leash.

To become individual selves is a part of our original nature. It is a part of our original nature to form societies not merely on the basis of instincts that flow in the same direction but also on the basis of recognized selfhood. Now, these two, the formation of a definite self and the formation of societies, are not in reality separate processes, nor are the results separate; rather, we have here two phases of a single process, two phases of a single achievement. For the achievement of a self is possible only in and through recognition of other selves, and what is distinctively human in society is precisely the organization of regard for individual selves as finalities.

Movement, effort toward this achievement, is natural to man—as natural as fleeing from a lion or pursuing a deer. Here is something in human nature that is superinstinctive, something that reflects upon, regulates, and uses instinct, and this something is in the profoundest possible sense both individual and social.[1]

The notion that human nature does not change. What has now been said as to the variability of habit within the scope of the instincts, and with respect to the naturalness of the correlative growth of self and society, has an important bearing upon that ogre's castle of social pessimism: "Your ideals won't work as long as human nature remains what it is." For now we can answer: "What do you mean by human nature?" The problem is by no means ended when we have recognized the fact that the instincts are hereditary, permanent, and fundamental to character. We must bear in mind, in addition, *first*, that no instinct is strictly univocal, but that every one has indefinitely many possible modes of expression that vary through a large scale; *second*, that habit forming is also human nature, and that it makes possible the fixing in human life, in an individual and through the generations by training, of either better or worse instinctive ways; and, *third*, that to become a self-criticising self, and to form self-criticising societies, are also a

---

[1] I content myself with this brief statement here because I touch upon it in other places in the present work, and because I have discussed it in my *Psychology of Religion* (see Index under "Social Aspects of Religion," and chap. XIV).

part of human nature, so that nature herself provides for taking the side of social aspiration as against what is unsocial in our instincts. "As long as human nature remains what it is," therefore, we may expect indefinite transformation of social life toward the highest ideals that we can conceive. The individual who in full health and vigor lies down under the weight of ancient wrong, saying that it is just human nature, does thereby make himself a critic of that nature, does thereby justify the opinion that he could hate ancient wrong a little harder, and that he could summon his neighbors not to surrender but to keep up the fight.

What if, moreover, self-conscious contemplation of our desires should give rise to new desires? How often, as a matter of fact, something like this certainly does occur. When I was a boy I thought it would be sport to shoot a meadow-lark—I thought so until a dead lark lay in my hands. I can see even now how its head hung limp when I lifted the beautiful body. At that instant one desire died and another was born. I saw myself having my desire, but defeated just because I had succeeded. I advanced to a new point of view, a new standard of values, a new arrangement of instinctive likes and dislikes. It makes little difference whether or not the new attitude can be classed under one of the instincts, for I *came to myself*, to a new self, to an unprecedented desire.

Society attains new mass desires in similar ways. When, rising above crowd action, and holding up our social habits to relentless scrutiny, we say: "This is our work, the result of what our community has done or neglected to do. Is this what we desire?" then we cringe before our old community self, or, as the case may be, we are inspired to excel ourselves. In increasing instances a community survey awakens community self-consciousness, and then and there men begin to support one another in having desires that they simply did not have before.

Social reconstruction is provided for in the nature of man. This is the reason why the likes and dislikes of men change so markedly between savagery and civilization. We simply could not enjoy some of the things that brought intense satisfaction to our early ancestors unless in some way we could be gradually trained backward. We are sunk enough, God knows, yet wants are better than they were. By giving attention to what we really want, and by training the impulses that we really prefer, we shall develop still other wants and the ways of satisfying them.[1]

[1] In chap. XIII of my *Psychology of Religion*, I have discussed this question at greater length.

CHAPTER XI

CHILDREN'S FAITH IN GOD

Children's notions of God are acquired as other notions are. To the question, How do little children get their notions of God? there is a simple, obvious answer: By instruction and hearsay, just as ideas of angels, fairies, hobgoblins, Santa Claus, and of historical personages are acquired. This "acquiring" of an idea includes, of course, a complex reaction. Language has no power to transfer a thought from one mind to another, but only to stimulate a mind to think. The meaning of the term God, and of any affirmation about him, has to be construed by imaginative combination of thought materials derived from the child's previous experiences. Nor does the idea, once started, continue "in one stay," but items from the child's growing experience are read into it and out of it.

The idea of God varies, therefore, from child to child, and from day to day, according to instruction or hearsay, the meanings that words (such as father) have already acquired, the characteristic experiences of the child (especially his experience of persons), and his usual methods of association and of inference. A boy not yet four years old who had had difficulty with "bad boys" in his back yard arranged there a house for God, saying: "He'll keep the bad boys out; nobody else can." This "house of God" was merely a large doll-house with some additions of the boy's own devising. When he was four years and eight months old he spontaneously made a drawing, in which God and Santa Claus, a Christmas tree, flags, home, and toys, which include a locomotive engine on a railroad-track, all figure. It is evident that this child, putting his own construction upon the words of others, had built up a notion of God far different from what his elders intended. On the other hand, the direct influence of instruction seems to appear in his argument with a playmate who had asserted that "If you do anything in a dark room God can't see it." "Yes, he can!" was the reply, "He can see you even in a dark room. He looks down through the stars, and I'm not going to do anything to get caught!"

Another boy of about the same age gave the following objective evidence of the Christmas story that he had recently heard. Of his own motion he devised for the entertainment of his parents and some guests a dramatization of the Star in the East. First, extinguishing other lights, he lighted a candle, which was to represent the sun. Then he placed an apple for the moon, and extinguished the candle in order to show that night had come. Finally, announcing that he was God, and was going to bring in the Star of Bethlehem, he marched into the room, bearing some sticks crudely fastened together with the apparent purpose of representing the conventional picture of a star's rays.

As an illustration of how the child's own social experience is read into his thought of God, the following case is instructive. "Mamma," said a boy a little older than those just mentioned, "do you know what I'm going to do the first thing when I get to heaven? I'm going to run up to the Heavenly Father, and give him a kiss!" Obviously this feeling-reaction to the idea of a Heavenly Father is due in part to experience in a human family.

Suggestion and imitation in childhood religion. Thus, both the fact that children have ideas of God, and the variations of these ideas from our adult notions are easily accounted for. That children really believe in God thus conceived is also obvious enough. They believe what they are told, and in this respect no difference is discernible between belief in God, in the Sand Man, or in the Black Man. The influence of mere suggestion upon children's beliefs is possibly more extensive and more prolonged than we ordinarily suppose. On a certain occasion, having told to a group of children a story of how I had seen a chipmunk store food, which included a muscat grape, upon the branches of a fir-tree, I remarked: "So there was a green grape growing upon an evergreen tree!" One of my listeners, a girl of about eight years, came to me some days afterward to inquire whether the grape really did grow upon that tree!

Just as children readily accept our instruction, so they willingly imitate our religious acts. The evening prayer, grace before meat, participation in public worship—these, under favorable conditions, are well liked; they require no compulsion. But they cannot, without further evidence, be regarded as clear signs of piety. Nevertheless, even such imitative acts may have immediate social value, and ultimate religious value. In a certain family that was accustomed to have brief devotions at the breakfast-table there was a girl who was still too young to commit the Lord's Prayer to memory. One morning, just after she had triumphantly learned to count up to eight, she joined her voice with the others when the Lord's Prayer was repeated by saying loudly: "One, two, three, four, five, six, seven, eight. . . . One, two, three, four, five, six, seven, eight!" I would hesitate to deny that even this crude participation in social worship contributed to religious growth. For the social situation was a religious one, and the girl's reaction, bare though it was of definite religious ideas, enriched her membership in the group, and brought her mind nearer to the meaning of the function then being performed.

These facts—the credulity of children's beliefs, the desultory associations that cluster therein, and the imitative origin of children's religious acts—go far toward accounting for the ambiguous or even negative attitude that largely prevails among adults with respect to the religious life of children. Besides, we are just now reacting against two types of religious work with them, the formal or catechetical type, and the revival or conversion-experience type. If these are the only practicable ways of promoting spiritual life in children, then indeed we must look for skepticism as to genuine spiritual life much before adolescence. It is not enough to show that children accept the idea of God, join in religious practices, and make an emotional response to revivalistic suggestion. The deeper question concerns a life of faith properly so called. This implies not merely belief and imitation, but also emotional satisfaction, and motivation of conduct without feverish excesses—in short, a personal realization or experience in a natural life. Does this exist in the small child?

Is there a special religious instinct? If children—adults, too, for that matter—are to have vital religious experience as distinguished from doctrinal assent, imitation, and emotional forcing, it must doubtless have a basis in instinct. Religious educators therefore have compelling reason to inquire whether there is a specifically religious instinct, that is, a universal inborn readiness to respond in some specific religious manner to particular, definable situations. If there is, then the work of religious education consists fundamentally in creating just these situations and placing children in them. On the other hand, if there is no specific religious instinct, but if religious response consists rather in a particular direction and organization of the various instinctive capacities for social living, then religious education does not have to create situations or invent special stimuli, but to utilize in appropriate ways the everyday human relations of the child. The alternatives may be roughly suggested by asking whether religious experience is *apart from*, or *a part of* our experience of one another.[1]

It is not possible in this place to go farther toward answering this question than merely to recite conclusions from the general psychology of religion. Of the naturalness of religion there is of course no question. It is not an invention; it is not an imposition of some upon others; its early appearance in the race, its universality, its persistence, and the way in which it is interfused with all sorts of human affairs, are conclusive on this point. This interfusion gives us, in fact, a clew to the sense in which religion is natural. It appears historically as a living out, intensely and insistently, of the interests that seem important, particularly the interests that gather about the life

---

[1] If my purpose were not merely to identify the thing, but also to define it with philosophical precision, I should of course suggest that our religious experience may possibly be, not a part of our experience of one another, but a whole, of which our human fellowships are parts or phases.

of men in societies, and as a tendency to organize and unify these interests. It is not an aside, or a luxury, or any other sort of addition to the common life, but just life most determined to fulfil itself to the utmost. There is here no trace of an instinct that functions by itself, but only of a tendency within the instincts taken as a whole.[1]

This general conclusion can be made more specific by reverting to the analysis of man's social nature in the last chapter. What is most characteristic of the religious consciousness is closely related, on the one hand, to the general tendency to become personal selves in a society of such selves, and on the other hand to the parental instinct, which plays such a distinctive part in individuating us and socializing us. Faith in God has impulsive roots in desires for a sufficient and certain supply of the things that men want, in the instinct that causes a man to identify his own wants and welfare with those of another, and in the human way of taking our ultimate values as our ultimate reals. What is most significant for our present discussion is that gods have been to their worshippers not only a security for goods of all kinds, but particularly. a security for the goods that are socially sought and enjoyed, and that gods have been likewise a spontaneous and last term in fellowship or social unity. In the divine the social principle itself achieves such objectivity and finality as the existing level of social life can appreciate. The tribal god, the national god, and the Universal Father, all have this relation to our fundamental social impulses.

The child's own parental instinct furnishes a natural basis for early appreciation of divine fatherhood. On the surface of the matter it is plain that whatever capacity a child has for responding to the Christian evangel of the fatherhood of God is at least parallel to filial attitudes toward one's earthly parents. We are now ready, in view of the last section, to say that it is not parallel, but identical. Moreover, in view of our analysis of filial affection in the last chapter, it now appears that children can make a vital response to the Christian God

[1] Readers who desire to pursue these considerations further will find them fully developed in my *Psychology of Religion*, especially chaps. IV and XIX.

because they themselves possess parental instinct. The yearning of the father toward the child, and the child's appreciation of this yearning are qualitatively the same. It is in the impulse to father somebody that the child's Christian experience begins. We love God only when we take his point of view, and we can take his point of view only through some experience of our own in which we actually exercise godlike interest in another.

In order to teach children of kindergarten age the love and care of the Heavenly Father, the Sunday-school teacher of to-day is likely to use as a part of her material the care of father-bird and mother-bird for their offspring. How does bird lore lead toward religion? Does the mind of such small children construe divine fatherhood analytically, by means of an analogy with feathered parenthood? Or, does an induction from different instances of parental care lead the heart up to universal fatherhood? Far different from either of these is the emotional logic of the kindergarten age. What happens is that the child instinctively assumes a parental attitude toward the helpless birdlings that have been brought to his attention, and thereby, nascently entering into the fatherhood purpose, he grasps the meaning of divine love.

It is easy, and educationally most appropriate, to awaken in small children a sentiment of gratitude to the Heavenly Father. What, then, is gratitude? Since it is an attitude that one can take toward another who is older, stronger, and not suffering, it appears at first sight to have no connection with the instinct that leads a child to fondle dolls and pet animals and smaller children. But A. F. Shand has shown that gratitude involves some realization of what the kindness of a benefactor has cost him, together with desire to requite this cost.[1] Gratitude is not mere jubilation; it contains also a tender element. This tenderness, as our discussion has shown, and as McDougall holds,[2] originates in parental instinct. McDougall is of the opinion that moral indignation originates at the same point.

[1] Chap. XVI of G. F. Stout, *Groundwork of Psychology* (New York, 1903).
[2] W. McDougall, *Social Psychology* (Boston, 1909), pp. 66–81.

No doubt it will seem odd to trace pity, gratitude, indignation, longing for justice and equality, and a child's fondness for dolls. and pets to one and the same source, even that in us that makes us see worlds in the smile of our own offspring. But thither the facts lead. They are of immense consequence for all moral and religious education. For in them we find not only evidence of capacity for moral and religious life in early childhood, but also the particular kinds of seed for which the young mind is ready.

Other instincts, of course, have a part. Fears drive the child to sheltering arms. Curiosity blends with the rest. G. E. Dawson infers from children's questions that the "instinct for causality" is a principal factor in child-religion,[1] and Earl Barnes looks upon the insistent who's and why's of the young mind as signs of a theological interest.[2] This interpretation seems, however, to be made under the influence of the outworn dogmatism that confuses religion with doctrine or philosophy. Whenever the causal interest is central in the child mind, the appropriate category is science rather than religion. This is the parent's opportunity to start the young intellect upon a correctly scientific analysis of the world. Religion gains nothing, but loses much, through the well-intentioned answer, "God did it," to questions that we adults answer to ourselves in terms of science.[3]

It has been said that children must first think of nature after the fashion of mythology. Dawson even makes animism an instinct of childhood.[4] If this be so, the precept, "Never

[1] The Child and His Religion (Chicago, 1909), p. 38.
[2] Studies in Education, II, 1902, p. 287.
[3] To Professor Dawson's precious collection of children's questions, I should like to add this one from a boy of about five: "Mother, who was my mamma before you were?" Lack of space prevents me from discussing the incautious use of the term "instinct" in Dawson's book, as "instinct for causality" and "instinct of immortality." The naturalness of child religion, moreover, seems to mean for him that religion is preformed, even to specific beliefs, whereas the growth of mind is not primarily from one set of definite ideas to another but from the indefinite toward the definite. On this point, see Irving King, The Psychology of Child Development (Chicago, 1903), p. 243. An analysis of Dawson's cases will show that, though the children in question received little or no formal religious instruction, they were nevertheless under the influence of the religious ideas of their elders.
[4] Op. cit., pp. 32 ff.

teach as true anything that must afterward be unlearned,"
is unwise, perhaps impossible of application. But I find no
adequate evidence that small children are incapable of employing the causal category in the same manner as adults. Least
of all do the facts indicate that there is a definite stage of
spontaneous animistic belief in Tylor's sense of animism.
Rather, we find a continuous mental movement from indefinite
toward definite ideas, and from emotional thinking toward
abstraction and objectivity. Not, then, from experience of
nature, mythologically conceived, but from the experience of a
present social reality in the family, should we expect the Christian idea of God to grow.

A child can, to use Bushnell's words, "grow up a Christian, and never know himself as being otherwise." Whatever be the case with other religions, the Christian religion,
which finds the whole meaning and destiny of man in divine
fatherhood and human brotherhood, is the flowering of a particular instinct that is active from infancy onward. To Ter-
tullian's argument that the soul is naturally Christian we may
now add that the child is naturally Christian. To the Christian idea of the All-Father the response (unless the child has
already been wounded and scarred by the unparental conduct
of others) is positive, free, and vital. Children love and trust
him; they struggle to obey him by kindly conduct; they desire
to help him in his work; they are grateful for his gifts. This
is Christian experience.

It is a tender thing, easily distorted, easily blighted. It
must have human fellowship in order to flourish. Only in and
through some human godlikeness that sustains what is parental
in us does any of us know the Father. Here is the deep meaning,
for childhood as well as for maturity, of the surpassing love
wherewith Jesus faced an unloving world. The spirit, the acts,
many of the words of Jesus appeal to little ones, to what is
elemental in them. Just as the Jewish children who heard him
say: "Let them come to me, for the kingdom of heaven belongs
to such as they are," must have clung to him and nestled in
his arms, so the children of to-day, imaginatively realizing him,

make him their actual leader, their helper, who saves them from their own unsocial impulses. The church, as far as in·its relations to children it is really the church of Christ, makes the same appeal to children and receives the same kind of response. The church belongs to children just as their fathers and mothers belong to them; and children belong to the church just as they belong to families. That is, ideally they belong to the church, from the standpoint of Jesus they belong to it, from the standpoint of their own social capacities they belong to it. But these capacities are as sensitive as they are beautiful; and there are contrary capacities, too; and habit-forming begins at birth. In order that a child may grow up a Christian and never know himself as being otherwise he must have co-operation from those who have the spirit of Christ. That is, the child must have social education upon the Christian plane.

CHAPTER XII

THE RELIGIOUS LIMITATIONS OF CHILDREN

The respective educational consequences of a theory of moral continuity in child growth and a theory of moral discontinuity. The view of child nature that has now been sketched is different from certain opinions that are widely held at the present moment. The last two chapters have shown that, though antisocial instincts are active in the early years, socially constructive ones also are present, and that even the particular instinct out of which spring the finest and most difficult things in social progress begins its functions in infancy. Here we found natural capacity for entering into the great and fundamental motives of the Christian religion, fatherhood and brotherhood, and therefore a natural basis for Christian education.

If this view is well founded, there is no necessary break, in moral quality, between the life of an adult Christian and that of a child who receives Christian nurture. The necessary difference between them concerns their respective range of experience, firmness of habit, and extent of foresight. An adult who is already well trained knows better *how* to be kind to a dog, a baby, a tuberculous family, a foreigner, a laboring man, a capitalist, a wife. With this wider knowledge of human relations there goes, of course, the possibility of profounder emotional appreciation of the character of God. Moreover, the well-trained adult Christian has so many times resisted his unsocial instincts, and indulged his social ones, and he has so often experienced the joy of Christian fellowship, that habit forming has borne its fruit in the weakened power of some temptations, the actual extinction of others, and relative ease in carrying high impulses into effect. This difference between childhood and maturity is great, but it is not a moral break. To attain Christian maturity, a child needs only to go on exercising more and more broadly, steadily, and intelligently certain impulses of childhood itself.[1]

But some voices are saying that childhood is essentially egoistic, and that genuine unselfishness must wait for adolescence. If this be true, we must postpone religious education in any vital sense until adolescence, while through childhood we allow motives to grow that must later be counteracted. This would be a saltatory education—education by a leap into society as contrasted with continuous growth within society as a member of it. The widest-spread doctrine of this type is the recapitulation theory that is taught by G. Stanley Hall and his pupils. Another instance, which it will be convenient to discuss first, is Ames's chapter on " Religion and Childhood."[2]

Taking religion to be identical with "the fullest and most intense social consciousness,"[3] which is about equivalent to the consciousness of the socially maturest persons, Ames finds children profoundly deficient in capacity for religion. He asserts: (1) That up to two and a half or three years human beings are non-religious, non-moral, and non-personal;[4] (2) That it is impossible for a child under the age of nine to pass in any considerable degree beyond the non-religious and non-moral attitude;[5] (3) That the child has no "religious nature";[6] (4) That "The social feeling of adolescence is original, inner, and urgent,"[7] and that in adolescence "Religion arises naturally, being an inherent and intimate phase of the social

[1] In some of my earlier writings I emphasized the notion that a child is not a diminutive adult, but something qualitatively as well as quantitatively different. Doctrinal systems, I said, even though abbreviated and expressed in words of one syllable, do not fit. A small child's spontaneous interest does not go out to the Trinity, but to dolls, dogs, hobby-horses, or a game of tag. Moreover, some human relations, as that of conjugal affection, one does not appreciate until the sexual instinct ripens. Finally, adult standards of right and wrong do not fit children, and attempts to make them fit do injustice by reason of the gap between rewards and punishments and anything that the child can understand. In this sense I still maintain that a child is not a diminutive adult, but qualitatively different. But this does not imply the kind of break in instinctive social capacities, and in social education, that is in question in the above paragraph.

[2] E. S. Ames, *Psychology of Religious Experience* (Boston, 1910), chap. XI.
[3] P. 197.   [4] Pp. 198, 209.   [5] P. 209.   [6] P. 209.   [7] P. 222.

consciousness."[1] "For the individual, religion originates in youth."[2]

If all this be true, man has a religious nature, original, inner, and urgent, which clearly makes its appearance with adolescence. It is denied of young children because of their supposed lack of capacity for social response.[3] If, now, we should discover that childhood is not set off from adolescence by any such social incompetence, it would follow that children also, in their measure, are religious by original nature. In a subsequent section I shall endeavor to show that the instinct of sex, which is the distinctive basis of adolescent phenomena, is not equal to the social task, which is nothing less than the social transformation of the mind, that Ames and others lay upon it. Meantime I would set over against the doctrine of the social incapacity of childhood the evidence, already adduced, of the early appearance of parental instinct.

The recapitulation theory is a special and recent form of an idea, long held, that there is some sort of parallel between child life and the "childhood of the race." That there is a considerable degree of similarity between them is clear. Both the race and the individual show a movement of mind from immediate ends toward remote ones; from immediate data of sense toward thought structures of greater and greater complexity; from the impulsiveness of instinct and of crowd action toward self-control and social deliberation; from a narrower to a broader range of social regard. A consequence for education is that young children take the freshest interest in, and are best trained by, objects and processes that correspond in simplicity and in sensuous appeal to the objects and processes with which early man occupied himself, and that as children grow older their ability to be interested in the complexities of civilization grows also. A child of six takes voraciously to Bopp's descriptions of primitive man's struggles with dangerous beasts; how old must one be, the teacher has to ask, before the struggles of the Roundheads with the Cavaliers arrest and hold attention?

[1] P. 249.   [2] P. 214.
[3] Ames's overcaution, not to seem to attribute a religious "instinct" to primitive men, suggests the possibility that I have taken too literally his statements concerning adolescence. See pp. 49, 50.

The special form that the recapitulation theory gives to this old idea is as follows: (1) The theory asserts that the growth of the individual mind shows a succession of definite forms that correspond in motive, content, and order of emergence to definite stages in racial evolution; (2) That this succession in the individual is not determined by anything in his environment, such as his associations, but is predetermined as a set of successively ripening instincts; (3) That the proper mental and moral food for each period of child growth is to be gathered from the level of the instinct then in action, not from later and higher levels of culture.[1]

The popular, and here and there the literary, interpretation of recapitulation runs to the effect that children, or at least boys, are different from adults in the same way that savagery is different from civilization, savagery being interpreted in terms of its coarseness and of its relative disregard for the pains and the pleasures of men and of animals.

Before examining the grounds for this theory, let us note its educational implications. At each period of growth, says the theory, feed the particular instinct that is then dominant. The child's goodness at the time, and his progress toward mature goodness, are to be measured by the fulness with which he enters into the spirit, the aims, and the characteristic activities of the lower order of society that his then dominant instinct reflects. That is—if we press the point to the utmost—we are to educate children for family, church, and state, not by enlarging as much as we can children's present participation in them, but by withholding and postponing common life on these levels. Social segregation of children with children, and of adults with adults, would then be the preliminary condition of educational efficiency. If we ask how, then, children are ever to acquire an interest in the higher social organizations and standards, and how adjustment to these standards is to be effected, the answer is that adolescence brings a spontaneous impulse to something like a conversion from egoism to altruism. This leap into the new life will take place through the innate,

[1] References to sources are postponed to the Classified Bibliography.

internal forces of the individual, it is assumed, if only appropriate material for these forces to act upon is present.

If nature has provided for social continuity in the growth of a child, then the process of social education can be sketched as follows, with the contrasting consequences of the recapitulation theory stated point by point.

(1) *Theory of continuity:* Social education first sees to it that the child is provided with wealth of human association, association with adults as well as with children. To this kind of experience various instinctive responses are made by the child, one or more of them social in a finally valid sense, that is, in the same sense in which the best conduct of adults is social. The teacher picks out these socially valid responses, and endeavors to give them such a distinctive place in the child's experience (by means of satisfactions associated with them) that they will have a permanent influence upon his character.

Theory of recapitulation: Provide the child with plenty of things, animal pets, and other children; this is the chief and essential educational service that adults can render at the beginning.

(2) *Theory of continuity:* The teacher now has the task of promoting repetition of these particularly wholesome responses, and of preventing repetition of the contrary ones. Therefore conditions are so arranged that discomfort accompanies the latter, and satisfaction the former, especially shared satisfactions, and these conditions are steadily repeated as often as the situations that tend to call out the responses recur. The result is the formation of certain social habits, and suppression of unsocial instincts by lack of exercise.

Theory of recapitulation: The instincts are given right of way, with no such careful selection by the teacher. For it is held that the exercise of an instinct on its own plane makes it not more attractive, but less so, at the next stage of growth. Let the teacher provide plenty of material for the expression of the instincts that are dominant.

(3) *Theory of continuity:* As the child's social contacts widen, his social responses become more and more complicated, and his capacity for continuity in social relations increases. The teacher carries into each fresh situation the same principle of selection and of habit forming as before, but attempts to organize the whole-

some responses in the form of more and more systematic and broad co-operation—co-operation of children with children, and of children with adults. Therefore the policy of the teacher is to admit the children to a part in adult social enterprises.

Theory of recapitulation: Organizations of children with children on their own plane are sufficient for social education. Let children settle their social relations to one another by the clash of opposing instincts.

(4) *Theory of continuity:* Since the problem of society is to produce free individuality rather than mechanized conduct, and also to improve society itself rather than repeat its own performances, the teacher does not stop with a set of habits that conform to a set of ethical rules, but goes on to awaken reflective intelligence with respect to what one is doing, why it should or should not be done, and how it can be improved, that is, made mutually more satisfactory. Thus, to instinct and habit, analytical reason is added, and genuinely voluntary purposes are formed. Material for this analysis, which proceeds by comparison, is drawn not only from child life and from cruder stages of adult society, but also from the best that is in contemporary social institutions. Thus, intellectually as well as affectively (in respect to satisfactions and dissatisfactions) the child is kept in growing fellowship with his elders.

Theory of recapitulation: The child's social insight will grow most certainly and normally if he is kept in rich intellectual fellowship with culture epochs of a lower order until the middle or later years of adolescence bring him face to face with the society that he is about to enter as a full member.

(5) *Theory of continuity:* The analysis of situations and of responses is so guided that it not only transforms instinct acts already habitual with the pupil into voluntary purposes, but also leads the pupil to ask what he himself really wants, and so to imagine and desire ideal good. An ideal is a more distant goal by reference to which we judge our particular purposes, and correct them. The process of idealizing, when it is not arrested in mere sentimentality, goes on to the identification of one's own weal and woe with the fate of the ideal, and thus makes the purpose of progress a constituent or modifier of all other purposes. Society thus trains her pupils to re-create their educator.

Theory of recapitulation: The upspringing of moral self-consciousness will be a part of the broad emotional agitation that ushers in the maturity of the sexual instinct. Youth will dream dreams, and see visions, and acquire reforming fervor as a phase of instinctive adolescent longing.

The contrast between these two conceptions of the attainment of moral self-consciousness is not slight. One of them makes it an achievement, the other makes it an eruption of volcanic fire; one makes it a discriminating attitude that accompanies analysis, the other makes it an emotional unrest that has yet to become acquainted with its appropriate objects; one puts at its disposal, in the whole gradual process of its upspringing, the moral experience of the race, the other lets the individual meet himself in the isolation in which fears, and conceits, and hasty choices are born.

This is the logic of the contrasting theories. To what extent the practice of teachers follows the logic of either theory is another matter. Let there be no misunderstanding as to the purpose of this analysis; it aims merely to make the elements of the problem stand out unmistakably. Another possible misunderstanding may grow out of the fact that the analysis is presented in the form of a numerical series. These five points in the theory of continuity do not represent so many successive steps, to be taken at successive periods of the child's growth, but five aspects of the sort of stimulus that society would continuously provide under the supposition that the social growth of the child can naturally be continuous rather than broken. The recapitulation theory implies that at each stage of growth the child leaves behind the self-and-society that was his at the preceding stage. But the theory of continuity, holding that the social growth of mind consists in defining what was at the outset relatively indefinite, in stabilizing what was relatively unstable, in differentiating what was relatively simple, and in bringing impulse under the control of permanent choices, implies that the child carries his self-and-society along through the years, enriching it as he goes.

The positive service that the theory of recapitulation has rendered to social education. There is no mistaking the fact that, coincident with, and under stimulus from, the spreading doctrine of recapitulation a great awakening began with respect to methods in the moral training of boys, and to a slight extent of girls. In the boys' departments of Young Men's Christian Associations, in Sunday-school classes and clubs, in the general boys' club movement, and in camps and schools for boys, we witness something that has not only the zest of newness, but also the zest of an obvious reality, or correspondence with life itself. I shall raise a question by and by as to the validity of some of the tendencies that have appeared, but without doubting that the new training is better than the old in point of freedom and spontaneity, in point of initiative and constructiveness, in the number of its contacts with nature, in its care for physical well being and for play, and in point of co-operation and of training therein.

Moral training of the individual through present group life on the natural level of the pupil—this is now axiomatic among educators of boys. It has become axiomatic with the practical workers largely because, under the influence of the glittering recapitulation theory, they undertook, as perhaps no teachers had ever undertaken before, to get the pupil's point of view, see through his eyes, feel with him, act with him. There was nothing new, to be sure, in the doctrine that the teacher must bend himself to the pupil's natural interests. But here was proclamation of a supposed law of the child's successive interests, a law that implied that children's social interests are even, for the time, opposed to those that are habitual with the teacher. Here was a challenge to the teacher to stretch his imagination and his sympathies as nothing in the general doctrine of interest and apperception had heretofore required him to do. Moreover, the study of boys' gangs as an instance of the supposed recapitulation results in an attempt to use the gang type of sociality as an educational agency. In order to use it, the leader had to become a member of it, and be obedient to laws not of his own devising.

This is too brief a statement to represent all the wide-spread effort to enter actively and sincerely into the realities of children's social motives, but it is sufficient to indicate ways in which the recapitulation theory has had an unquestionably vitalizing effect upon moral training. We need not stint our recognition of this effect if we go on to inquire whether we have reached the end of the matter. Is it not possible that if we rigorously apply the recapitulation theory we shall fix children in immature social motives? Granted that fellowship is the basis of social education, does it follow that fellowship is possible only on the basis of children's crude instinctive social interactions, and not also on the basis of adult enterprises? The teacher must reach down, no doubt; is it certain that children should not be expected to reach up?

Does the social life of children instinctively recapitulate the social evolution of the race? The only sense in which an answer can here be attempted is that of an enumeration of points involved, with some indication of sources in which the positions here taken are discussed at greater length.

(1) The theory took its start from supposed traces of bodily recapitulation in the embryo. But "the view . . . that embryonic development is essentially a recapitulation of ancestral history must be given up."[1]

(2) With reference to the brain in particular it does not hold. "Man's brain in general follows in its growth a course enormously unlike that by which it developed in the race."[2]

(3) Where comparison of the two mental series, racial and mental, can safely be made, "what little is known is rather decidedly against any close parallelism of the two."[3]

(4) The sex instinct, which presents in its late ripening the supreme case of a social acceleration of the individual that is both marked and fairly universal, ripens early in the race, but late in the individual.

(5) Further—and this has peculiar weight against those who have relied upon adolescence for evidence of recapitulation— whereas in the race the sex instinct does not appear until it is physi-

[1] Adam Sedgwick, "Embryology," in *Encyclopædia Britannica*, 11th ed.
[2] Thorndike, *op. cit.*, p. 255.
[3] *Ibid.*, p. 256. Thorndike's whole chapter should be read. An extended analysis of both the biological and the psychological evidence will be found in Davidson, P. E., *The Recapitulation Theory and Human Infancy* (New York, 1914).

ologically employed, in the individual it appears, and begins to influence social groupings, long before reproduction is possible.

(6) Parental instinct, as we have seen at length, does not coincide, in its appearance and growth, with procreation or with capacity therefor. Here again an instinct that has tremendous social significance appears earlier in the individual series than in the racial series.

(7) If any one should hold that, even though other evidence for recapitulation be leaky, common observation of boys shows them to be little savages anyhow, whereas in adolescence they attain to something like civilization, the following answer could be made: "The" boy, who figures so largely as the living demonstration to the popular mind, is a socially neglected boy. He is the boy on the street; or the boy in a boys' school, removed from normal family relationships; or the boy who goes to extremes because he has been misunderstood and mishandled; or the boy who has simply lacked sufficient fellowship with older persons to show what he is socially capable of. Social capacities do not sprout in a vacuum, much less under thumb-screws. Nor does a child's possible social reach appear until he has something to reach toward. We need sorely to realize that *what* to reach toward can be revealed to a boy only through acquaintance with those who are further advanced. A boy who lives in a good house surrounded by wholesome things, the roof of which covers also refined and affectionate parents, may nevertheless be socially neglected, that is, lack opportunity to take the part that he is capable of taking in the doings of his elders. Over against the results of all these kinds of neglect stands a multitude of boys who have grown up in co-operative fellowship with adults, and as a consequence have conducted themselves in such a civilized way that they have not attracted attention to themselves. In short, the argument from current observation unintentionally picks its cases, and then attributes to original nature social limitations that arise from deficiencies in boys' social opportunities.

(8) The evidence from current observation that is adduced in support of the theory of recapitulation is derived almost exclusively from boy life, scarcely at all from girl life. Why? In part, we need not doubt, because girls, being kept in closer contact with adult life in the home, and having more opportunity to co-operate with a parent in important duties, develop earlier the social capacities that are common to boys and girls.

The social significance of adolescence. That adolescence brings changes in the child's social capacities and spontaneous interests, and that these changes are of momentous consequence for social education, no one will question. But that undue reliance has been placed upon the socializing influence of the instinct that now ripens may be asserted without hesitation. Adolescence offers fresh, unique *opportunity* for social education; but instinct does not do the work of educating. The opportunity is unique because: (1) There is instinctive effort to please persons of the opposite sex. This regard for others *may* be extended beyond the courtship process.[1] (2) The fact of loosing oneself from dependence upon parents to begin independent life is of itself an assertion of individuality; it *may* become an incentive to reflective weighing of life's ethical alternatives; it *may* be the occasion of great choices. (3) The general state of restlessness, excitement, and general emotional susceptibility (as for beauty in nature and in art) makes it comparatively easy to acquire new interests and enthusiasms, which *may* be highly idealistic and social. Adolescence tends to make the human soil mellow, but mellowness of soil does not determine whether the harvest shall be wheat or tares. (4) More or less parental tenderness, obviously instinctive, mixes with sexual instinct in the attitudes of lovers toward each other. On this compound instinctive basis family life on the highest ethical plane *may* be built, and this life *may* radiate into community organization and into world society.

What an opportunity is this for social education! But the same thing that makes it an opportunity for education makes it also an open road to evil. The period of adolescence, and the magnetism of its characteristic instinct, fasten upon the individual the worst faults that the race has developed. That criminality here gets its chief entrance into the mind is a serious enough fact, but it is not the most serious one. The profoundest and the most prolific of all evils in the world is the selfish use of the sex instinct.

[1] Under the term "courtship process" I include not only the consciously intended preliminaries to marriage, but also the preceding years of taking an interest in, and making oneself interesting to, persons of the opposite sex.

There is no need to dwell upon the phases of this evil that are prominent in the public mind. There are in addition momentous phases of it that the public thinks nothing about. Even aside from all question of social vice, social idealisms that sprout in childhood and blossom in youth are largely shrivelled by conjugal experience following an undisciplined adolescence. Selfishness in this relation means arrest of social capacity, a hardening of the personality that is likely to affect all the relations that one has with one's fellows. It inevitably affects the children in the family, though they know nothing of its existence. For selfishness in the conjugal relation is *per se* the drying up of tender regard for the personality of another, and tender regard springs from parental instinct. One cannot henceforth be a whole parent to one's children, much less train them for future parenthood.

The canker of this selfishness spreads directly also, not merely through one's children, to relations between persons in the larger social units. Tender regard for the personality of another, which is none other than justice in one's soul—this, wrought into habit by self-discipline in the most intimate association of husband and wife, forms an excellent background and preparation for the recognition of personality in business and in civic affairs, while absence of this soul's justice at home bodes ill for the world outside. Granted that there is no absolute guarantee that a social quality that is habitual in one human relation will be transferred to different relations; granted that we are bundles of inconsistencies; nevertheless it is a safe assumption that what my family is to me can easily affect my valuation of the family life of my employees, and that in the by-and-large this effect will occur frequently in a large society. Justice in the conjugal relation will tend, in the long run, to inject domestic considerations into the wage problem, the problems of civic betterment, the problem of industrial disputes, and the problem of war.

When we consider all this in addition to the vice and criminality that get their impulse from the adolescent condition of mind, we shall see that incalculable evil and incalculable good depend upon the direction that is given to the instinct that comes to maturity in this period. The sex instinct is not self-directing toward the ends of just society—this is evident. Like all other useful instincts, it requires training. It requires training more, possibly, than any other, and not merely in the way of restraint because of its possibilities for evil, but also in the way of positive development into a defined and noble social purpose. Reliance for the right social fruitage of adolescence is not to be placed upon even the fine spontaneities of youth, but upon educational foresight and skill.

The social limitations of adolescence appear, too, from the fact that it accomplishes its full instinctive work under various social systems, under any system, in fact, that permits between the sexes the relations of courtship and marriage. The primary impulses of youth find outlet under any form of government; at every level of social organization, from the savage tribe to the great modern state; under social institutions that range through the whole scale from slavery to industrial democracy. What kind of society we shall have depends in no appreciable degree upon the sex instinct as such, but upon the place it occupies in a great complex of instincts, habits, assumptions, and ideals.[1]

The relation of adolescence to childhood's social habits. The irruption of a fresh instinct that profoundly stirs the whole psychophysical organism offers a specially favorable opportunity for the basal educational process of habit making and habit breaking. One notices things not noticed before, reacts to them, experiences satisfactions and dissatisfactions of new varieties, and presto! the youth has "taken to" fiction, poetry, history, pictures, natural scenery, sport, good clothes, education, business, politics, or what not. Most certainly of all, he takes to some social circle, which may easily be one unknown and undreamed of in his childhood.

So rapid and so radical are the shiftings of adolescence from the personal groupings of childhood, and so positive is the de-

---

[1] The significance of adolescence for religious conversion will be considered in the next chapter.

sire not to be a child any longer, that the observer can easily get an impression that what occurs is not only a social quickening but also a social break with the individual's past. This impression is deepened by reactions made by youths who encounter parental opposition to the laying aside of childhood's dependence and subordination.

Before we commit ourselves to the opinion that adolescence is such a break, however, we should remind ourselves that a peaceful river, if it is obstructed by a dam, may break the barrier and become a destructive flood. Many a parent, blunderingly preferring that his child should remain a child, and resenting the individuality and the new social attachments that youth brings, produces the social refractoriness that he blames upon the hot blood of youth. That is, the break in such cases is not brought about by growth into adolescence any more than by resistance to such growth.

Educators, moreover, should have no illusions as to the relation of the laws of habit to the adolescent period. It is a truism when one speaks it, and yet it needs to be said, that provision must be made for forming, not social habits (for some social connections will be made anyway), but the particular sort of social habits that is required by the democracy toward which the Christian purpose aspires. Adolescence can produce snobbery more easily than democracy. In fact, no small part of social education at this period consists in widening out the purposes of groups already formed upon the basis of a narrow and exclusive regard of a few for a few. Here again the indicated educational method is admittance of the young to social groups and to social practice that are more mature than youth itself would spontaneously devise.

The theory of recapitulation, when it asserts that childhood is essentially egoistic, and that genuine altruism must wait for adolescence, seems to assume that selfish habits, made strong by exercise through the whole of childhood, somehow become null and void when one passes from childhood to youth. Is this true? We have already seen that the sexual instinct is not, of itself, unambiguously social except in a narrow sense;

it can easily mingle with itself other impulses so as to form a complex whole that is tender and beautiful as well as strong; but it can also be cruel, hard, blind, savage, weak. The particular complex of social attitudes that are henceforth to prevail is not at all predictable from anything in this one instinct. Just as in childhood, so here, the personality is formed by a multitude of particular experiences that bring multiform instinctive satisfactions and dissatisfactions. The bonds that are now formed with one's fellows are bonds of habit as well as of instinct.

Not only must habit forming still go on; the whole of it will be affected by preadolescent social experience. Nothing occurs that can at a stroke wipe old selfish habits off the slate. On the face of the matter, how can one suppose that instinctive attraction for the opposite sex will reverse an already firm habit with respect to one's own sex? Even a youth's attitudes toward the opposite sex are like the householder's treasure, which contains things new and old. The kind of mother a boy has associated with for more than a dozen years; the way his father has treated her, and the way she has responded to this treatment; the sort of sex distinctions that have been current in the boy's social environment; the amount and the qualities of the comradeship that he has had with girls; the treatment of women to which he has been witness everywhere, all these leave in his mind a sediment so firm that it seems to him to be bed rock, nature itself.

These social assumptions are not necessarily affected by his new emotions toward girls and women. He can adore a female without stopping to ask whether women should be treated as equals or as inferiors; and he can actually treat the adored one as an inferior without ceasing to adore. He can even magnify the virtue of his affection on the ground that he, a superior creature, bestows himself upon an inferior! By the complementary process, too, girls can come to prefer such male attentions to any other. The whole instinctive adolescent process can run its course between the fences of almost any social system. To change the figure, the social attitudes of a youth are not like a garden bed of plants just breaking through the soil, and all springing from freshly planted seeds of one and the same variety, but like a bed in which annuals, biennials, and perennials mix, the tender shoots standing side by side with plants that are fibrous and stiff from years of growth.

It follows that educational methods that segregate children in such a way as to narrow their social experience tend toward permanent arrest of social growth. It may well be that for particular purposes boys should practise co-operation with boys, and girls with girls, but a general policy of sex segregation, placed within the actual historical setting of the present, cannot fail to leave permanent marks of social impoverishment upon both sexes, an impoverishment that makes both of them unready for certain essentials of democracy. Again, the segregation of younger children from older ones, and the segregation of children of any age from adult companionship and from adult thought and enterprise, leave some social capacities undeveloped, and harden the remaining ones into a dominant life attitude.

Of course gradation of pupils and of material is essential for certain purposes, but the nature of proper gradation is easily misconceived. Pupils are often graded down to that which is easy for them instead of being graded up toward the most advanced of their interests; or the average performance of an age group is taken as a satisfactory standard for each member of it, whereas there are wide variations within such groups; or an assumption is made that the interests and capacities of an individual go up like an elevator, all at once, whereas their ascent is uneven, like that of a band of children frolicking up a stairway. If the possibilities of co-operation between younger and older are found in a given case to cover only a narrow area, we must not conclude that co-operation within this narrow area is educationally unimportant. This particular readiness of a child may be an open road toward a valuable social habit; experience at this point may awaken further interests; the joy of achievement here may raise the level of all his work.

The cordiality of our recognition of social values in new

types of boys' club work must now be tempered by reserve as to a single point. As far as these clubs take boys out of educationally wholesome homes; as far as parents are encouraged to transfer their educational responsibility to the boys' work specialist; as far as this specialist conceals the man in himself in order to be a boy with the boys; as far as he binds the boys to himself rather than to the social order; to the extent that he encourages not only the processes of tribal society but also its social standards—to this extent social arrest will mix with social growth.

CHAPTER XIII

THE STRUGGLE WITH SIN

"Sin" is a social conception. When I was a boy I was taught that sin is a relation, not between me and my neighbor, but between me and God. Subsequent reflection has led me to regard the distinction here made as not valid. The intimacy of the two Great Commandments to each other is too close. The dwelling place of the Highest is not apart from, but within, the brotherhood, which is the family of God and the kingdom of God. I find neither psychological, nor ethical, nor metaphysical footing for the idea that I can have relations with God in which he and I are isolated from all other society. My very being as a conscious individual is bound up with that of my fellows; a divine judgment upon what I am and upon what I will to be is *per se* a judgment upon my reciprocal human relationships. Nor can I judge God otherwise. The only meaning that I can give to his supreme goodness, the only ground that I can assign for bowing my will to his, is that he enters into the human social process more fully, more constructively, than I do. The need for any such term as sin lies in the fact that we men, in addition to constructing the human society in which God and men are both sharers, also obstruct it and in some measure destroy. We must now as educators face the fact that we do, individually and collectively, oppose, resist, and undo our own work of social upbuilding. We must inquire into the ground in human nature for the slowness, the delays, the backsets, and the defeat of ourselves by ourselves that are so obviously a part of the process of establishing the democracy of God.

The lodgment of sin in the individual and in society. In the light of our previous analysis it is possible to go at once to an inventory of the negative factors with which we have to reckon.

164

(1) *We have anti-social instincts.* They have been enumerated already. What needs to be noted in addition is that they are not so many isolated impulses, but factors that by various mental processes are built into the personality and into the structure of society.

(2) *The exercise of anti-social as well as of social instincts is pleasurable.* The satisfaction of grabbing; of greedy possession; of venting envy, jealousy, and wrath; of hunting, fighting, and mastering, as well as of sexual license—this satisfaction is what makes all of them hard to resist. Only psychological blindness and educational folly could teach that the pleasures of sin are a delusion. Some sinful pleasures are evanescent, it is true, but not all. Some bring pain in their wake, but not all, and there are great possibilities of foresighted calculation and prevention of disagreeable consequences. Social impulses have a way of disturbing the dreams of selfishness, it is true, but then, social impulses can be quieted!

(3) *The laws of habit formation are indifferent to social values; therefore a child who experiences satisfaction in his anti-social acts has in himself no protection from anti-social habits.* A particular child may be so situated that the constructive social instincts, being called out oftener and yielding greater pleasure than the anti-social ones, counteract them. Such situations the educator deliberately arranges, and he also attaches dissatisfactions to the anti-social reactions. But there is nothing in the child's own habit-forming mechanism that does this for him. In the absence of help from others, or of some fortunate chance mixture of conditions, he forms anti-social habits as spontaneously as social ones. As a matter of fact, education has not yet perfected its control of the habits of even one child. Every one makes anti-social instinctive reactions, experiences pleasure from them, as a result repeats them with added vigor, and thus becomes a victim of habits which education has to devise methods for breaking.

(4) *One's habits of conduct reflect themselves in one's social thinking, sometimes as a formulated premise the truth of which is assumed, sometimes as a control of attention whereby social facts*

*of some sorts are noticed and evaluated, while social facts of other
sorts are not. Thus, in a perfectly natural way, anti-social principles and rules of conduct mix with social ones.* A thing tends
to be defined in our thinking by that which we habitually notice
in it. A pine-tree is not the same sort of thing to a lumberjack
as to a John Muir. Just so, "human nature" is, in the thinking
of each of us, that which we habitually notice in our fellows.
Now, what we habitually notice is that which we have to take
account of in carrying out our own purposes and lines of conduct. Many of us not only initiate our plans from our own selfishness, but in the execution of them awaken self-regarding
impulses in others. Thereupon we judge that human nature
is rootedly selfish! You will find no one so doggedly certain of
this as the man who makes profits by stimulating other men's
cupidity. On the other hand, you will find no one so certain
of the inherent nobility of human nature as those who make
opportunity for such nobility to show itself.

Thus it is that anti-social instincts, confirmed by habit, become a basis of anti-social thinking. Probably most persons
suppose that the order of psychological dependence is the reverse of this, at least in part. Justifying their habits by their
thinking, they imagine that their habits are a product of reason. Socrates, indeed, held that the reason that we do wrong
is that we do not clearly see what is right. Aristotle, on the
other hand, took the position that practice is itself one of the
sources of insight. Without going into some fine questions
thus raised, we may say that psychology justifies, on the whole,
the tendency of Aristotle's thought at this point. Thoughts
about what is worthy of approval do not begin until we have
already approved and condemned many things. It is by reflection upon these judgments, already made, and by reaffirming
some of them, that we arrive at principles for future conduct.

Sin gets control of our thinking, then, as follows: First we
experience enjoyment in some anti-social reaction; the enjoyment stimulates to repetition of the act; a habit is thus started;
we cherish the memory of the experience; then relate it in
thought to other things so as to make a system, and to provide

for unlimited repetition; this thought system in turn becomes a habit, and now, behold, the unsocial principle that has been derived from instinct is henceforth taken as an axiom of social life.

(5) *Anti-social instincts, habits, and ways of thinking are intrenched in social institutions, in customs, and in public opinion. Society expects selfishness from individuals, and to some extent actually rewards it.* If we look at society in historical perspective, we perceive that it is, on the whole, an evolutionary process in which we are working out the beast, and training ourselves to have regard for what is humane. The organized faults that are in society did not, of course, originate in any fall from a perfectly organized common life; they are simply parts of our instinctive endowment that, confirmed by habit and by being made premises for thought, restimulate themselves from generation to generation by informal education.

The social conditions into which a child is born actually train him, though unintentionally for the most part, to be selfish within these conventional limits. It is true that society praises unstinted generosity; it admires, though with more reserve, the fine and sturdy justice that asks for only a democrat's share, and endeavors to secure as much for others. But it takes for granted that these will be exceptional. A general low average of self-seeking is socially expected. Success, in common parlance, connotes getting something for oneself, and the mass pays homage to success. At the crucially important point of sex morality, young men who are willing to make the fight for character cannot yet count upon effective social support from either men or women.

When a morally thoughtful parent or teacher witnesses the generous and trustful impulses of childhood, or the glowing idealism of youth, he sighs to think of the disillusionment that is to come when, "getting into the world," one meets its hardness, and is in turn hardened. The withering of ideals as the dews of life's morning are dried up by the heat of competition, of greed, of political self-seeking, and of licentiousness, is the continuous tragedy of education. Sin, that is to say, has social organs by which it is transmitted through the generations, positively preventing the young from even attempting to follow out in maturity their best social impulses. Generation after generation social capacities that are certainly here are wasted by society itself.

Sin, then, is rooted in instinct, confirmed by habit, and propagated by informal social education. Let us have no illusions with respect to the cost of democracy. Education for democracy has to face, not only unsocial traits in the child's original nature, but also a social system that brings them out, sustains them, justifies them in popular thinking, and rewards them when they "succeed."

The possibility of success in educating for democracy lies in the fact, first of all, that in our selfishness we are not at one with ourselves, but are stirred to unselfishness also by instinct, and by the habits and institutions that have arisen therefrom, and second, that selfishness and brotherliness do not have equal capacity for organizing themselves. Love of one another produces a degree of co-operation, which is the massing of human energy, that is impossible to greed, licentiousness, and the lust of power. Selfishness tends to disorganization and ineffectiveness in the long run. Temporary equilibrium may be attained in some cases by balancing the selfish interest of one person against that of another, but permanent stability is not attained in this way. Have we not learned the lesson that the massing of individual self-interest into a group selfishness is the way of class struggles within a nation, and of wars without? Massed selfishness tends thus to be anarchic, and to pull itself down in the ruin of its competitors. But love builds and destroys not. Unwise love may destroy, but it is the unwisdom, not the love, that is responsible. What the friends of democracy have to do is to put administrative experience and scientific analysis into the service of the brotherly purpose, and to train children in the resulting concepts and methods as well as in the love motive.

The psychological approach to children's faults. What has just been said as to the extent and the firmness of the lodgement of sin awakens echoes of the old controversy over total depravity. Echoes only; for our problem is different, and our approach to facts is different. Belief in total depravity was a dogmatic belief, that is, one accepted upon authority that was supposed to be that of divine revelation. The procedure was a priori, the conclusion being first accepted, and facts then being used merely to illustrate and confirm it. Illustration and confirmation, too, consisted, not in analyzing children's conduct, or in tracing it to its causes, but in contrasting it with a fixed standard of adult or even divine perfection, and then taking all deviation from the standard *en bloc* as defect of child nature. Even though less deviation had been found, or none at all, the doctrine would have stood nevertheless.

The whole landscape is changed as soon as we go at the facts in the spirit of science. We recognize in children multitudes of reactions that are social in the same sense in which some of our maturest Christian conduct is social. We perceive other reactions that are anti-social in the same sense in which some of our mature badness is anti-social. But we perceive also that neither sort of reaction has as yet the woody fibre of adult character. Moreover, we see that children's ways are not simple, as the theory of depravity makes them out to be. We do not have just "good children" and "bad children" to deal with, but personalities already complex because of the influence of preceding experiences as well as because of the variety of the instincts that are always at work. If we are to understand these personalities, we must analyze their conduct into its elements; we must see the relations of these elements to one another and to the particular stimulus that awakens each of them on each occasion; and in all this we must persistently trace each specific item to an equally specific cause. The following questions, which may appropriately be raised when faulty conduct, or conduct that seems to be faulty, occur, will illustrate this psychological approach.

How much in the conduct that is regarded as faulty is a result of physiological conditions such as imperfect nutrition, digestive disturbances, adenoids and mouth-breathing or other diseased conditions that lower the vitality, defective sense-organs, and nervous instability produced by fatigue, lack of sleep, over-stimulation, or other causes?

.How much of the faulty conduct is an imitative reproduction of the conduct of others, whether children or adults? How much of it constitutes an attempt to adjust oneself, protectively for example, to persons who are stronger?

How much of it is a matter of habit, and how did this habit arise? Note the distribution of the child's pleasures heretofore. Has he repeatedly experienced pleasure in acts of this kind, and if so could his elders have controlled conditions so as to deprive such acts of their pleasurable quality? What satisfactions have been provided for conduct of opposite social quality? In short, have his elders arranged conditions heretofore so that social acts on his part have regularly brought satisfaction, and anti-social acts discomfort?

What is the situation that called out this particular unsocial act? Our reactions do not occur in a vacuum, but in response to specific incitement. What are the specific elements in the situation that the child was reacting *to*, and in particular what was each of these elements *to him* at the time? Do not define the situation merely as it looks to an adult; do not define it in merely general terms, but make sure how the particular features of it looked to this child at this time.[1]

What are the instinctive roots of the reaction? Avoid for the time being all such blanket or cover-up terms as badness, naughty child, selfishness, wilfulness, obstinacy, disobedience, heedless-ness, untruthfulness, cruelty, and guilt and innocence. Find what specific impulses were in play at the moment and immediately before it, and see how each responds to some particular incitement in the situation.

---

[1] A child of six was told by his mother to perform a certain small service that would take him temporarily from the room. He started to comply, but paused inside the room, and he remained unmoved even by the second command. A third command brought this rejoinder "But, mother, I shall miss the story!" For at the moment he was a member of a conversa-tional group in which a story was just then in progress. The mother, promptly perceiving that she, rather than the boy, had strained the mother-child re-lation, gave permission to remain to the end of the story, whereupon the child cheerfully performed his duty. What would have been the educa-tional effect if the mother had insisted upon instant compliance regardless of the elements in the situation to which the child was at the moment respond-ing? How can we expect to make children social minded by insisting that we are right when in fact we are blundering?

It will then at last be time to ask which of these impulses, if any at all, needs to be suppressed. We shall often find that the chief difficulty is in an immature application of an instinct that has permanent value.

Analysis like this usually discovers that the chief factor in the faulty conduct is some physiological condition or else some previous and continued failure of the child's elders to provide conditions favorable for the growth of social habits and of social intelligence. Even the nervous causes of children's unsocial conduct are most often a product of adult neglect. The "depravity" that the child exhibits, therefore, is commonly not that of his own heart, but that of remediable faults of adult individuals and of adult society.

Educational guidance of self-approval and self-condemnation. Though the causes of a child's misconduct be thus traced to us his elders, the misconduct is nevertheless his own, and he needs emancipation from it. His act is bound to leave some deposit in the self that he is now forming. The educator's task is to see that childish faults, whatever their cause, are so handled as to leave a socially constructive deposit. The fact that a child is not "really bad" does not imply that he should be let alone. In some instances, doubtless, the best thing that can happen is that his misconduct should be minimized and forgotten, especially misconduct that involves no immediate danger to others, and misconduct that is not in serious danger of becoming habitual. But in the by-and-large some realization on the part of the child himself that something is wrong, and that it must be corrected, is most important both for constructive social habits and for constructive social thinking. If a child who is already able to communicate by language is merely wheedled or coddled into being amiable, the best that can result is a blind habit, probably a habit of waiting for the wheedling or the coddling, whereas he needs to grow in self-reliance, in self-guidance, and therefore in discriminative judgment upon his own conduct. This implies that:

(1) *Things to be done and things to be avoided must be defined in the child's own mind with sufficient clearness to enable him to*

know whether or not he has acted correctly. This means that
there must be rules, but it does not imply that rules are to be
imposed by authority that to the child must seem arbitrary.
In some matters, especially those that concern health and physical safety, rules must be enforced whether the child understands
the necessity of them or not. But every effort should be made
to have every requirement, as far as possible, a mutual understanding between the child and his elders. Moreover, rules
must not be so difficult as to discourage efforts to obey. Rather,
rules should be made so easy that the child will have the joy of
meeting the standard and of triumphing over his own weakness.
To children, as to adults, the consciousness that one knows
just what is expected, and just how to meet the expectation,
gives a sense of power.[1]

(2) *The child must be made aware that other persons, if possible
both children and adults, approve acts of his that comply with the
standard, and disapprove acts of his that violate it.* Every child
is entitled to such social support and correction for his judgments upon himself. Social approval and disapproval hold
his attention to the point, enable him to look farther ahead,
and to some extent help to keep the mind objective and to
counteract self-sophistication and self-importance. The power
that others thus have over us by strictly psychological means
is elemental. Our response to the approvals and disapprovals
of others is instinctive and emotional. Here is natural education, the power of which is little less than marvellous. Children as young as four years who persist in passionate attacks
upon playmates in spite of repeated physical chastisement by
parents have been known to struggle for self-control and to
achieve it as soon as their playmates unitedly expressed their
attitude by withdrawing from the passionate children's society.

Here lie the instinctive roots of the sense of guilt, and in
general of what is popularly called conscience. Whatever

---

[1] "How do you do, M.?" said some neighbors to a very small boy who
was playing in the front yard. He answered: "Pretty well, thank you," and
instantly ran into the house to ask his mother whether he had made the correct reply.

sensitiveness we attain toward abstract right, or duty, or ideals, or God, takes its rise in sensitiveness toward the approvals and disapprovals of human beings. The range of this influence has no natural limits. The most exalted sense of obligation is psychologically continuous with the inner impulsion that makes us conform to social expectation in such trivial matters as the style of our shoes; and the self-approval of a good conscience is similarly related to the puffing up of ourselves when we learn that one of our thousand ancestors ten generations back was distinguished for something or other! Obviously a power like this needs to be used by the educator with discrimination. Both the objects that are to receive social approval and disapproval, and the emotional intensity of the experience of social opinion must be regulated. Hence:

(3) *These approvals and disapprovals must be so expressed that the attention of the child is kept upon the grounds thereof, that is, the thing that is good or bad, and why it is so.* What he needs is to form a like opinion, or to see some fact in a new light, yes, even to desire something that he did not desire before. If, when he is condemned, he fixes his mind upon the disapproving persons, he may resent their attitude because it hurts him. He then condemns their condemnation instead of condemning the act that they disapprove. He may even stiffen himself in his misconduct by associating his discomfort with the disapproval instead of with his own fault. Moreover, the emotional effect of condemnation, especially if it is not tempered to the child's individual sensitiveness, may easily be depression and discouragement, paralysis of action, the withering of initiative. Here, again, the persons who condemn get themselves between the child and his proper goal.

When he meets approval, as well as when he meets disapproval, something depends upon the direction of his attention. If he does not think of the grounds of the approval, but rather forms a mental association between his own enjoyment and the approvers, he will indeed be drawn to them in a sort of fellowship, but the attachment will be that of the clique, not that of a generous sociality. Cliquism consists essentially in admiration for persons without discriminating what is admirable or otherwise in them. If discrimination were practised, the traits that are really likable in the members of the clique would be found outside as well as inside it, and unlikable traits would be found inside.

The sum of the matter is that the educational effect that is to be sought from social approvals and disapprovals, whether from other children or from adults, should not be the strengthening of purposeless social likes and dislikes, but increase in the child's intelligent co-operation with other children and with adults for specific objective ends.

(4) *Condemnation must not be administered so often or made so emphatic, and approval must not be so rare, that the child becomes convinced that he is really and rootedly bad, and accepts himself as such, or concludes that misconduct is not a serious thing after all.* The approvals and disapprovals should be of such a kind, and so distributed, as to awaken in him a discriminating judgment upon the tendencies of his conduct, a realization that there is something for him to struggle for, and a hopeful attitude in the struggle. Joy is the handmaid of vigor; depression conspires with weakness. If frequent repetition of condemnation does not bring depression, it brings nevertheless another evil. As the skin defends itself from undue pressure by becoming thick and callous, so constant fault-finding renders the mind insensitive to its faults. The child must be trained to notice differences; therefore his elders must do so. They must express their appreciation of even feeble efforts toward improvement, and they must so habitually show their confidence in him that his habitual notion of himself will be that of improvement. This policy fits the spontaneous interests of children. They know that they are children; they aspire to grow; they know that they are faulty; they like change; they are proud to become stronger both mentally and physically, and they are quite capable of the joy of self-conquest. What a pity that our own insensitiveness to the child's capacities for changing himself should create conditions that dull these capacities instead of using them.

(5) *In order to educate for democracy, there must be free reciprocity of approvals and disapprovals between children and their elders.* We cannot make democrats of children by treating their judgments as of no account. Merely beating down another will, or flattening it down by constant pressure, whether the will of a nation, or of a man, or of a child, is the mark of an autocracy that is bent upon perpetuating itself. A child does not increase in virtue by absolute submission to anybody or anything. Not training in such submission, but practice in intelligent, voluntary co-operation, is the thing that will make democrats of children.

This principle is violated in self-governing groups of children whenever the public opinion of the group suppresses individual judgment, or leaves no scope for making it effective. The principle is violated by adults whenever, in their relations with a child, they assume to be infallibly right. The assumption is grotesquely untrue anyway; it is always untrue; the wisest parent or teacher is wise only in spots, and no one is competent to locate with precision the boundaries between his own competence and his own incompetence.

Even when the judgment of an adult is precisely right, it should not be merely imposed upon a child. The way to make the child a democrat is to make him a convinced and therefore free participant in true judgments. Children must be encouraged, then, to weigh what the educator says and does. Amendments proposed by children are always in order; that is, the educator must be sincerely willing (not merely make a pretense of being willing) to reconsider and modify his own plans. The formation of a genuinely common will by deliberation—this is the problem of democracy not only in election campaigns and in the halls of legislation, but also in every schoolhouse, in every home, and in every church school.

This will involve children's approval and condemnation not only of what we invite their judgment upon, but also of what they take it into their heads to have a judgment upon. One of the things in which they will take the keenest interest is our own personal conduct. Here, as well as in child life, they will find objective material in which they can discover and define moral differences. Here they will find fellowship in their faults as well as in their virtues—that is, if we adults have the truly democratic humility, the high educational wisdom, to let children help us in our moral struggle even as we help them. This is democracy in moral education, and it is moral education toward democracy.

Socialization by means of punishment. What has been said of social disapproval, which is a kind of punishment, contains almost everything that is essential in a general theory of punishment except certain warnings as to what it is not. In the strict and proper sense of the word, to punish is to express disapproval by means more emphatic and generally more painful (though not always so) than words. The disapproval, the personal relationship, is of the essence of it. Punishment, then, is the use of pain as a means of improving the child's social attitudes. The test of it in any instance is the contribution that it makes to the formation of a genuinely common will of the deliberative type. If it puts persons farther apart instead of bringing them closer to one another, it not only fails to be socially educative, it becomes anti-social education.

Much that is called disciplinary punishment is condemned at once by this test. Here belong:

Punishing in anger or as a means of relieving one's own irritation.

Punishing to even up things, under the barbarous theory of retaliation—if you hurt us, we will hurt you. A refined form of this theory holds that abstract justice requires that wrong be expiated by pain, and that right be rewarded by happiness. Here the presupposition is that each individual will act upon purely individualistic motives. Such punishment tends to intensify such motives. It separates the punished from the punisher instead of uniting them.

Punishment that compels to the performance or the avoidance of a particular act without regard to the relations between persons that are involved in the whole matter. When the punisher steps into the situation he makes the personal factor prominent, whether he intends to do so or not. He may imagine that he is merely adjusting the child to the proper use of material things, or to playmates, whereas he is also changing the relation of the child to himself and to other adults. Unless this change in personal relations is a wholesome one, the punishment is to be condemned.

In view of these strictures one may well ask whether, then, any punishment can be socially constructive. Must not the deliberate infliction of pain inevitably separate persons even though it secures the performance or the avoidance of a particular act? The disciplinarian, whether parent or teacher, should not flinch at this point. The cement that binds individuals into society is ultimately the satisfactions that they have in one another's presence. Something to be enjoyed in common is the genuinely constructive factor, and the only one, in any part of social education. All that the infliction of pain can possibly do is to clear the way for increased social enjoyment. Here, then, is the proper test and control of all punishments. Under some conditions pain deliberately inflicted can, as experience shows, heal a child's mind of one or another social defect just as truly as the painful process of filling a tooth may stop toothache. Let us note some of these conditions:

When a child is carried away by some excitement of the moment so that he is unable to use his judgment, as when hilarious play becomes dangerous or cruel, a moderate pain inflicted in good nature may break the spell, "clear the air," and restore him to himself, a self that he actually approves and prefers.

Young children often produce pain in others without quite realizing the fact. Inflicting some similar, but harmless, pain, with appropriate explanation, may be the most effective cure.[1]

What is past and gone cannot be corrected; it can only be used to secure some future good. The reason for punishment is not past misconduct or present perversity of will, but the happier

---

[1] A small boy had bitten his still smaller sister. "Come here," said the mother, "I want to show you just how you have made sister feel." Thereupon the mother's teeth, applied firmly and painfully to the lobe of an ear illuminated the small boy's social thinking and strengthened his social motive toward his sister without separating him from his mother's love.

future that punishment may bring nearer. The amount of pain, and the method of administering it, must be determined with a view to turning the child's attention toward this better future. Pain that draws attention to itself only can hardly promote self-control or social self-guidance. The consequence of this remark with respect to the severity of the infliction is obvious enough. Not to stop reflection, but to help it, is the proper purpose; not to compel or crush, but to assist toward the realized freedom of self-control. In short, punishment is good when it actually guides the child's attention toward a possible good, the desirability of which he himself sees. If at the moment of the smart he cannot see, the smart must be preceded and followed by deliberative processes that assist him to do so. Many a child has found, and promptly, the sweetness of clarified insight and improved self-control produced by an attention-arresting pain accompanied by calm and friendly discussion of its purpose.

But increased pleasures *of a social sort*, that is, shared pleasures, must be provided by the very hand that inflicts the pain. It is a terrible thing for a child to think habitually of any human being as a pain-bringer. Not fear, but love is what does all the constructive work. The punisher and the punished must have so many pleasures that they share with each other that the child himself will realize that the pain is only an incident of an unbroken fellowship.

As soon as we reach this point we see that we must go one step further if punishment is to be socially constructive in the highest measure. As the ordinary relation of the punisher to the punished is that of pleasure-sharing, so their relation, when occasion for punishment comes, is that of pain-sharing, and this must be realized by both. The only way by which the punisher can avoid separating himself from the child is to cause the child to know that the two suffer together. The punisher is not to triumph over the child, is not to be happy while the child is in woe, but to maintain at-one-ment alike in pleasures and in pains.

Turning-points in character. We have seen in preceding chapters why the educator should aim at continuous moral growth rather than rely upon any breaks provided by original nature. In the present chapter we have dealt with another sort of continuity, for again and again we have come upon the fact that the conduct of the young is bound up, in a remarkably close way, with that of their elders. But neither sort of continuity implies either that moral growth can be equally rapid at all times, or that all parts of the complex moral experience can grow at the same rate, or that it can be free from crises, that is, such collocations of internal and external conditions that the child's particular reaction at this time gives a permanent direction to future conduct, or in other words a "set" to character. As a matter of fact, all these kinds of unevenness occur. At one time we find acceleration of moral intelligence and of social motives, at another time slowing down; interest now in this phase of conduct, now in that; the costliest errors at critical points, and also decisive and permanent victories for right character. Let us consider the educational significance of the most marked of these deviations, the crises.

The turning-points that one can remember as one's own are almost exclusively those of adolescence or of maturity. Consequently we form a habit of thinking of crises of character in terms of issues defined at the time and involving decisions of greater or less deliberateness. But a set toward or away from a particular human relationship, or a particular mode of reaction, may be established whenever an overwhelming emotion occurs in connection with it. Shocks occur in childhood that produce permanent timidities of one sort or another, with their paralysis of action and of initiative. Set revulsions or attractions toward individuals, or set attitudes toward the opposite sex, are also started now and then in childhood. Moreover, the ground tone of one's subsequent social existence may be determined by early experiences that awaken trust or distrust. Thus we come up from childhood sometimes with permanent scars upon the mind, sometimes with a permanent outreaching impulse toward some social good, neither of which we recognize the source of. With respect to these things the wisdom of the educator will consist not only in providing abundance of wholesome social relationships, but also in the habit of noting children's emotions, and of preventing children from being isolated and merely self-involved upon the occasion of any overwhelming experience. The sharing of one's emotions with a sympathetic, steady, and social minded friend is the surest road to balance. Moreover, if the passing of the years reveals the presence of an unfortunate set, again the task is to induce the victim to share this particular side of his nature and experience with such a friend, to share memories, hopes, fears, victories, and defeats.[1]

That adolescence has a peculiar relation to the establishment of the final set of character is evident from a variety of facts. The general psychophysical condition renders the formation and reorganization of habits relatively easy for a few years, after which there comes the relative non-plasticity of maturity, and its absorption in the compelling grind of existence. In this period the new capacity for affection makes possible fresh and profounder ethical appreciation. The general maturing of self-dependence opens the way for a final commitment of one's purposes to some life principle or ideal. Hence the tribal custom of adolescent initiation; the custom, in various denominations, of confirming children just as adolescent interests begin to be pronounced; the great relative frequency of adolescent conversions in denominations that cultivate this experience, and the frequency with which a lifelong interest or ambition takes its rise in this period. On the other hand, the significance of adolescence for character is equally clear from the great number of criminal careers that have their rise here, and from the vastly greater number of persons who are pursued through life by vicious habits, such as alcoholism and licentiousness, that are formed at this time.

[1] We are here at the edge of the morbidities that require psychotherapy. We should find, if it were possible to go into them in this work, that social education and psychotherapy are at many points continuous with each other. Two points in particular may be mentioned. Less reliance is placed than formerly upon the corrective power of mere suggestion, and more upon a re-education of the will in which the patient deliberately co-operates with the suggestions of the physician. Here habit formation assisted by the social support of the physician is the essence of the healing. The other point concerns the value of bringing one's secrets to the light and sharing them with another. Psychoanalysis has many aspects and angles that cannot here be mentioned. But its relation to social education appears in its method of establishing normal attitudes toward society at large by first securing complete co-operation between physician and patient.

When, alongside these considerations the recapitulation theory placed its doctrine of the natural and necessary egoism of childhood, the inference was drawn in certain circles that conversion in the sense of a reversal of character, or in the sense of the beginning of genuinely personal religion, is a standard religious experience for adolescents. We have already seen, however, how the theory that childhood is doomed to egoism, and that adolescence is spontaneously altruistic, overlooks, oversimplifies, and distorts facts. A policy of religious education that postpones the beginning of personal religion of a social sort till adolescence, relying upon the chance that a conversion experience will reverse the set that childhood has given to the character, is a fatal policy. It has not worked in practice. For parallel with the stream of adolescent conversions are two other streams that issue from the Sunday schools, a stream of youths who come into full church-membership without a conversion, and a stream of those who go on into mature life without taking any religious stand at all. The constant aim of elementary religious education should be to make conversion unnecessary.[1]

Nevertheless, the peculiar plasticity of adolescence does make it the scene of many a decisive experience. It contains the main turning-point of many a character. Social education has here a distinctive work to do. On the positive side it is threefold: To meet the spontaneously enlarging social craving by providing wholesome social experience both with one's own sex and with the opposite sex; to guide this experience toward intelligent ideals of marriage and of the larger society, the democracy of God; and to train the individual specifically for the attainment of his "majority," the assumption of full and independent citizenship, and entrance upon a life occupation.

On the other hand, here is opportunity, such as will never

[1] One of the evils that result from assuming that an adolescent conversion is normal is weakening and confusion in the term "conversion." It should not be used for any and every sign of religious interest, but only in the New Testament sense of a reversal, "about face," in the principle or policy of one's life.

I have discussed the psychology of adolescent conversions at considerable length in chap. X of *The Psychology of Religion*.

recur, for correcting unsocial sets that the personality may have acquired. These sets are of many kinds. In one case a particular anti-social habit has to be conquered; in another case there is needed an awakening from indifference, or from mere drifting with a social current; or the thrall of an unwholesome social connection may have to be broken; or an already organized self-centredness may have to be undone; or one may have the problem of consecration to a particular life work. In this list we have youths who require conversion in the strict sense of the word, but we have also cases of a milder sort to which the term conversion cannot be applied without confusion. But in all these cases alike educational methods are required— the making and the breaking of habits, the practice of co-operation, the enlargement of ideals, the culture of worship, the increasing control of conduct by knowledge. That is, even turning-points in character that involve a profound reversal are to be included under the notion of religious education, and they are therefore to be planned for, controlled, and tested, by educational standards.

Considerable unsteadiness and confusion exist at this point. Many persons persist in thinking of education as identical with instruction—persist in it to the point of perversity. Even some who know that education has to do with the forming of a will, do not clearly see how much it involves besides habit formation. The most fundamental thing in education is its constant reconstruction of purposes. Christian education, when it is really social, is through and through an incoming of the higher life, a renewing of the mind, a laying aside of lower selves. If, then, one of our pupils has already formed such perverse purposes that his present need is conversion, we are still to proceed as educators. We should never turn an adolescent over to uneducational evangelism.

Evangelism is uneducational to the extent that it is characterized by any of these things: Separating the act of surrender to God from devotion to men; inducing a decision so general or so indeterminate in its content as to separate it from the specific decisions involved in the previous and the subsequent education of the youth; awakening aspiration without providing immediate outlet for it in social living; separating conversion from habit formation on the one side and from intelligent analysis on the other; occasionalism, or postponing specific dealing with the adolescent's purposes to a particular occasion, and then crowding this occasion with appeals so that mental assimilation is impossible; finally, such use of suggestion and of emotional incitements as prevents rather than promotes the self-controlled organization of purposes.

CHAPTER XIV

THE LEARNING PROCESS CONSIDERED AS THE ACHIEVING OF CHARACTER

Various senses of "moral character." In the present chapter certain questions that are fundamental to the problem of method in social education will be opened, particularly questions that have to do with the pupil's awareness of social issues, and with his self-consciousness as related thereto. What are the effects, on the one hand, of shielding a child from knowledge of the issues that we are training him to meet, and on the other hand of letting him know what he is moving toward? What is the educational value of moral self-consciousness as compared with unreflective adjustment to social situations? How shall we conceive social character in individual terms, and what sort of individual consciousness is involved in the achieving of such character? In order to clear the ground for these questions, it is necessary to note that each of the main terms involved—character, learning process, and self-consciousness—has several senses. Let us begin with the concept of moral character.

To have a good character means, of course, to be steady rather than merely impulsive in one's conduct, and to pursue lines of conduct that have, or are worthy to have, social approval. But both the steadiness and the worthiness may be of different kinds. Good character may mean, and actually does mean, any one or more of the following things: (1) *Negative goodness*, or abstaining from acts that are forbidden by the code that is acknowledged by the society in which one moves, whether this society be a club, a church, one's profession, or the world of business. (2) *Conventional goodness*, or habitually doing the

184

acts that are positively prescribed in such a code. (3) *The inner determination* that involves self-discipline in addition to habit. This keeps one true to standards in difficult situations. (4) *Steady devotion to a cause or social ideal that outruns the conventional social code, and perhaps requires that it be revised.*

If we are to establish the democracy of God, we must, it is obvious, cultivate character in the fourth sense. Just at this point religious education finds its peculiar function and its peculiar difficulties in respect of method. Society as it now exists is quite willing to support an educational policy that makes for negative goodness and for conventional goodness; society would go as far, if it knew how, as to produce in its children the "rock-ribbed" fidelity to principle that constitutes character in the third sense. Up to this point religious education includes, or fuses with, whatever there is in "general" education that effectively socializes children. But beyond this point there lie, not the highways of social conformity, but the mountain trails of social reconstruction. Not the will that is conformed even to what is good in conventional social standards, but the will that is transformed into the likeness of the divine democracy that is far beyond and far above, is the character that Christian education has to produce.

From many points in the valley of conventionality men are blazing trails up the steeps of social idealism. The love of mankind, confidence that human nature contains high possibilities, the gleam of a universal justice that may yet be—these are alluring many men of many minds toward the heights. With these men religious education that is based upon the ideal of a democracy of God has a special affinity. We may agree or not with this or that program of social reform; we must doubtless make many experiments before we shall secure control of essential conditions of democracy, and some of these experiments will fail; but through all the give-and-take of debate upon social programs, and through all the practical measures that succeed or fail, religious education will have the distinctive task of producing men whose motives steadily and uncompromisingly reflect the will of the Father that we should make ourselves brothers. The democratizing of the heart is the fundamental and the most difficult part in creating effective democratic institutions. Democratic character will be formed, of course, only by participation in specific purposes of democratic quality, and it will go on to require democratic institutions for the fulfilment of itself. No esoteric goodness will suffice. But our specific mission will be to put sufficient heart, and a sufficiently radical character, into this work, even the heart and character of God.

Various senses of "to learn." To learn means either (1) *To form a habit;* or (2) *To acquire information;* or (3) *To attain skill in a particular operation or occupation;* or (4) *To become wise.* No one can mistake the fact that we have to learn wisdom, or the further fact that learning to be wise, though it depends upon and includes the three other sorts of learning, is not quite the same as either of them or as all of them together. Becoming wise implies acquiring better desires, reconstructing one's purposes, self-conquest, and placing oneself effectively within some foresighted scheme of society that awakens social approval. Wisdom is more than intelligence; more than craftiness, however successful. It is more than good habits, which reproduce good life but do not transform the good into the better. It is more than skill, for one can be skilful in getting what one wants, and yet be unwise in wanting it. Social education, then, must somehow, at some time, or perhaps through all periods of the child's growth, induct him into this individual relation to ideals. It must inspire in him an original foregrasping of social good, even the faith by which alone we can be saved to our highest possibilities.

Various senses of "moral self-consciousness." Everybody is familiar with, and everybody who reflects disapproves, the following forms of moral self-consciousness in children and youth as well as in adults: (1) *Moral priggery,* or habitually thinking about one's own goodness, habitually bringing it to the attention of others, and conforming to standards for this self-centred reason. (2) *Moral snobbery,* or looking down upon others because of their supposed moral inferiority. (3)

Moral hypersensitiveness, which shows itself in scruples, hesitations, and doubts when action is required; in self-condemnation so intense or so prolonged as to interfere with moral vigor; in longings for an abstract and contentless perfection; or in failure to co-operate in practical affairs because of the imperfections that inhere in all social adjustments (which is, practically, insistence that others should always adjust themselves to me).

In contrast to all this, we admire a child who does his duty as a matter of course; doesn't cry too much over spilled milk, but goes ahead, endeavoring to do better next time; and doesn't bother his head about the degree of his virtuousness. This is sometimes called moral unconsciousness, which is then contrasted with moral self-consciousness. No one will question the justice of this judgment, but the grounds for it are not always clearly seen.

What is the precise nature of the evil in the moral self-consciousness that has just been described? It is that the child obscures the moral goal by looking at his moral self. Just as a golfer is required, in the act of driving, to fix his attention upon the ball and not upon his club, so moral conduct is in general most effective when one's attention is upon what is to be accomplished, and not upon one's faults and virtues. It is this objectivity of mind that we praise in one child and deplore the absence of in another. We praise objectivity of mind because it is a condition of objective efficiency. Moral self-consciousness in the sense thus far defined connotes in the end moral clumsiness, actual defects in objective social relations.

But a distinction has to be made, and the possibility of another sort of moral self-consciousness has to be considered. Does the misfortune of the children whom we have in mind lie in the fact that they judge themselves to be good or bad? Hardly, for the so-called morally unconscious child, too, is by no means unaware of his proper classification. If my fellows approve me, especially if I am approved by those who are older and wiser than I, how can I help approving myself? The trouble lies partly in misjudging oneself, and partly in failure to organize one's judgments of oneself into a social scheme.   To be good, to achieve a moral status, is not a moral finality. I am a good boy, or a good man, am I?   Or perhaps a bad one? Well,,what of it?   What difference does it make?   That is, what persons are affected by it, and how are they affected? How is the social world in which I move either better off or worse off because I am what I am?   When I thus make my judgment upon myself, a part of a more general judgment upon social welfare, social justice, or the progress of world society, my self-consciousness is healthily objective.   The self-consciousness that stops short of this objectivity becomes self-involution, and "foozles the ball."

Self-involution is, in fact, a better name than self-consciousness for that which is common to moral priggery, moral snobbery, and moral hypersensitiveness.   Self-consciousness, in the stricter and more proper sense of the term, is present whenever what is actually desired is distinguished from something else as an alternative or contrary object of desire.   That is, self-consciousness is inseparable from the facing of any live issue, in other words, one that involves mutually exclusive or mutually limiting satisfactions.   This statement is not intended as a general definition of self-consciousness in distinction from any other sort of consciousness, but only as an indication of the route that is taken in the progress of a mind from instinctive reactions toward those that are required by membership in a deliberative group.

Moral self-consciousness and deliberative group consciousness are correlative—they are two aspects of the same experience.   There can be no deliberative group the members of which are non-deliberative.   The weighing of alternatives takes place within each individual, who then compares his scales and his results with those of other members.   Thus each has to be aware both of himself as this particular self and of others as those particular selves, each self being characterized by the alternative that it cleaves to.   Self-consciousness is thus an essential factor in the evolution of society.   Social education, accordingly, must bring children to moral self-consciousness.

Neither instinct, nor any mere drifting into social habits, is sufficient for the life of deliberative society.

It is true that much, very much, that is socially valuable is acquired by imitation or in response to verbal suggestion. Moreover, constant social pressure by the massing of pleasures in one direction and of pains in the opposite direction produces a large measure of conformity without deliberation. Such conformity is natural, is economically produced, and is admirably "unconscious." It is an essential part of moral education. But its educational capacity has several limitations:

First, Even in the fundamental matter of habit formation self-consciousness plays a most important rôle. In many spheres habits are most easily formed, and are most accurately adjusted to specific needs, when at the beginning contrasts are noticed, alternatives faced, and the first acts in the series are fully voluntary rather than imitative or otherwise suggestive in origin. This is the way to acquire skill. It is the best way to acquire various social habits, such as punctuality at school, neatness in this or that work, proper self-control in eating and drinking, and constructive charitableness.

Second, Imitation and other forms of social suggestion, taken by themselves, transmit the imperfections of society as well as its virtues.

Third, Imitation and other forms of social suggestion contain within themselves no provision for situations in which society is divided against itself. Shall one go with the majority or with the minority? "Unconscious tuition," valuable as it is, makes little contribution to a problem like this. Non-conformists, stubborn minorities, are vital organs of progressive society. How, then, shall the pupil be trained to deal with them? By the use of suggestion we can make him a partisan, often an active and efficient partisan, of any party with which he has happened to associate during his growing years. But partisanship does not solve the problems of society. A genuine social solution is never merely a resultant of moving bodies that collide. Society, because it is co-operation, can resolve its strains only by making individual minds feel both of the opposing interests that cause the strain. When any citizen does this, he becomes socially self-conscious. Now, this part of a citizen's duty does not fulfil itself by any fresh impulsive outburst upon the day that one becomes qualified to vote. Nay, it requires long, persistent, preliminary training—training, that is to say, in social self-consciousness.

But self-consciousness of this kind is the precise opposite of self-involution. Self-involution sets me in the centre of a group every member of which is gazing at me; wholesome moral self-consciousness, on the other hand, consists in so controlling my eyes that they shall surely see some object other than myself toward which the eyes of my fellows are looking—shall see it *because* they are looking that way. Selfhood of this type is objective-minded because it is social-minded, because it sees through other eyes as well as its own.[1]   In the end, then, moral self-consciousness is not so much a preliminary to democracy, or a part of the machinery of democracy, as it is democracy itself realized in an individual will.

Ambiguities in the debate upon "direct" versus "indirect" **methods in moral education.** The conclusion that follows from the last three sections is, in a word, that, though the guidance of instinctive action by deliberate prearrangement of pleasures and pains, and the development of wholesome instinctive conduct into habits without premeditation on the part of the child are fundamental essentials in moral education, sound method requires also specific measures for promoting premeditation, the weighing of social standards themselves, and the fully conscious taking of one's position with respect to these standards. If, now, any one asks whether this conclusion supports "direct" methods in moral education, no simple yes or no can be given in reply. For the terms "direct" and "indirect" have no single or uniform meaning in the writings of those who have debated this question now for several years.   A veritable medley of conceptions, some expressed, others im-

---

[1] Compare what was said in the last chapter about keeping the attention of children upon the grounds of social approval and disapproval rather than upon the approvers and disapprovers.

plied, gathers particularly around the "direct methods." Thus, one or another writer thinks that:

> The direct method consists in telling children what is right and what is wrong, or how to act.
>
> It consists in ethical instruction as distinguished from moral training.
>
> It consists in setting aside a particular period in the school program for morals as a subject of instruction.
>
> It consists in causing children to single out and define the ethical aspect of situations as distinguished from causing children to deal with each situation in its concrete totality.
>
> It consists in causing children to reason about ethical principles, and trying to make them act from ethical reasons rather than from simple and wholesome impulses.
>
> It consists in inducing children to dwell upon their own moral excellences and defects.
>
> It is an attempt to secure good conduct by exhortation or by emotional pressure.
>
> It is moralizing, or contemplating goodness by itself, in the absence of any occasion for exercising the kind of goodness that is under contemplation.
>
> It consists in imposing our moral notions upon children, or in securing good conduct from them by pressure from without as distinguished from action from within in response to a situation that the child himself appreciates.

On the other hand, the designation "indirect" is given to methods that are variously characterized as follows:

> The use of suggestion, rather than either compulsion or reasoning, to secure good conduct.
>
> Reliance upon school organization, classroom management, playground supervision, and the personality of the teacher, as supplying both material and method for moral education.
>
> Getting moral reactions by means of actual moral situations as distinguished from the imaginary situations of mere instruction. More fully expressed, moral growth through solving the problems that arise in one's own social experience.
>
> Discussing moral problems when they arise in the pupil's actual

conduct rather than according to a systematic plan—that is, "incidental" moral instruction.

Training for the larger society by bringing the school curriculum into closer relation therewith, and in general by getting the school out of its social isolation.

That there is some fundamental difference between these two bundles of conceptions one easily feels. But just what the difference is when it is traced downward to its psychological assumptions, or upward to details of practice, is not always so obvious. In respect to practice, we find ambiguities like this: An argument against direct instruction is coupled with an argument for training the pupil to analyze situations so as to pick out the moral element in them. As an example of correct method an instance is given in which a principal dealt with cheating in school work by explaining to the pupils that they were dishonest, and that cheating is stealing. Where lies the indirectness in this case? The principal went directly at the pupils and at the ethical problem, and he did it analytically, not by suggestion. Some writers treat story-telling as an instance of direct method; others classify it as indirect.

What is needed here is a more strictly psychological approach; that is, we need to ask what happens in the pupil's mind. What are the two things that are to be either directly or indirectly related to each other in the pupil's experience? Himself and his teacher? Or himself and another pupil? Or himself and the larger society of which he is to become an adult member? Or his ideas on the one hand and his acts on the other? And what is it for any of these to be either directly or indirectly related to the other? It is directness as compared with indirectness in the pupil's own mind that we have to deal with.

Method in moral education follows the general principles of good teaching. The polemic against "direct" methods in moral instruction and training is at bottom a part of the general campaign for better teaching. The defects of the old practice, whether in the teaching of arithmetic or of morals, have their roots in these assumptions:

(1) The intellectualistic assumption with respect to the relation of knowledge to life, namely, that thought first grasps reality and then adjusts life to it. The new education reflects the contrary view, that the adjustment process and the cognitive process are not two but one. Jesus intimated that up-reaching conduct is a condition of knowing the higher things—those who put something divine into their acts are the ones who know the things of God. Just so, modern educational reformers in a long procession have proclaimed that we learn by doing, that experience of the real world is the basis of vital instruction about it, that participation in the elements of industrial processes is essential to education, and that character grows by fulfilling one's functions in some social group.

(2) The undemocratic assumption that to teach is to impose the teacher's thought and will upon the pupil. Here is social bias of the most serious import. It ever seeks to justify itself by considerations drawn from the incapacity of children for self-guidance. But it is ever self-condemned because there is lacking in it any provision for bringing pupils to genuine *self-guidance*, especially to the union of co-operation and liberty that are essential to popular government. The old type of teaching assumed that the use of authority is simply to control others for any good end; the new type assumes that the use of authority is to bring others to self-control, emancipating them from external controls. The only authority to which the teacher has any right is that which is continuously extinguishing itself.

Accordingly, the reform that is now demanded in school practice insists not only that pupils shall be active rather than passive, but also that they shall act from within, and shall organize their activities through their own reflection. Instruction in the natural and physical sciences, for example, now aims, not merely to transfer a given amount of biology or of physics to the pupil, but to bring him up to perform scientific processes himself, and if possible, to make him an independent investigator. Just so, the moral aim of the school requires that the pupils be led, not only to hold correct views of conduct, not only to accept loyally and to act upon the superior wisdom of their elders, but also to perform among themselves, each for himself, here and now, the actual processes of social living under freedom.

These processes are not to be mere applications of what the teacher tells or prescribes. The teacher, instead of giving solutions, which are then to be merely illustrated by pupil experimentation, engages the pupils in a genuine trial-and-error method of learning to live. This is the method by which society as a whole has evolved. Education is able to make the process a short one, abbreviating it into the score or so of years during which the school has the child, by making available the rich social materials that have been deposited by the experience of the race. The art of the teacher consists, in no small measure, in making obvious, at the right moment, the applicability of this or that part of the social inheritance to the present purposes of the pupils. In this way waste of time and of effort is reduced, and conformity to social standards is most certainly produced. Conformity, that is, from the heart, because it is self-induced. But by this method conformity is secured through freedom, and it carries with it the training in objective moral criticism that is necessary to social progress through revision of social standards.

Sound method in moral education, then, will cause children to face, directly and analytically, their relations to one another, to their teachers, and to the larger society. It will not build up a structure of moral ideas apart from moral action, nor will it be content, on the other hand, with conduct, however appropriate, that does not grow into reflective self-control and weighing of standards. Just as the best teaching of arithmetic, or of manual processes, or of physics causes the child to realize what he is doing, why he does it, what the results are, and how it can be improved, so in morals it is open-eyed, forward-looking, and in this sense self-conscious, practice that counts most for the formation of a democratic character.

The relation of ethical thinking to **virtuous action.** From every point of view the lines of our discussion converge upon the

conclusion that the learning process with which moral education is chiefly concerned is an achieving process—the process of
achieving character. But character, not as something static,
already accomplished; rather, character conceived as making
oneself count for objective ends. Here we find a touchstone
for the curriculum aspect of any scheme of moral or religious
education.

What value does this touchstone reveal in curricula that
divide and subdivide and arrange lesson material according to
a schedule of the virtues into which good character can be
analyzed? If we ask what a good man is like, we get from such
curricula the answer that a good man is truthful, industrious,
persevering, kind, and so on. Therefore the pupil is made to
study in succession the virtues of truthfulness, industry, and
all the others. There are curricula that appear actually to
assume that if a pupil thinks about industry he will become
industrious. But the teaching profession as a whole condemns
the implied method on the ground that it separates thought
from life, substitutes ethical instruction for character formation, and tends, by reason of its abstractness and its dryness,
to create actual dislike for moral standards. If, in order to
create like instead of dislike, admiration-awakening examples
are used, the objection is made that such separation of ethical
emotion from moral action creates a habit of feeling rather than
of action, and actually substitutes sentiment for character.

In order to avoid these pitfalls, suppose that, in connection
with the study of each virtue, we provide opportunity for the
practice of it. There is going on, in fact, considerable hunting
up of things that children can do in the way of, shall we say,
practice work in goodness? That this search will uncover some
really vital things in the moral reactions of children we need
not doubt. But the artificiality of the point of view is at
best only alleviated thereby. For any such practice is merely
added to life. What is added to life can be subtracted upon
occasion. It is too like an excursion in a captive balloon; the
balloon returns to earth.

The whole scheme rests upon the fundamental fallacy that

virtuous character is made up by combining virtues, whereas, the virtues, one and all, are abstractions, mere thought-things, and therefore static only. Our concern is not that the pupil should possess virtues, but that he should have virtue, that is, strength in right causes. Here two conceptions are essential, firmness of action, and discriminated, objective ends. Now, objective moral ends or "causes" are those that arise in inter-actions between individuals. In fact, only through social give-and-take do ends of any sort—whether wealth, science, or artis-tic production—become anything more than self-involution. Ethical ends, such as charitable relief, follow the same law. As long as my charitable act is simply an outlet for me, a mere doing *for* another, it contains a fatal ethical defect. Real charity, or love, is doing *with* another. Moral character im-plies, then, that one has found something important to do that requires the union of several wills, and it implies also that one is firmly devoted to getting this thing done.

The consequences for moral education are these:

(1) The primary material for moral analysis is to be derived from the child's experienced relations with persons, that is, from his ordinary, every-day social contacts with both children and adults, whether in the school, on the playground, on the street, at home, in church, in buying and selling, or wherever.

(2) Imaginative material, whether historical or other, is to be selected on the basis of its continuity with what the child has already experienced in his relations with living persons, and it is to be so used as to assist in the analysis of these relations. To this point I shall return in a subsequent section.

(3) The natural growth of these contacts from the family hearth outward yields a principle for the gradation of material. Home, church, school and playground, local community, national community, world community—these form a natural ascending order of social contacts and of social interests and functions. But this is an order of increasing complication: it is not a stairway in which each step is left behind in the act of reaching the next higher. We are not to graduate from the home, but deeper and deeper into it, nor from the school, but

further and further into the system of education until we take upon ourselves full responsibility for the schooling of others.

(4) In all this material the centre for the pupil's attention is men and women, particularly what they do, why they do it, what the results are, and how perhaps something better might have happened. What father and mother do, and why it needs to be done; what each family helper does; what the grocer, the postman, the physician, the policeman does; what the mayor, the councilman, the police judge does; what a school, a fire department, a library, an art museum, a natural history collection does; how charities are organized and what they accomplish; why the Child Labor Association exists and what it is doing—it is unnecessary to finish this inventory, for already it must be clear that in the actual organization, work, and purposes of persons as social agents, all the way from preparing the family breakfast to promoting world peace, we have the concrete material for enabling the pupil to form definite social purposes of his own. In subsequent chapters we shall see how this principle applies to the child's relation to the church.

With a large proportion of the persons involved in this inventory children can have some personal contact. The most significant thing about a grocery is the grocer, not his goods. Guide the child's knowledge of the goods so that it shall include acquaintance with the purveyors of them, and let buying and selling be guided so that it shall be mutual service between buyer and seller. Treat institutions in the same way. The library clerk and the doorman at the museum, for example, are to be discriminated from the things that they handle, and are to be recognized as persons with whose acts the child's own life is bound up.

(5) The irreducible factors in a morally educative situation, whether it is encountered in experience or only in imagination, are persons in their concrete individuality. The presence of persons is what makes a situation ethical. Because they are individual, irreducible, present as persons or not at all, a child's moral progress consists, not in achieving one sort of moral goodness now, another next year, but in increasing control of whole

personal situations. Thus, in abiding relations like the family, he will show a firmer will to co-operate (ability to act socially under greater strains), and ability to co-operate in more ways. In addition, as his social relations grow more complicated, he will put into them one after another the same intelligent, constructive good will. Progress like this is not likely to correspond with any possible serial order of virtues or qualities of character. Progress does not consist in any increase of a quality, but in achieving ends in "real life." One phase of such progress can be measured by testing the changes that occur in the pupil's ideas concerning social relations, but only one phase. The full measure of any method of moral education is the part played by the pupil in actual social relations.

Imagination and character. Social education by conscious effort at adjustment to social reality describes the platform that we have now reached. What, then, of story-telling, and what of the world's treasure of imaginative literature? What relation has imagination to the realistic educational processes that are fundamental? This problem, looked at from the psychological angle, is wider than it is ordinarily supposed to be. For the contents of imagination are not at all restricted to what is called imaginative. Historical characters and events are made concrete to me by the same process that enables me to grasp a fairy-tale. When I read the morning paper, too, imagining events that the paper describes is what puts me into touch with the real world. Yes, it is imagination that puts me into touch with myself and with my immediate environment. It does it by holding before me my own yesterday, or my own hour-ago, and also by holding before me the picture of some possible future good. Here, moreover, we have not only a reproductive, but also a productive, inventive, creative process, and it is productive most of all where fresh adjustment to reality is taking place.

A child's imagination is a stage upon which programs of possible action are rehearsed, with himself always as one of the actors, albeit he is also a spectator. Small children do their thinking largely in story form, their thinking even of situations that to grown-ups are prosily literal. This is a necessary part of the trial-and-error method of learning to live. The trial-and-error method, when it is educationally used, is no mere lunging about until one happens to hit upon success, but the following of programs of action previously discriminated from other possible programs, and then noting the results. In the imaginative rehearsals that are so characteristic of children, particular parts are assigned, distinctions of social quality are recognized, relations of social cause and effect are to some extent noted, and *the imaginer himself assumes a character*. This assumed character may, under favorable conditions, persist as an attitude or special readiness for action after the dramatic rehearsal is over. An attitude is an initial stage in actual conduct; there is momentum in it. Thus it is that the imaginary can control the actual with children and with adults.

This rehearsing can take place in a story that a child is listening to as truly as in one that he invents. It is safe to assume that any child, when he listens to a story in which the actors display contrasting social characters, takes one of them as himself. In a certain kindergarten a story was told of a wild duck that protected her ducklings from a pursuer by hiding them among rocks along a shore, saying: "Don't one of you stir, don't one of you make a sound, don't even whisper." Then the story went on: "Not one of them stirred, not one of them made a sound, not one of them even whispered." At this point a boy was heard to gasp: "I couldn't do that!" The child who made this remark was the one of all the group who was having the hardest time learning to think twice and to await his turn. Obviously this listening child was at work upon his own social problem, upon realities, and it is equally obvious that to arrive at such a true judgment upon one's faults is a natural step toward correcting them.

The social experience and experimentation that produce social growth can be extended, then, by imagination. There is no necessary break between a fairy-story, an incident in the life of a historical personage, and to-day's playground experience. It is the teacher's business to select and to use imaginative material, fiction as well as history and current events, so that there shall be in it no break with real life. The matchless power of Jesus as a teller of educative stories lies in part in the utter continuity of the life process in his tales with that of his hearers. If only the actors in stories for children are made to act from simple motives in situations that are not too complicated or far-fetched, continuity with child life is possible in material that is derived not only from child life, but also from adult life, animal life, and the realm of myth, folk-lore, and fairy-tale. Plant life, too, and even inanimate objects can be used by endowing them with human motives. Mountains can break forth into singing, and the trees of the field can clap their hands.

Parents and teachers of very young children have the special problem of helping their pupils to grasp the difference between fiction and history. The clew to this problem lies in the truth that there is no necessary break between fiction and "real" life. The distinction is not that between stories that are true and stories that are not true. There is nothing in any language more true than, say, the fictitious narratives that Jesus told. The difference between one of his tales and history lies in the sphere in which the event takes place. The story sphere is human motive; the historical sphere adds the full, socially complicated bodily expression of motive; both spheres are real, and they are continuous with each other. "Thou," said Nathan to David, "art the man." The Priest, the Levite, and the Samaritan are realities within our own breasts. Santa Claus, the spirit of Christmas giving, is a blessed reality, and so are the other good fairies.

Under favorable conditions, I have said, an imaginatively assumed character may persist as an attitude in overt action. Probably the part that one plays in one's imagination invariably has some tendency toward conduct of like quality. But the tendency may be greater or less, and it may be more or less thwarted by the setting that it has in the imaginary event. The teacher has the task, not merely of causing the pupil to rehearse imaginatively some sort of good act, but also that of arranging the other factors in the rehearsal so that a particular attitude shall persist and pass on into the child's relations with some actual human being. Before stating what this positively requires, we may well pause to consider some methods that fail, and why they fail.

Moralizing, or telling children what the application of the story is, interferes with the educative process by drawing attention away from the concrete and particular to the abstract and general. It interferes likewise by injecting the teacher's personality into the situation. If the story is an appropriate one appropriately told, connection with life is already there as the child listens. To introduce a new vehicle to carry him over from the story into life is to create distraction. Nor is this the worst of it. For moralizing creates a new attitude of the pupil toward the story as a whole. A moment ago he was living in the story; now he sees that the story has no reality to the teacher, but is only an extended way of uttering an abstraction; so the imaginary becomes for him the unreal; and the goodness and the badness in the story cease to be live issues. A healthy child is very likely, under these circumstances, to form a habit of regarding moral rules as prosy impositions upon life, dull things.

A method much in vogue in sermons to children is teaching by analogy. A sensible object is presented, or a physical or chemical experiment is performed, or an event in external nature is described, and the attention of the children is then invited to the similarity between this thing or process or event and life issues of right and wrong. The method is apparently an attempt to take advantage of children's spontaneous interest in sense-objects and in sensible happenings, and to move the child mind on from the sense-level to the level of ethical thought and appreciation. But the device rests upon a fundamental misunderstanding. Analogical thinking is not characteristic of children. They must have a larger range of identities between the things that they compare, going from person to person, say, with ease, but not from the properties of physical things to qualities of character. When children hang upon the preacher's words as he expounds an analogy they are likely to be attending to the physical side of the analogy only. A minister once illustrated "Thou desirest truth in the inward parts" by holding up a watch and calling attention to the effects that would follow if the little wheels inside it got rusty. A small boy reported the minister as having said that "If you tell lies you'll get rust in your stomach." In such cases the child's attention fixes upon the symbol so intently as not to move on with the preacher from the symbol to the thing symbolized. In short, the imaginative material by means of which children get control of actual social situations is that which has a large rather than small number of elements, and particularly motives, that are continuous with those of the child's social experience.

The positive conditions under which a dramatically assumed moral attitude is most likely to pass on into conduct are in general those that favor "transfer of training." The fact that a child has been trained to neatness in his arithmetic papers does not of itself guarantee that he will be equally neat in his map-drawing; the fact that a man is truthful in certain relations or with certain persons does not prevent him from being untruthful in a different set of relations or with a different set of persons. The transfer of neatness, or of truthfulness, or indeed of any habit, from one situation to another depends upon such conditions as the number of points in which the two situations are identical with each other, and the definiteness with which one has faced and understood and accepted as one's ideal the principle that is involved in the good habit in question. A large part of the present chapter has a bearing, as a matter of fact, upon the transfer of moral training. For we have been occupied with the difference between particular good habits on the one hand and readiness for moral discrimination on the other, and between the exercise of good will upon conventional levels on the one hand, and on the other hand the carrying forward of good will into reconstruction of standards. The particular application of the principles of transfer to the use of stories, history, current events, or other material of the imagination, is as follows:

> There must be many rather than few elements in the imagined situation that are identical with elements in social situations already experienced by the child. By identical elements in social situations I mean, not the externals of life, but persons, their char-

acteristic interactions, and consequences of conduct as they are determined by laws (natural laws and laws of the state) and custom.

The imagined situation should be so constructed and presented as to contain a social problem of a type that the child has already encountered, together with at least some steps toward the solution. Something unsettled, suspense, light coming from the consequences of conduct, these consequences occurring not arbitrarily or by chance but in accordance with the actual laws of life—all this should be in the imagined situation itself, so that the teacher does not need to translate anything into a different language.

It is not enough, however, that the material should represent important laws of life; these laws must be made to seem important. There must be perspective. This is to be had, not by telling the child what is important but by the selection and arrangement of details, as in climaxes, and by such methods as emphasis, repetition of key-phrases, and tone of voice. Discussion of the story by the pupils under suggestive guidance from the parent or teacher, and dramatization under such guidance, add still further to the production of perspective as well as to depth of impression.

Whatever be the proportions of pleasure and pain, joy and sadness, in the personal experiences portrayed in the story, these experiences must be so organized and presented that the child who listens will imaginatively side with the right against the wrong, and get pleasure from doing so. Not, indeed, pleasure without cost, not the pleasure of passivity, for this would be untrue to the realities of the moral life. Struggle, pain, failures, sacrifice must not be slurred in the content of the story, or in the pupil's imaginative participation in it. He must be led at times to take sides with what is hard and disagreeable, and even this taking of sides in imagination will cost him an effort. Yet there should be here also the joy of winning, some realization that the socially right alternative is more agreeable than its opposite. It is easy to dislocate the pleasure of the listening child; the story may be very different to him from what it is to the teacher. "Children," said a clergyman in a talk to a Sunday school, "when you get to heaven, whom do you want to see first?" A ten-year-old boy, being pressed for an answer, replied: "Goliath."

When an actual situation subsequently arises that involves a problem that has already been at least partly solved in a story, the skilful use of a phrase from the story, or a mere allusion to an event in it, may help.   But not if reminding constitutes nagging, and whether it does constitute nagging or not depends upon the pupil's attitude toward it, not upon the teacher's intention.   But we must not forget that a normal child who lives in wholesome social relations desires to be helped.   He wants to achieve.   No concealment is necessary, no subterfuge.   The effective reminder is the one that brings him this help, and makes him feel that doing right is made easier.   Here is another instance of the law that in moral training the major keys of pleasure must predominate.   This is the reason why humor is so valuable both in story material and in direct relations between teacher and pupil, humor, that is to say, that enables the teacher to laugh with the pupil, not at him.

PART IV

THE ORGANIZATION OF A SOCIALIZED
RELIGIOUS EDUCATION

CHAPTER XV

THE CHRISTIAN REORGANIZATION OF THE FAMILY

The family as a determiner of the social type. When does a human being make his début into society? When he is born into the common life of mother, father, and child. A family is a society, and it is an educational institution of the very first significance. "Where was he educated?" is often asked, and the answer is given: "In such or such a college," or perhaps: "In the public schools of his State," whereas the most that school and college are likely to have contributed to him is some sort of superstructure built upon foundations of social character already laid. Just as it was said of Peter, "Thou also art one of them, for thy speech maketh thee known," so any observant teacher sees in a student's manners and in his use of language an index of his home life. And deeper than words and accents, deeper than manners, is a substratum of social presuppositions and social attitudes that home life has already made firm.

The reason why family life has peculiar influence in respect to the social substratum of the character is this: The long dependence of the child for so many of his satisfactions upon the same few persons, and the intimacy and continuity of his relations with them. In this intimacy with persons he deals with what is elemental and final in the ethical and the religious life. Many parents believe that the social experiences of small children are insignificant, mere time-fillers that are to pass away with the time that they occupy, whereas these experiences form firm notions of what a person is, of what is due from one person to another as a person, and of what concerns in life are im-

portant or unimportant. These notions become the presuppositions of future thinking on social relations. They are wrought
into habits, too, and are bound up with whatever life purpose
or ambition a child or youth forms.

The family, moreover, is not an isolated society, for into and
out of it flows the life-blood of civilization in the large. Through
his parents the child is under the tutelage of the traditions, customs, and economic conditions that have made his parents to
be what they are. Thus it is that a social standpoint, high or
low, Christian or un-Christian, may, through the personal intimacy of parent and child, become to the child a self-evident
and even sacred thing. No child merely plays around the outside of society. In the intimacy of the family every member,
younger or older, is a feeling part of social processes. He is
included within a network of concrete relations between persons—between the stronger and the weaker, between male and
female, between buyer and seller, between the employer and the
employed. The child is not prepared to weigh these relations.
He knows not how to sift out the wheat that is always there.
He may even accept injustice to himself as something that belongs within natural and proper social relations.[1]

**It is the fundamentals of social justice that are at stake
in the child's experience in his father's family.** Family
government, to begin with, tends to fix one's ideas as to the
basal rights of men. Consider the educational difference between a family in which each child, however young, has rights
that the older and stronger members respect, and a family in
which no child is aware that he has any rights that are respected
by his own father and mother, or by older brothers and sisters.
Genuine parental affection can be mixed with caprice and self-

---

[1] The educational power of family intimacies is well illustrated by the
almost universal regard for family honor. There are few things that awaken
anger and resentment as uniformly as opprobrious remarks about one's family.
A still more remarkable illustration is the rarity of incest. There is nothing
in our instinctive endowment to make incestuous relations unattractive.
Yet a traditional standard, passed down from generation to generation merely
as a presupposition about which almost nothing is said, holds instinct in
complete control, nay, has all the force of a negative instinct or impossibility
of desire.

will, and genuine self-sacrifice may lack real respect for the personality of the one on whose behalf the sacrifice is made. Even a firm, steady, and genuinely benevolent family government may fail to produce in the children any heartfelt respect for law simply because the government to which they are subjected is an autocracy. Thus it is that out of the same domestic spring may come water both bitter and sweet—regard for some rights, disregard for others equally basal; respect for persons in one classification, disrespect for persons in another; tenderness in some human relations, callousness in others; sincere belief in the Christian ideal of brotherhood, sincerity in conduct that obviously defeats it.

Here is the explanation of the paradox in a rather common attitude of men toward women. Almost every child experiences tender maternal affection; hence almost every man retains through life some capacity for noble emotion with respect to his own mother and with respect to motherhood in general. Men who have this emotion commonly assume that they hold an exalted view of womanhood. Yet many of them regard marriage as properly the subjection of a woman to a man. Many of them are willing to accept profits that depend upon risks to the health and the morals of working women. Men glorify motherhood in one breath, and in the next buy from a hundred girls their capacity for competent motherhood! Moreover, how is it that reverence for womanhood "because one has had a mother" can exist in the same breast with acceptance of prostitution as a matter of course? The key to this situation is this: Boys—and girls too—acquire in the family a second sort of presupposition with respect to womanhood, a presupposition based upon the habitual attitude of the males in the family to wife, daughter, or sister. How far would one overshoot the truth if one should assert that rarely does a boy acquire in his own family a firm presupposition that girls are his equals? It is because boys grow up as intimate parts of actual sex inequality that men fail to see the grotesqueness of the assumption that one sex has an inherent right to determine the "proper sphere" of the other. Is there not, in fact, a trace

of condescension or patronage even in the common glorification
of "mother"? Admiring tenderness is easier, too, than justice.

Thus it is that fundamental social assumptions and habits—
those that concern the valuation of the individual, personal
liberty, social classifications, the relations of the sexes, the right
of property, the nature of law, and the sphere of government—
flow from the large society into the small family society, and
thence back into the large society. If we desire to reform any
one of them, there can be no more effective measure than to
induce parents to reorganize family life. If the Christian
churches really believe in universal brotherhood, with its
inevitable corollary of a world-democracy, let them begin now
to form democratic presuppositions and habits at the source.

On what conditions can family life educate for democracy?
The general answer is, By being, in its measure, a co-operative
group of the deliberative type. The family is to prepare children for democracy by being itself a democracy. On the
face of the matter, is it not absurd to think that inequality and
arbitrary rule within the society in which an individual spends
his most plastic years can prepare him to labor toward a society
that is based on exactly contrary principles?

It will be objected, of course, that any attempt to make the
family into a deliberative group will hit upon the rock of children's incapacity for deliberation, the discontinuity of their
attention, the fact that it is child nature to act immediately in
one way or another. Does not the practical impossibility of
suspense and postponement render it necessary for the father
and the mother to make decisions for the child, blocking the
way to harmful acts, and moving him by their power rather
than his own into wholesome ways? To argue thus, however,
is to miss the main point of the problem, and to act thus is to
miss an opportunity for the social education of the young.
The main question is, What sort of experience tends to make the
child into a socially deliberative individual? What is the most
certain and the most rapid way to enfranchise him? To provide the conditions for this sort of experience is the base-line of
social education. Upon this basis the family must present to

the child opportunity for fellowship in fundamental, outgoing brotherhood. An outline of some of these conditions will indicate the direction in which the Christian reorganization of the family has to move.

(1) *Abandon the doctrine and the practice of the inequality of the sexes.* If children are bred in the assumption that even among the persons with whom they have the most intimate and affectionate relations nature itself has established a permanent, impassable division between the rulers and the ruled, the served and the servers, if children go into the world saturated with any such assumption, the males, already accustomed to the individualistic satisfactions of a superior caste, will tend to lord it wherever they can, and the females, unaccustomed to free initiative, will withhold from society services that they are by nature well qualified to render. It is hard to imagine a way in which Christianity could more decisively promote appreciation of humanity as such, which is the spirit of brotherhood, than the abolition of the sex caste in Christian families.

Tender, admiring, reverential affection, ennobling though it be to the one who feels it, is no proper substitute for the recognition of equality. Not seldom tenderness contains in itself the unrecognized but cruel poison of wanting to keep its object, whether wife or child, permanently dependent and inferior. On the other hand, the recipient of such regard is often pampered thereby into selfish receptivity, or else beguiled into a narrow, almost slavish devotion which in turn pampers the man who accepts it. Thus, love itself, acting under the assumption of permanent inequality between the lovers, arrests the growth of the social capacities of both. Even within the family this arrest often manifests itself in hypertrophied demands of either lover upon the other. Whether or not children witness such marital infelicity, they have no experience that enables them to see the social significance of the inequality in the midst of which they live. They take this inequality as a matter of nature, as something self-evident. They accept the satisfactions that it brings, or accommodate themselves to the limitations involved, and so go into the world with a fundamental defect in their faith in man and in their preparation for a world brotherhood.

(2) *Develop capacity for deliberative group life by respecting and effectively utilizing any such capacity, however slight, that any member already possesses.* The right to be heard, the right to have one's ideas and desires weighed by others, is the reverse side of the duty to listen and to be ready, when the common good requires it, to waive one's wishes. The reciprocal relation between rights and duties holds not only as between adult and adult, but also as between adults and children. Parents who do not listen and weigh ought not to be surprised if their progeny is heedless and stiff-necked. Parents who never "own up" to a fault, and never make open amends, may expect to encounter the same sort of infallibility in their children. The difficulty of developing a democratic family organization lies less in children's limitations than in the stiffness and unadaptability that are fostered by current conceptions of parental, dignity and authority. Children like to talk things over seriously when they know that the outcome of the conversation has not been arbitrarily predetermined. An artificial class-distinction exists in many a family because parents underestimate the thought-capacity of their children. What surer way can there be to create in children a class-consciousness that is unsympathetic and impervious to parental authority? Anything that prevents the honest, serious, and effective utilization of childish capacities tends to stunt them. To be a listening parent implies much more than giving attention to complaint or clamor when it arises; it means also consulting children, sharing with them the really important problems of the family, and letting them participate in working out solutions. It means, too, that this consultative relation between parent and child is to be extended and developed as fast as the child's mental grasp increases.

(3) *In a democratic family each member will perform regular, defined, personal services for the maintenance of the common life.* This innocent-looking proposition is full of sharp points. Each member will contribute *personal service*, which is a thing that

money cannot buy and that cannot be done by proxy. Personal service may take the form of earning money for family use, but there is much "supporting one's family" that does not include giving oneself. Providing plenty of "servants" is not at all the same as contributing personal service. *Every* member of the family will be in his own person a servant of the family, being made thereby conformable to the Great Servant who has revealed in his own person the great God. Here child and parent will meet on the truly democratic plane of industry, useful labor, done co-operatively for the common weal, and with no compensation except the common weal. Finally, the service that is required of each individual will have a *defined sphere*, beyond which one may indeed give but no one may demand. When the service of love, freely given, becomes subserviency to unregulated, and hence unsocialized, calls for service, the result is little more than slavery. Its undemocratic character is not relieved by the fact that the slave loves the master and willingly obeys.

(4) *In a democratic family each member will have a defined sphere in which he is entitled to initiative, and likewise one in which his own judgment is final.* Dependence of a child upon the decisions of others is to be reduced as rapidly as is consistent with physical safety, health, and the continuance of his education. Doing for oneself all that one is competent to do is a significant contribution to the common weal, and it is highly educative. Self-reliant experimentation must be encouraged even though we are certain that errors will be made, and from the uncomfortable effects of his errors a child must not be too much shielded. The important thing is not to get the most perfect possible immediate result, but to promote growth, to develop individuality that is both independent and co-operative. A good example of the principle is presented by certain parents who grant each child a regular allowance of money, require open and accurate accounting, increase the amount with growth, and require each child increasingly to purchase his own clothing from his own income, first with aid from the parent in the way of explanations as to colors, durability, style, etc., but

later without consultation. What a blunder it is to keep on deciding everything for a child up to young manhood or young womanhood, under the expectation that then, by some hocus-pocus of benevolent nature he will suddenly acquire good judgment! And the worst thing about this policy is not that it puts upon young men and young women tasks for which they have not been prepared, but that it leaves their social capacities uncultivated. To keep children dependent-willed as long as possible is to isolate them into a social class even under their father's own roof. Denying them the experience of progressive co-operative judging, it fits them for none but arbitrary social relations thereafter.

(5) *Democracy in the family is to be promoted by providing common pleasures.* Not long ago I learned of a family in which the father as well as the mother takes part regularly in the children's daily story hour preceding bedtime. In another instance a father and mother provided a combination dining-table and billiard-table, and evening after evening played interesting matches with their children. It is a sinister sign if father, mother, adolescent boy, and adolescent girl must all go out of the home and away from one another in order to have a good time. The sign is sinister even if the diversions that are sought are unobjectionable in themselves, for the absence of common pleasures is the absence of a most important social cement. When a parent and a child frolic together they become acquainted with each other. Each finds in the other personality riches that would otherwise, perhaps, be unsuspected. Family life is famishing for want of deep acquaintance between parents and their own offspring. And not only do common pleasures reveal one to another, but—under the basal law of habit formation that satisfaction in an act tends to prolongation and repetition thereof—they help toward the deep and permanent attachments that hold through adversity as well as through happiness. Thus it is that playing together; enjoying literature, music, and pictures together; making family excursions into the open; going together to places of amusement, and even common indulgence in jolly nonsense have the deep ethical value of joining person to person in a society of reciprocal good will.

(6) *The unity of the family cannot be made perfect until family consciousness is fused with a wider social consciousness, particularly through participation by all members of the family in remedial and constructive social enterprises.* The mere fact that the children, when they marry, and in the social acquaintanceships that precede marriage, link their own family with others is of itself sufficient to prove that regard for one's own flesh and blood is an expansive principle. The weal of my family is inextricably bound up in a thousand ways with that of others. Children of different families play together, go to school together; infect one another with disease germs, with smutty ideas, with bad habits; later they employ one another or are employed, they bargain with one another, they vote for or against one another, they determine the sanitary and moral conditions of the community. The child of wealth who was infected with a fatal disease by wearing a garment made in a sweat-shop illustrates a solidarity that no individual or family can escape. There is simply no possibility of fulfilling love in a narrow circle except by treating the circle as a section of the total social sphere. The exclusive family is the self-undermining family. Therefore the building up of deliberative group living in the family must be continuous with the building forth of the same thing in the community. It is not enough that the father should contribute of his substance and of his energy to the outgoing social enterprises of the church or of the neighborhood— the family as a family should talk them over, weigh the needs, form a united purpose, and work together for the fulfilment of it.

Even young children can participate from the heart in great social enterprises because the greatness of a social enterprise grows out of the elemental character of the human need that it seeks to meet. There is perhaps no defect of society that does not inflict hunger and sickness upon children, and this appeals to any child. Moreover, children's imaginations easily seize upon some point of difference between better and worse social conditions—between good and poor school buildings and grounds; clean and unclean streets and alleys; sanitary factories and unsanitary sweat-shops; humane and inhumane conditions in industries and in housing; war and peace, and much more. When the missionary enterprise is clearly conscious of its social calling, it comes home to children with the force of reality, and not as an abstract propaganda. The participation of children in the social movement should, of course, be graded; new enterprises will allure as power of analysis and continuity of purpose grow. But this does not mean that small children can have a vital part in none but small enterprises. The elemental character of their social attitudes joins them directly and simply with their elders in great undertakings. And besides, fellowship with a parent in doing something that the parent feels to be important brings its own delight, its own sense of the reality of the matter.

Finally, a noble common purpose, and united labor and if need be suffering for another, are essential to the full realization of intimate affection. If we go back far enough in the evolution of marriage we find that mating is a temporary affair, not yet marriage in the proper sense. How is it, then, that such fleeting sex attraction has grown as far as it has already done toward lasting conjugal affection? In spite of prevalent defects in marriage, and of the great underworld of infidelity on the part of both the married and the unmarried, the world already contains numberless instances of unsullied, lifelong affection between one man and one woman, and, moreover, in the presence of a standard like this the world does not condemn the standard but itself, or at most seeks excuses for the despite that it still does to such love. What has brought this about is the presence of children who needed long years of care. Thus, historically considered, conjugal affection is not the prius of parental love, but just the reverse. It is the child who binds the parents together. Love grows rich enough to defy time and the fluctuations of sexual desire because there is common work for the lovers to do, yes, because their fondness for each other goes out and takes in a third. This is not an isolated fact, but a law of life. Idle affection grows stagnant. Our friendships, our social circles, our churches, and our families find life for themselves only as they bestow life upon others.

(7) *These conditions cannot be met without the domestication of private property.* Family life is psychophysical. Affection between its members is embodied, incarnate. The family table is not only its symbol, but also one of its important instruments. In the fellowship of eating and drinking the domestication of private property is taken for granted. "If any provideth not for his own . . . household, he hath denied the faith, and is worse than an unbeliever." But if this is so obvious, why do we not see that upon the same principle *all* the property that any member of the family has should be domesticated? For what is property if not means for human life? And what is the right of property if not a call to the enlargement of life? And what is the family but partnership in life and in the promotion of living? And how can there be the supreme fellowship of a common, outgoing purpose if one member of the group is the autocratic master of the means whereby the group itself lives and of the means whereby the group might enrich other life than its own? The reservation of such mastership as a right, even though its actual exercise be liberal, is simply incompatible with the thorough domestication of the master's will.

Christian teaching has long recognized that there is a cleft between property as a legal right and property as a moral obligation. The law sustains me absolutely if I withhold my goods while my neighbor starves; it protects the sharp bargains whereby I accumulate goods at the expense of others; and, as to the family, it lays upon me only the mild obligation of feeding, clothing, and sheltering wife and children, leaving to my sense or my whim the feeding or the starving of their other capacities. Our religion constantly admonishes us to be better in these respects than the law requires us to be. But at the centre of the problem of private property, which is the family hearth, there is as yet no clear interpretation of the Christian law of brotherhood. The common assumption is that God requires nothing more of the individual in whom the legal title inheres than a certain arbitrary benevolence toward the members of his own family. The admonition to even this modicum of virtue is not vociferous! This assumption lacks, too, the definiteness of the legal right to withhold—a right that individualistic love of power guards with jealousy, and even confuses with moral right.

Here, in short, is an ancient wall of division within the family itself, a class distinction, a fundamental denial of brotherhood. Property comes between persons. It is, to be sure, a wall of glass only; any member of the family may look through it at the good deeds wrought by the member who is on the other side, but one may not reach one's hands through so as to share in the doing of the good deeds. In how many churches do husbands and wives make contributions as equals? How many holders of the purse escape being infected with the silent assumption that those whom one "supports" are dependents, inferiors, persons to be controlled by giving and withholding, or perchance favorites who are to be attached to oneself by largesses?[1]

This is not the atmosphere of democracy, and children who are brought up in it are not being adequately prepared to take the full part of a Christian in the great and growingly acute economic struggle. To be merciful and to be moderate will not be sufficient to reconstruct our social order. Something far more sacrificial will be required of us if the distribution of goods, which is the distribution of power and opportunity to live, is to become brotherly. Even if we are not yet certain which of several forks of the road to take in the legal revision of economic inequalities and injustices, there is no reason why we should not set to work at once to give love full sway in family education. This will involve, first and foremost, the beginning of economic enfranchisement for married women by the voluntary act of husbands. It would be a great step if a stated amount were to be received by each married woman as her *earnings*, to be disposed of with freedom equal to that of the

[1] What unconscious irony there is in the frequent boast of men who insist upon the inequality of the sexes, "We hold women to be our superiors." What a cheap and tawdry homage is this! "You are a goddess!" Tagore makes Kumo's husband say, but she replies: "No, no, no! I am not going to be a goddess any longer . . . I am just an ordinary woman." *The Hungry Stones* (New York, 1916), p. 169.

husband in the disposition of his own earnings or income. But beyond this will come partnership between husband and wife as equals in stewardship of the entire family income. The constant problem will be how to do the most good with what we have, and not seldom there will be the added problem of how we shall increase this our power to do good—that is, the wife will not be an outsider to any of her husband's business concerns. What this implies in the training of girls and young women is evident. It will make for a sturdier domestic character in women—and in men, too. And—here is our present concern—it will introduce the children, both boys and girls, to the democratic spirit in actual operation, and it will furnish a standard whereby they will be able to detect the various tyrannies that creep, under other titles, through modern society.

Finally, the domestication of property will include the gradual economic enfranchisement of each child. That is, he will be given control of property, but held to social responsibilities. By "social responsibilities" is meant not only one's share of domestic labor, but also one's share in studying (which should have economic recognition as productive labor), and one's share in social enterprises in church and community. The whole should be treated from the beginning of the child's experience of money, not as private gain from being good, but as participation in the family's enterprise, and thereby as participation in the life of the community. In short, in the family the child's experience of property can and should be an experience of something that binds men together, not of something that keeps them apart.

The interest of religion in the economic status of the family. What has just been said assumes the existence of what may be called well-to-do living conditions such as:

Housing that is not only sanitary, but also adequate, in space and in furnishings, for happy group life, and for distributed home duties.

Culture material, such as books and music and pictures.

Opportunity for each child to have schooling as far as his abilities and his interests can carry him.

Sufficient leisure on the part of parents to enable them to spend considerable time in the company of their children.

Sufficient freedom from fatiguing labor to make it possible for parents to play with their children.

Sufficient income to enable the family to take part in community affairs, such as religious, philanthropic, recreational, cultural, and civic enterprises.

Every one of these conditions is important for the religious education of children in the family. Yet families whose place in the economic scale is below that of the "middle class" are *ipso facto* excluded from one or more of these conditions, in multitudes of cases from all of them.

That many beautiful characters bloom out of domestic deprivation; that suffering itself sometimes brings the sufferers close to one another; that much improvement of home training is possible even under the conditions that prevail below the "middle class family"—all this is true and important. But it is not an appreciable offset to the economic depression that is upon multitudes of families, upon them not merely as an occasional emergency, but upon them permanently as the unescapable grip of an economic fate. Our glorification of the higher life—the life of persons united with one another by good will—is ignorant mockery if we do not see that deprivation of nutrition, of the company of parents, of the physical things whereby knowledge and beauty and good will are communicated from man to man, is deprivation of opportunity to be a person, deprivation of opportunity to form a good will.

Therefore the cause of social education in the family is all one with the demand for improving the economic status of the family as such. Every Christian church and every Christian family may be expected to identify themselves, as a matter that involves their own life or death, with such movements as these:

To abolish child labor;
To shorten the hours of labor for men and for women;
To improve the sanitary and moral conditions of labor;
To increase the income of most families;

To forestall unemployment, and to provide for accident, sickness, and old age;

To improve housing conditions;

To provide playgrounds, wholesome amusements, and cultural opportunities for every community;

To remove the saloon, the haunts of vice, and degrading amusements;

To keep the organs of the community life—local and other governmental officials—responsive to the needs and views of the masses;

To improve the human stock by adequate supervision of health, by preventing the propagation of obviously unfit strains, and by inducing wiser mating;

To provide a diversified education that, keeping close to the people, shall be adapted on the one hand to their industrial needs, and on the other hand to bringing out and developing to the full whatever special talent individuals may possess.

There are various ways of putting on the harness of a cause like this. Three of these ways that have a particularly close relation to religious education may be mentioned: (a) Religious education in the Sunday school may well include participation in these movements at the points where they most obviously touch child life. (b) The family can reinforce the Sunday school at these points, feeding during the week the interests that are aroused on Sunday, or even anticipating the Sunday school by taking social problems to it. (c) Most communities contain families that are depressed by the conditions that have just been analyzed. Here pastoral visitation may well include an inquiry into the child life of the community, and groups of adults may well undertake community surveys, and then adopt such community programs as the conditions seem to require.

The problem of family worship. For some years there have been complaints that family religion is declining. The old customs of family prayer, catechizing, and direct, personal religious appeal from parent to child have largely disappeared. The reasons for this disappearance are found partly in industrial and other conditions of modern society that separate the members of the family for many hours of the day, and partly in sheer parental neglect. The remedy that is most often attempted is

mutual incitement of ministers by one another to arouse parents
to re-establish "the family altar." In spite of untoward conditions, it is said, time can be found for devotions, and if necessary some sacrifice of other interests should be made in order
that children may grow up in the knowledge and the practice of
religion.

That agitation of this kind has had little practical effect
would probably be admitted by all. The so-called secularization of the family—even of church families—goes on apace
even though we continually declare that the issue is a vital one
for our religion. Is it not possible that some elements of the
problem have been left out of the account? For example, has
not the accusation of parental neglect covered, in addition to
infirmity of purpose, a certain bewilderment for which parents
are not responsible? Two generations back there was relatively
little question as to the sort of religious ideas that should be
presented to children. Almost any part of the Bible might be
read at family worship, for it was all alike the word of God.
No caution was necessary as to the impression made upon children by a biblical passage, for a particular interpretation, imposed by authority, was the sovereign antidote for all errors.
How to pray was clear, for the outline of the dogmatic system
needed only to be rephrased in order to appear as worship.
Catechizing was the simple process of drilling certain finished
ideas or verbal formulas into the memory. Even personal religious appeal could follow an easy and uniform tradition as to the
lost estate of man and the conditions of salvation.

It is scarcely necessary to say that neither the content nor
the method of such family religion can be restored. The duty
that is before us is not restoration, but revision and reconstruction from the foundation upward. Parents are bewildered because they do not see what sort of reasonable religious life can
be shared in any vital way by parents and children. The preaching of religion as life in distinction from dogma, and the proclamation of the social content of the gospel, have not made
sufficiently clear as yet what these things imply with respect
to the domestic circle.

Let us come at once to the core of the matter. The reconstruction of fireside religion will require the formation within the family of common social purposes so deep that they reach the level of worship. The principle that underlies the discussion, in an earlier chapter, of the church as an organization of worship applies to the family also. Not by saying: "Lord, Lord" shall we introduce children to Christ, but rather by giving them a share in Christly enterprises, and then letting the motive thereof come to full consciousness as fellowship with Jesus and with the Father. Here will be found a guide for the selection of biblical passages that are really appropriate for family worship, passages that will be luminous to children as well as to adults. Here, too, will be found a language for prayer that parents and children can use in the same sense. The common joys of the family will utter themselves in gratitude, and so will the joys of others with whom the members of the family feel their unity. Conjoint confession of sin will have meaning because the contrasts of life will be revealed in the enterprise of social living. From the same vital source will spring the inextinguishable social aspiration that is the heart of intercession, namely, the identification of our claim upon life itself with the claim of others. Children will realize the presence of God, just as their parents will do, in the "love that will not let us go," the love that is at once command, and condemnation, and reconciliation, and the power of a higher life.

Education for married life and for parenthood. The sort of sex-consciousness that refuses to face the conditions essential to the rational—that is, socially foresighted—control of one of the primal factors in social weal or woe is an immodest "modesty." The essence of the immodesty lies in making self prominent in the thought of sex. Once we take the social point of view with respect to it, the whole perspective changes. Frankness then becomes natural and wholesome wherever discussion of the physiological and the ethical laws involved in the sexual life can contribute anything to a better society. Specific preparation for marriage and for parenthood then becomes a fundamental interest of religious education. In the divorce evil we are reaping tares that were sown while Christian education was asleep to its social calling. While it distributed among the youth maxims of private goodness and of individualistic salvation, the conditions of modern life were loosing the family from its old moorings, but providing it with no chart or compass for its voyage. The prevalence of divorce, moreover, is only an acute symptom of a general failure to reorganize the family upon a higher social plane when the old, semi-patriarchal basis began its inevitable crumbling.[1] The churches have before them the task of transforming life in church families in accordance with the social principles of the gospel. This implies far more than fresh legislation on marriage and divorce, far more than palliation of strains that arise in a family that lacks a clear, outgoing social purpose; it implies nothing less than instructing and training children specifically for marriage and parenthood as the first and foremost sphere for the deliberate organization and control of society as a democracy of God.

Not only is sex-instruction necessary as a part of religious education, but the level of this instruction must be made utterly social. The avoidance of harm to oneself must be simply a phase of a positive purpose of good for others. All the "Thou shalt nots," which have been presented hitherto as laws of one's own individual perfection or righteousness, are to be transformed into parts of an ambition to marry, to contribute to the happiness of a spouse, to have healthy, happy children, and through them to contribute to the larger society. Here is the point of view that should prevail with respect to prostitution. A purpose to keep oneself uncontaminated is not enough. There is needed the truly Christian identification of one's own interests with those of others, with the interests of every harlot and of every girl who may yet be tempted, of every male victim and of every boy who is in danger.

---

[1] It would be interesting if one could arrange in parallel columns the resolutions of ecclesiastical assemblies with regard to marriage and divorce, and the sermons and Sunday-school instruction upon the same subject within the same communions. It would be found, I surmise, that as yet the churches have scarcely begun to use the power that they possess for preventing the evils that they urge the state to rectify by legislation.

Thus it is that problems of personal purity open out into a wide social perspective. They open out toward the family, and toward all the economic conditions that depress its life; they open out toward the causes that unduly postpone marriage; to those that keep white slavery going—both the social and economic causes that add to the force of instinct, and the political causes that give power to the organization of vice. The question is truly as wide as one's outlook for the race. The question of the eugenic regulation of mating is, with all the rest, a part of the problem of a possible democracy of God. In short, religious education must deal with the whole sexual life as a sphere for deliberate, constructive, social purpose. It must instruct parents as to their part in unfolding these high and holy things to their children. It must support the state and other agencies in every enlightened effort to spread knowledge and social standards. It must itself instruct, inspire, and train the young with marriage and parenthood frankly in view, and it must be ready to assist inexperienced parents with the best knowledge that is anywhere available.

CHAPTER XVI

THE CHURCH SCHOOL

Popular education is the central function of a church. If the church were simply a purveyor of spiritual goods, a sort of "general store" of the soul, its educational work would not necessarily involve much more than the training of the ministry. But if the church is an agency for developing in the people a certain sort of self-control, especially one that is difficult of achievement, then popular education becomes a fundamental ecclesiastical necessity. It is a necessity because of the ineradicable difference between the plasticity of childhood and the relative fixity of maturity. True, maturity is only relatively rigid; modifications of character occur at any age, and conversions that reverse the whole current of life are scattered through the history of the church. Our religion glories, and should glory, in its power to rescue shipwrecked characters. But the supreme test of its power lies in the prevention of wrecks. To put the matter in terms of construction rather than in terms of disaster, the predominant function of the church is to get Christian motives into control of the growing powers of children and youth. This function predominates in religion precisely as sanitation and hygiene predominate in matters of public health. More than this, the educational function must predominate in Christianity because of what Christianity is. For:

(1) *The church can maintain the spirit of prophecy within itself only by educating the people.* The priestly function of dispensing benefits can be handed on from priest to priest without intervention of the people, but prophetic insight into life's problems, and prophetic zeal for truly divine justice come

"up from the burning core below," up from the "common" people, not down from any privileged class. If the ministry desires to avoid stagnation, let it keep close to the people; yes, let it train the people to make great demands upon the church. If the church is not to be a belated follower of the social conscience, a sort of "me too" among philanthropic societies and organizations for reform; if the church is to be a perpetual inspiration to the human longing for a humane life, a perpetual organ for the manifestation of the God of love—if this is to constitute the very life of the church, then it must continuously stimulate the fresh spirits of the young to make greater and greater demands upon life. Not to keep human vitality in prearranged grooves, but to enlarge its desires, widen its outlook, make it more critical of things as they are, and more ready to pay the cost of social reconstruction—this is religious education upon the prophetic level. It involves of necessity ever-renewed criticism of the church and of its ministry from the standpoint of human need, and ever-recurring necessity for inner reconstruction of ecclesiastical life and purpose. This is what it means to maintain the spirit of prophecy. This spirit is the divine love-impulse circulating upward from the needs of the people, and pouring itself wherever it can into the hearts of those who can help.[1]

(2) *Education of the people is an indispensable means for correcting the faults of the church.* Errors of learning, defects in standards, and inefficiencies in methods, all require as their corrective one or another sort of democratic judgment. Errors in learning are corrected by the methods of science, which is the democracy of the intellect. Scientific method spreads before the whole world every esoteric doctrine. Here hoary prerogative has no standing; here every one must become as a little child who gazes unabashed upon anything whatever, and

---

[1] In *Is Christianity Practicable?* (New York, 1916), William Adams Brown has given striking evidence of this spiritual law of the church's life. The powerlessness of the churches everywhere to avert the present world calamity, and the dominance of church consciousness by nationalistic assumptions in all the warring countries, point back to failure to educate the commonalty in the world outlook that is inherent in the Christian principle of brotherhood.

tells without reserve what he has seen. The emancipation of the church from its chief ancient errors with respect to the Scriptures, for example, came about, not by exercising any self-sufficient ecclesiastical prerogative, but by opening ecclesiastical doors to democratic scientific methods that were already prevalent outside.

This represents a general law. The church can save itself only by the help of those to whom it is sent; it has a vital interest in stimulating them to the largest use of their native capacities. Even in respect to standards of conduct ecclesiastical self-sufficiency is self-delusion. That the church's officially proclaimed standards can fall behind those of church members and of outsiders we all know right well. It is necessary time and again to convert the church as one step in a social reform. Nor is this anomalous; it represents a law of the growth and decay of institutions. Self-involution on the part of any institution involves decay of its social value. Granted that the church is the inheritor of imperishable truth; does it follow therefrom that she always understands and uses the riches that are under her hand? Nothing, in fact, but the cry of the people for a richer life can keep her awake to the exhaustlessness of the treasure that she carries.

If this is true of standards of conduct, how much more true is it of methods of work. It is a trite remark that institutional procedures that arise in response to a particular situation tend to perpetuate themselves regardless of changes of situation, and therefore regardless of efficiency. Institutions tend to measure their duty by their own past performances. Hence the necessity of popular judgments, unhampered by habit, by vested interests, or by pride of official consistency.

Thus, on all accounts, the church needs a policy of unreserve in religious education. Does some one suggest that the churches are embarrassed at the present moment by popular criticism? Or that religious education should therefore adopt a defensive policy? The reply is that the danger to the churches from the prevalent popular criticism arises from the fact that it is not thoroughgoing enough; it demands too little of us, not too much; it tends to beget in us a multitude of insignificant accommodations instead of a more fundamental, more creative, purpose. The social deficiences of the religious education of the past are thus returning upon our own heads through the paltry demands that the people make upon the church.

(3) *Through popular education the church makes its chief contribution to the community life.* What has just been said concerns the maintenance and the improvement of the church itself as an organ of divine inspiration. The conclusion that we have reached may be summarily stated as follows: As it is the character of God to give himself forth into human life, and as self-forgetting service is the great law of individual vitality, so ecclesiastical institutions can escape institutionalism only through the influence of an awakened commonalty. The church must educate the people, then, for the sake of its own perpetuity and self-improvement.

The power that the church should desire to have is power to transform the common life, and this means the community. Religious education must be outgoing as truly as foreign missions. "Come unto me," said Jesus, but when men had come to him he said to them "Go." This is the spirit of enlightened Christian education. It seeks to lay upon pupils a mission. It does, indeed, say: "Come into the church fellowship," but it adds: "Let us go." There is no denying, however, that the "Come" has been far more in evidence than the "Go." Religious education has had too prominently in mind membership in the church, and not prominently enough membership in the community. Both the church and the community have suffered as a consequence.

But an awakening is upon us. As never before, proclamations of the Christian religion as social reconstruction issue from pulpits and from ecclesiastical assemblies. But these proclamations are addressed for the most part to mature men and women whose social habits are already formed, and whose occupations and stations in life have already enmeshed them in social unrighteousness. The most that can be expected directly from these persons is some amelioration of bad conditions.

To their children will be left the more basal parts of social reconstruction. Just here is where the church will make its chief contribution to the common life—by providing a constant and increasing supply of young people who have social outlook and purpose before they cast their first vote, and before they enter upon their life-occupations.[1]

The idea of a department of education in the local religious society. The clergy of to-day, if we may judge by conditions that are prevalent in the churches, commonly look upon education as an adjunct of the church, an appendix of the ministry, which requires only such strength and such means as may be left over after other things are attended to. If this looks like a harsh judgment, test it by instituting a survey of the twenty churches nearest to you, a survey that will compare expenditure for religious education with expenditure for other things in three respects: (*a*) Hours per week given to religious education by salaried officials as compared with hours given to other interests; (*b*) A similar comparison of annual fiscal expenditure, salaries included; (*c*) A comparison of the space used for religious education with that used for other purposes, a comparison that shall include both amount of room and degree of adaptation.

It would doubtless be unjust to charge any one with stupidity in this matter. Ministers, like the rest of us, are made what they are by social conditions. It is impossible, too, not to sympathize with pastors upon whom there falls such a multiplicity of burdens that no strength is left for the improvement of parish education. Yet it must be said that this heaping of

---

[1] From the sporadic attempts at whirlwind reforms that one witnesses here and there, one might suppose: (1) That social wrongs like the saloon, white slavery, unemployment, seven-day labor, child labor, poverty, and war, are discontinuous parts of the social complex, each of which might be cleaned up by itself once and for all. It is not so. Social wrongs not only intertwine, they are continuous with one another, like teeth, æsophagus, and stomach. (2) That, after certain reforms are accomplished, the church will be able to devote itself wholly to its more particular work. Again, it is not so. The particular work of the church *is* the radical transformation of society. The fundamental difference between the church and other institutions is the radical character of its social principle, a principle within which is included Christianity's limitless hope for each individual.

miscellaneous duties upon one another occurs because of the lack of an adequate organizing principle for the pastoral office. The question that needs to be answered is not, "How can I possibly do more things?" but "What is my perspective? Which things are large, and which ones small? What is fundamental, and what accessory? Which sort of labor brings the largest returns?"

In view of present insight into the church's duty to the community, and in view of the agitation for religious education that has been going on for years, one might say, without uncharitableness, that the minister *of the future* will indeed be stupid if he permits himself to be made a pack-horse, or an all-'round handy man, when he is called of God to be a prophet. The spirit of prophecy, when it comes among us, will doubtless manifest itself in many ways, but one of them will surely be the organization of genuine departments of religious education.

As a rule, departments of religious education do not yet exist in our churches. Instead, we have a heap of unrelated organizations and activities—a Sunday school, a young people's society, a junior society, clubs of boys and of girls, mission-study classes, week-day religious instruction, classes of catechumens, sermons to children, and, apart from them all, the isolated efforts of church members at religious education in the home. The results are:

(a) Overlapping and duplication, as in Bible study or study of missions.

(b) Gaps, such as: Lack of social or other activities appropriate to a particular age, or to one sex at a particular age; lack of regular educational procedures for inducting the young into full membership in the church; lack of missionary training for one or another group; lack of connection between all these activities and the ordinary functions of laymen in the local society. At present the fact that one has been trained in a Sunday school rarely guarantees that he is fit for skilful churchmanship.

(c) Indefiniteness of purpose, and consequently lack of standards. Because the young people's society doesn't quite know what place belongs to it in an educational scheme, the upper age

limit is often left undefined, so that men and women of almost
any age are found among the "young" people. Moreover, many
a young people's society, instead of training its members in churchmanship, has become a competitor of the church. Similarly,
clubs of various sorts pursue their way, according to chance conditions or chance leadership, with little or no vital connection
with the church or with any distinctly religious purpose. The
Sunday school, in turn, not seldom assumes that it is efficient simply because the school machinery hums. That is, it compares
itself with itself instead of judging itself by the ascertained progress of its pupils toward some defined goal. The lack of a defined
goal subjects the school, further, to the whims of individuals.
For the same reason there is much jumping at fads, or standing
"pat" on already discredited methods.

(d) In a word, there is no guarantee that any person will receive genuine, continuous pastoral care through his childhood
and youth.

The gaps and the overlappings in a local society, or in a
denominational programme, can be graphically presented by
making a table like that shown on the opposite page.

The respective provisions for the two sexes may be made
still more graphic by using black ink for one, and red ink for
the other. The table here given is only a suggestion. In many
churches additional items would have to be inserted, and in
some cases a different division would be advisable. Thus,
church doctrine might be separated from church usages, or
usages and worship might be combined. If the conditions in
any church were adequately presented in the present table, the
following queries would arise: Why duplicate Bible instruction for just these ages; in fact, why duplicate at all? Does
instruction in church doctrine and usages begin early enough
and continue long enough? Does mission study begin early
enough, and why is there so much more for women than for
men? Why does training in worship stop while the capacity
for worship is little more than infantile? Why is there training in giving for women and not for men, and why doesn't this
training run all the way through the Sunday school? Why do

DISTRIBUTION OF RELIGIOUS EDUCATION IN..........

Provision for males is indicated by continuous lines; for females by broken lines

Age	3 TO 4 5	6	7	8	9	10	11	12	13	14	15	16	17	18	19	20	21	22	23	24	25	26	27	28	29	30	etc.
Instruction in Bible:																											
In Sunday school..........																											
In Young People's Society.....																											
In Junior Society, etc.........																											
Instruction in Church Doctrine and Usages:																											
In Catechumen's Class, etc...																											
Instruction in Missions:																											
In Sunday school..............																											
In Mission-Study Class, etc...																											
Training in Worship:																											
In Sunday school, etc.........																											
Training in Giving Money:																											
In Sunday school..............																											
In Mission-Study Class, etc...																											
Instruction and Training in Social Service and in Social Righteousness:																											
In Sunday school..............																											
In Sermons to Children, etc.																											

men receive instruction and training in social righteousness while women do not, and why are the socially important years of early and middle adolescence left blank? In general, why is middle adolescence less richly provided for than other ages? Finally, is this church promoting and supervising home instruction and training?

A department of religious education, on the other hand, would provide all-'round pastoral care for children. For, in contrast to the present jumble of agencies, and the hit-or-miss methods that are so common, it would have the following features:

(a) It would include as pupils all the children and youth over whom the church has oversight.

(b) It would include, and unify, everything done by the church with these pupils. Labor would be economized by omitting useless activities and duplications, and by increased specialization within the activities that remain. Every class, club, or society that might be needed would then become a real organ of the central purpose.

(c) Such a department would have for the whole a definite plan, out of which, in connection with accumulating experience, would grow definite standards and tests of the various organs and procedures. Of the nature of standards and tests more will be said presently.

(d) Because of this definiteness of purpose, of functions, of standards, and of tests, specialized training would be provided for the workers, and they would be appointed, transferred, promoted, and relieved, on impersonal, educational grounds, not, as happens so often at present, for personal considerations, sometimes even irrelevant ones.[1]

(e) Such a unified whole would have unified supervision that reaches to every part and to every activity. Somebody must

---

[1] The smart that so many Sunday school teachers and officers now feel when they cannot have their own way is due in large measure to the fact that irresponsibility has become a presumption of one's office. When there is neither standard, nor test, nor supervision for my work, how can I help being hurt when anybody else assumes authority over me? The way out of this medley of arbitrary prerogatives, with the touchiness that results, is not increase of arbitrary power, or more decisive use of it, as by a superintendent,

know just what is happening, and must be competent and ready to assist any and every worker to do his best.

Wherein supervision consists. The proposal to establish thorough supervision in religious education, and to appoint, transfer, promote, and relieve teachers and officers solely on the ground of efficiency will seem to many persons to involve extreme difficulty. For supervision is popularly supposed to imply one or more of these disagreeable things: Secret spying upon my work; concocting plans with respect to me behind my back; subjecting myself to a boss who may not understand my problems, or difficulties, or limitations; encountering fault-finding, and possibly sarcasm, when I have done the best I know how. If such fears were well founded, supervision would be essentially anarchy—the anarchy that lurks in every autocracy. Teachers are justified in being sensitive at this point; no foreign invasion of their work or of their personal dignity can be justified. But supervision, properly understood, is the exact opposite of the wrongs that are feared. Thus:

(1) *Supervision is sharing the burdens, and the blame, that might otherwise fall upon an isolated individual.* One of the worst vices of the traditional Sunday school is that it isolates the worker with his work. How few teachers and officers can say: "There is one person who understands my problems and difficulties, is ever ready to help me with them, and if things go wrong will share with me the responsibility for the error"! As a matter of fact, the gibes to which Sunday school teachers have been subjected in recent years have been made possible, for the most part, by lack of supervision. If a pastor or a director of religious education were known to be implicated in the faults that seem-worthy of castigation, he would

but the exaltation of impersonal educational standards—standards sufficiently technical to do honor to those who attain them, without dishonoring those who do not. Besides, when a church as a whole takes religious education in a sufficiently serious way, the very largeness of the problem sobers those who realize what is happening. It is then possible to appeal to the deeper religious motives of the workers—motives that will make one glad to have the best possible work done, and even, out of loyalty, to acquiesce in decisions the wisdom of which one doubts.

be the more shining mark for the darts of scorn, or at least his share in the chagrin would make the teacher's share easier to bear. Simple fairness requires some stated provision whereby each worker may talk over his problems with some other person who will take the trouble to understand them and to assist in solving them. This conception of the matter puts upon the supervisor, on the other hand, an obligation to co-operate understandingly and sympathetically with each worker—to make him succeed if this is possible. The supervisor is not to be a slave-driver, or a mere task-setter, or a mere measurer and appraiser; he is not to be outside the work at all, but inside it; he is to be "touched with the feeling of our infirmities," having been "in all points tempted like as we are."

(2) *Supervision limits the arbitrariness of every worker, the supervisor himself included.* Supervision does imply that I surrender my arbitrary will in every detail of my work, but that to which I surrender is not another arbitrary will, but the common cause. Moreover, every other worker does the same, so that we meet one another upon a truly democratic basis. *Every one* is to take this humble position.

Probably no workers receive less supervisory assistance than Sunday school superintendents, though in the nature of their work no one needs it more. Their duties are complicated, to begin with. Administration, conduct of worship, selection and supervision of teachers—all these fall to their lot. For lack of supervision the best powers of many a superintendent are never called into use. Lack of supervision means isolation. Having no one to go to with his problems, and no one to show him his faults or how to improve, he stumbles along, forms habits of stumbling, becomes set in his ways, and very likely arbitrary. There are many superintendents who think of themselves as specialists in Sunday school work, whereas they are merely mechanized. Again, the many superintendents who assume that they have a sort of prescriptive right to their office, those who are ready to make a row if they are deposed, most of the martinets and the autocrats, are victims of the injustice that is inherent in every unsupervised school. They have been made what they are by the situation in which the votes of others have placed them. Gradually, gently, irresponsible superintendents must be made over into responsible ones, or else displaced. The same principle applies to the pastor and the director of religious education.

The fundamental idea in supervision is intimate sharing in burden-bearing. This implies that the group of workers is of the deliberative sort. Every one has a right to be heard. Every one has the duty of making available the facts that only he knows; every one's experience contains some illumination; every one must form judgments of his own as a part of his contribution to the common enterprise, and these judgments must concern, in some measure, the acts of the supervisor himself. He will make a serious blunder if he assumes to be a self-sufficient fountain of either wisdom or executive power. For he will almost certainly discredit himself by his obvious fallibility, and even if, by personal attractiveness or by sheer energy, he gets himself accepted at his own valuation, the result will be a mechanized school which, lacking the unity and the self-perpetuating capacity of a living organism, will fall to pieces when his hand is withdrawn. The way of the wise supervisor is that of humble seeking for light; it is that of openness of purpose, and great frankness with every worker; it is that of spreading his own policies and acts before the staff of workers so that they may not only be instructed but also become his instructors.

(3) *Supervision implies that there is a definite organ for maintaining the unity of the school.* The present isolation of the worker not only increases his own burdens, it adds to the burdens of others also. Take as an example the problem of cultivating reverence in pupils. The conduct of a pupil in the common worship of the school often depends upon the attitude and the habits of his teacher. The thoughtless influence of many a tardy, inattentive, disorderly teacher pulls against the superintendent's efforts to lead the children into a worshipful frame of mind. On the other hand, cases are not lacking in which a superintendent's slam-bang ways in the assembly of the school beget irreverence that the teacher cannot over-

come. Consider, likewise, the burdens that teachers must
bear because of poor work done in lower grades. The fact is
that the parts of a school are interdependent, whether we plan
to have them so or not. But interdependence is not the same
as unity. Nor is unity achieved even by having a common
purpose in all the parts unless the community of the purpose be
specifically represented in some official who acts upon every
part from the standpoint of wholeness. The supervisor is, in
fact, the organ whereby the school assures itself of a *system* of
religious education.

(4) *Supervision develops standards of educational efficiency
for every office.* The very fact that a school has a supervisor
should mean emphasis upon results, or efficiency, as distinguished
from going through certain movements. For example, the office
of secretary will involve not only filling in certain blank spaces
in record books, but also such use of the records as helps to
educate the pupils. The secretary will be, in his own way, an
educator. A long vista of attractive possibilities opens up for
this ordinarily prosaic office—a vista of analyses that shall
show the strong and the weak points in the school; reports that
shall stimulate pupils, teachers, parents, and the church board;
exhibits that shall be a tonic for everybody. Similarly, the
office of the teacher in each grade will consist primarily in producing certain ascertainable results in pupils—not in saying
certain things, not in "going over" certain pages in a text-
book. So it will be through the whole school. The superintendent, as well as his colleagues, will be answerable for producing definable educational effects in pupils. Not "What have
you done?" but "What have you got done?" will be the
primary question for each.

When each office comes to be defined thus by its educational
function, then and then only the person who holds the office
is put into true perspective. We have then the antidote for
the substitution of personal attractiveness for skill; we have
the corrective for both faddishness and traditionalism; and we
undermine every claim to hold an office as a personal perquisite.
Here is the beginning of the cure for discontinuity of work

through changes of personnel. As long as the present fogginess of standards prevails, we must expect that, as workers come and go, there will be interruptions and disruptions of function. But clearly understood standards, administered by a recognized supervisor, will tend to stabilize the whole school, and to produce continuity of life at every point.

(5) *Supervision develops tests of efficiency.* A standard is some point that we set out to reach within a given time; a test is any fact by which we can judge whether we have moved toward this point, and how far we have moved. If the standard is that every teacher should be on time every Sunday of the year, the test is the facts of attendance counted one by one each Sunday. If a standard for the fourth grade is that each pupil should by the end of the year know the Bible stories up to the David cycle, then the test is some piece or pieces of work done by each pupil in which he uses these stories.[1] If a standard of the secondary department is that every pupil, *as far as possible*, should be brought into full or confirmed membership in the church by the age of sixteen, then the test will include, in addition to counting those who are and those who are not in this relation to the church by the age of sixteen, such a study of each remaining outsider as will reveal why he remains outside. Only so can we judge whether the obstacle was or was not removable by our efforts.

The distinction between standards and tests is important. For high standards do not of themselves prove much as to the effectiveness of the work that is actually done. Many a worker, in fact, deceives himself by measuring the quality of his work by the motives with which it is done, or by the hopes that are entertained for it. There is no end to the possibilities of bungling on the part of those who mean well. Generally the standard itself is somewhat hazy until tests are devised, so that standards

---

[1] This is not the same as saying that an examination is necessary, at least if "examination" is used in the ordinary sense. The formalistic examination that still lingers in day schools and colleges bears witness, not to thoroughness of teaching in these institutions, but to a low level of teaching methods. Here and there a Sunday school needs to be warned against adopting in religious teaching the defective methods that progressive educators are struggling to put an end to in other schools.

and tests, though they are distinct, are practically reciprocal. The tabular view on the oppsite page will suggest the relations here involved, and also some general notions of the sorts of standard and of test that will be found appropriate in a church department of education.

Most of the theory that underlies this table has already been stated. The proposal to utilize in administration all the available powers of pupils may, however, need a word of explanation. Let us recall, then, two features of the outlook that we have already reached. The first is that the basal process in the teaching of religion is social experience on the Christian plane, or common purposeful life on the part of teacher and pupil. The second is that we are to educate for democracy. These two principles taken together imply that the ideal school is not the one in which there is an impervious governing class placed over the class of the governed, but the one in which there is no plane of separation at all between the governors and the governed. That is, though diversity of function must exist, so that one person uses his judgment in one sphere, another in another, children themselves at all ages have real functions in school management. Alternatives are constantly to be provided, and the choice of pupils between such alternatives is to be final.

By the time pupils reach the secondary school age they are experienced enough to form a student council made up of representatives from their various classes. Such a council, as experience has already shown, may well consider, and in many cases settle, serious problems. When such a body is not a make-believe one, devised by adults simply for getting pupils to accept what has already been decided, but a body that is seriously consulted and really used for improving policies and methods, the members of it show surprising capacity—surprising to any one brought up under a contrary type of education— for appreciating the purposes of the school and for contributing a valuable element to the administration of it.

Relation of the families of the church to the church school. Thus far I have spoken of the department of religious educa-

STANDARDS
AND
TESTS
FOR THE
CHURCH
SCHOOL

STANDARDS AND TESTS OF ULTIMATE RESULTS

The Standard: Progress of the Democracy of God, Progress being Defined from time to time by the Right Settlement of Specific Social Problems.

The Test: Statistics of Social Conditions, including the Church and Missions, our own Local Community, and the Larger Society—Nation and World.

STANDARDS AND TESTS OF PROXIMATE RESULTS

The Standard: Intelligent Consecration of Every Pupil, according to his Capacity, to the Christian Purpose, which is promotion of the Democracy of God.

The Test: Varies with the Age of the Pupil. With Younger Pupils, Observation of Conduct by Parents and Teachers; with Older Pupils, Activities in Church and Community. "By their Fruits."

STANDARDS AND TESTS OF PROCESS

TEACHING

The Standard: The Principles of Teaching as Scientifically Determined.

The Test: Observation of the Teacher's Work by the Supervisor, and Self-observation by the Teacher, with written Reports.

ORGANIZATION

The Standard: (1) Every Function of a School of Religion to be Definitely Assigned to some Individual. (2) Economy of Human Energy by Avoidance of Duplications and of Useless Enterprises. (3) All Work to be Supervised.

The Test: (1) Comparison with other Schools, Religious and Secular. (2) The History and Theory of Religious Education. (3) Direct Study of Results of this School. Hence an Adequate System of Records and Reports.

ADMINISTRATION

The Standard: (1) All Available Power to be Utilized, including Powers of Pupils. (2) All Workers to be Trained. Provision to be made for Growth after Formal Training has Ended. (3) Selection, Promotion, etc., on Basis of Efficiency only. (4) Search for the Best; Experimental Attitude; Readiness to Improve. (5) Humane, Co-operative Relations between all Persons Involved. Expressions of Appreciation.

The Test: (1) Annual Report from Each Worker upon His Own Part of the Work. (2) Annual Summaries and Statistical Exhibits that show where both Strength and Weakness lie. (3) Democratic Council of Workers for Digesting this Knowledge and Planning Improvements.

tion, or church school, as though it comprised only the activities that have their centre in the church building. But a broader conception is possible and necessary. All members of the church who have growing children should be accounted members of the staff of instructors, accounted so not merely in sentiment, but also administratively. Upon the birth of the first child the parents' names should be recorded as teachers, just as the child's name should be recorded as a pupil in the Cradle Roll or Font Roll department. And not until all their living children have graduated from the church school should the names of such parents be dropped from the roll of teachers. In the meantime they should be given continuous supervision; they should make annual reports just as other teachers and all officers should do; and training classes and departmental staff meetings should be provided.[1]

The evils of isolation are nowhere more in evidence than in the semichaotic condition of religious education in church families. Here are multitudes of parents who would like to know how to rear their children to be Christians, but no one tells them how. The chief trouble is not that knowledge on this point is limited (as it certainly is), but that there is no organized method of spreading the knowledge that is available. And one reason why our knowledge on this point is so limited is that there is no organized method of observing and recording the experience of families. Beginnings of the right kind have been made in the distribution of material by the superintendents of

---

[1] In my own thinking, what is here suggested has its place in a comprehensive conception of a working church. The notion of a church as a congregation to be talked to, or as a fellowship in anything that does not include co-operative labor, does not of itself go far enough. What does it mean to the people themselves that they are members of churches? Doubtless it means refraining from certain sorts of wrong conduct, going to church, and leading a life of prayer. It ought to mean, in addition, a specific, defined, and supervised sphere of labor for the promotion of the democracy of God. Is it too much to hope that the time will yet come when every member will be recorded in the books of the church as a worker in a certain department; when each of these departments will have plans and policies that bear specifically, not in any merely generic and hazy way, upon actual conditions that confront its members; when businesslike supervision will be provided for every worker; when every worker will render regular reports of his activities, and when progress or decline in his department will be annually ascertained and recorded? This, I conceive, fairly represents what the church is here for.

Cradle Roll and Font Roll departments, and in the holding of parents' meetings and parents' classes in various Sunday schools. But these are only a drop in the bucket; they are only a mild palliation of an enormous waste.

The problem of getting time enough for effective religious education. When present inefficiencies are pointed out, few remarks are more common than this: "Well, how much can you expect from a half-hour's instruction once a week? We must have more time." Thereupon there is casting about for either some method of getting religious instruction into the public schools, or for establishing week-day religious instruction by the churches themselves. The problem is a real and pressing one, and it is not less serious than it seems to be; yet the time-situation as a whole has never yet, I believe, been correctly analyzed in print. Reserving for a subsequent chapter the relations of state education to religion, let me describe in blunt fashion the present situation within the churches.

(1) *The churches are wasting a large proportion of the precious half-hour for religious instruction on Sunday.* They are wasting it by curtailing it for trivial causes, such as speeches by strangers, a superintendent's dawdling, the intervention of unimportant "special occasions"; by interruptions, as by the secretary; by unnecessary distractions; and by failure to supervise the teacher or to train him so as to get the best possible work from him.

(2) *It is not true that only a half-hour is available for religious instruction on Sunday.* In most Sunday schools the period for class instruction could be lengthened fifteen minutes by adding to it the time that is now wasted or ill used. The school begins late, protracts the opening exercises without reason, makes clumsy transitions because system and team-work are weak, and takes the time of the general session for various things that could be attended to at least as well otherwise. To test the applicability of this analysis to your school, take your watch in hand for a few Sundays, and write down the number of minutes spent upon each procedure, being sure to include any items like those mentioned in the preceding sentence; then write out your judgment as to the time needed,

on educational grounds, for each of these procedures. Was the prayer too long, or not long enough? Did the superintendent do any unnecessary talking? Etc., etc.

(3) *Every minute of the Sunday school, not merely the class period, should be made educationally effective.* Why talk as if church education were shut up to a bare half-hour, when perhaps thrice this time is already available? Our greatest weakness is not lack of time, after all, but lack of effectiveness in the use of what we have.

(4) *It has not been demonstrated that a longer Sunday session is impracticable.* We need experiments with, say, a two-hour session, which shall include, besides a period for worship and one for recitation, a period for study (under supervision), and a period for planning and administering enterprises of social helpfulness.

(5) *When week-day instruction is entered upon, as it must probably be sooner or later, it should be an organic part of a general plan for the church school, and there should be unified administration.* That is to say, the time problem is not an isolated one. The question whether we ought to have more time is bound up with the question of what we would do with it if we had it. Agitation for week-day instruction has only too often proceeded as if, granted the time, we would be ready to go ahead, whereas such matters as the content and method of instruction and the relation thereof to the Sunday instruction, and the whole problem of administration have hardly begun to be considered. Nor has the problem of securing competent teachers for week-day classes even approached a solution as yet.[1] I would not imply that these problems must all be worked out in advance of experiment, but only that any experiment that is made should proceed from a competent grasp of educational principles. We should hesitate, we should refuse, to establish another isolated, falsely self-sufficient agency.

(6) *The problem of securing a sufficient proportion of the pupil's*

---

[1] I have presented concrete instances of these problems in "A General View of the Movement for Correlating Religious Education with Public Instruction."—*Religious Education* XI (1916), 109–122.

time is bound up with that of securing a sufficient proportion of the teacher's time, and this problem is bound up, in turn, with the injustices of our economic order. We should not put ourselves in the position of asking for additional time in which to do poor teaching; but when we ask for more of the teacher's time in order that he may fit himself for more skilful work, we confront, in a great proportion of cases, the grim fact of economic pressure so great as to leave insufficient time and energy for the necessary study. A large part of the work of religious education is being done at the present moment with only the fag ends of human energy. All honor to the housekeepers, the factory operatives, the stenographers, the salespeople, and the bookkeepers who are giving a considerable proportion of their free time to uncompensated and often unhonored labor in the Sunday school. Many of them are bravely, but with great handicaps, struggling to secure adequate training for their work. The spectacle is more noble than it is pathetic. But most of all it is a challenge to the church to realize how her very life is being drained by the economic order against which she has only feebly protested. The long working day, and the high-pressure methods that now prevail are not necessary to feed, clothe, house, and educate all the people, nor are the products of the people's industry distributed upon any such principle. Let us face the fact that the great problem of time in religious education is identical with the problem of the consumption of the time of the many in heaping up possessions for the few.

The financial support of the church school. That the church school should be supported by the church should be rather obvious from the principles that have been stated. There are two great objections to the common practice of paying the expenses of the school by collections of money from its pupils: *First*, the pupils' contributions can be made far more educative by a different plan, and, *second*, when the school pays its own expenses the church lacks an important reminder of its function as religious educator, and is practically invited to let the school go its own way. Let us consider these two points in reverse order.

Having the school regularly in the church budget is more than a matter of paying bills. It is an outward and visible sign of the church's inward and spiritual comprehension of its central task. Something is gained when the school merely appears along with the minister, the janitor, the choir, the coal man, and the insurance agent. But the relative amounts appropriated for these various items reveal something of importance. Here is a church with a budget of twenty thousand dollars for local expenditures that appropriates for its Sunday school the same amount that it pays to one janitor, namely, seven hundred and fifty dollars.[1] This is one-fifth of the amount appropriated for church music. A budget like this is a veritable window into the local ecclesiastical mind. Well-to-do churches are buying for their Sunday schools printed matter that is educationally as well as commercially cheap. There are wealthy churches that "cannot afford" to employ a director of religious education, and when the payment of teachers is suggested ask: "Will not paying the teacher interfere with the spirituality of his work?" We need, then, for the sake of the church as a whole to keep the Sunday school in the church budget, and to keep on increasing the appropriation until the church wakes up to the greatness of its task.

On the other hand, the pupils in the school need to be trained in giving. Ordinarily, it appears, the "authorities of the school" decide where the pupils' money shall go, and then approach the pupils with little more than "Give, give!" One child is reported to have been under the delusion that he was giving to his teacher! Real training in giving requires: (a) Intelligence as to the object for which money is solicited. (b) Comparison of one object with another so as to judge how money should be apportioned between them. (c) Free choice

[1] It is to be assumed, of course, that a part of the salary of both pastor and janitor, and a part of the expenditure usually listed under lighting, heating, insurance, repairs, etc., are devoted to religious education. But even when these are added to the item for the Sunday school the total bears no fitting relation to the fundamental place and the proper cost of religious education. It would be well for every church to make a budget that would show for whom (children or adults) all moneys are appropriated.

between alternatives. (*d*) The development of co-operation in judging causes and in supporting them. (*e*) Continuity, the habit of giving, sustained loyalty to a cause. (*f*) A report to the giver as to what has been done with his contributions, and what they have accomplished.

The pupils in the church school should be led, in accordance with these principles, to support the local church, to give to missions and other church enterprises, and to support philanthropies. To exploit a school in the interest of a financial need, to "work" it as a source of increased revenues, to play upon children's untrained sympathies and impulses—this is degradation. Every financial transaction in which a pupil takes part should be educative to him. If we seek first this educational righteousness, we need have no fears that the contributions of the pupils will be niggardly, but if we do not train them thus to intelligent, discriminating, systematic giving, we need not be surprised if they make crotchety and ungenerous givers in maturity.[1]

[1] These principles may be worked out by various methods. The duplicate envelope system offers a great advance over traditional ways, but much more than the envelope is needed. I look forward to a time when every church will report all its receipts and expenditures to the pupils in the Sunday school, and when the great church societies also will give an account of their stewardship to the learners. In the Union School of Religion each class has its own treasury, out of which it votes its contributions after studying various causes. These contributions fall into two classes, those made to causes that the school as a whole is helping to support, such as a missionary enterprise and a local philanthropy, and those which the class itself, with the help (but never the dictation) of the teacher, chooses as its particular sphere of helpfulness. When a class gives a contribution to one of the general causes, the class treasurer pays over the amount to the school treasurer.

CHAPTER XVII

EDUCATIONAL RELATIONS BETWEEN STATE AND CHURCH

The social significance of the modern secular state.
The term "secular state" is here used as the most convenient designation for a political society in which organized religion as well as individual religious attitude is an altogether voluntary matter. This implies, of course, that the financial support of organized religion is voluntary, not a matter of taxation, which is a form of legal compulsion.

The tendency of modern states to become secular is unmistakable. First, the civil power, refusing to accept dictation from the ecclesiastical power, holds itself to be co-ordinate therewith. Next, the state takes over ecclesiastical functions of many kinds, such as charities and education. Disestablishment follows, and finally even patronage is withdrawn. Only "free churches" then remain—free in the same sense as a literary society or a golf-club.

This growing separation of church from state is a phase of the growth of popular government. The necessity that such government should have an intelligent electorate has caused it to assume the duty of educating all the people. Here, more than anywhere else, we shall find the nerve of the secular state. Here civil society procreates itself, so to say, in the thought and the conscience of children. Just here is where the separation of the churches from the taxing power is most difficult in both theory and practice. Long after disestablishment occurs, the two powers remain entangled in the matter of education.

If we desire a disentanglement that shall be in the interest of a socially adequate education, we must look at the state school itself (which we of the United States commonly call the

248

"public" school) as an expression of certain great social aspirations. We must realize, to begin with, that the secularization of the state, and therefore of state schools, has been necessitated chiefly by the social inadequacy of ecclesiastical traditions and practices. The state, not the church, has been the decisive defender and guarantor of fundamental liberties, such as the right to think, to speak, to associate with one's fellows, and to stand before courts of law as the equal of any citizen. The conception of indefeasible rights, which no authority, whether it speaks in the name of man or of God, may abridge—this conception may almost be said to have given birth to the modern state.

The free state, moreover, rather than any church, has been the chief practical realization of the unity and the solidarity of men. The Jews, for example, becoming free citizens, find in the state a human recognition that the dominant religion of the western world had never, in any of its main branches, accorded to them. The great mixer of races in this country has been the civic rather than the ecclesiastical community, and before all else the public school.

Without doubt what is humane and democratic in the modern state owes a large part of its inspiration to religion. Within Christianity from the days of Jesus there has been the leaven of democracy. Though this leaven has been for the most part, to use Jesus' own word, "hidden," there has appeared from time to time evidence that the germ is not dead. Not only have individuals here and there seen and declared the incompatibility of the spirit of Jesus with all oppression, exploitation, and denial of equality of opportunity, but minor groups of many sorts have endeavored to live the brotherhood that they professed, and some phases of liberty have been espoused by whole denominations. On the other hand, many a prophet of the rights of men has been an "infidel," and certainly the secular state has actually brought men together as no religious organization has done.

One might maintain, with considerable show of reason, that the socially integrative power of religion has passed to the state, even the secular state.   During the rise of popular government, the populace has been divided on religious grounds, divided not only as respects the great historic religions of the world— Christianity, Judaism, etc.—but divided also into apparently irreconcilable parties within the dominant religion.   Indeed, so bitter has been religious partisanship at times that the civil power has had to step in to preserve the peace.   Religion has had to be protected from religion by the secular arm.   On the other hand, the secular power has had to guard against allowing its prerogatives or its funds to come under the control of one or another religious party.

In short, then, the secular state, particularly in its schools, is our highest social achievement in these two respects: (1) The securing of freedom and equal rights for individuals, and (2) The organization of authority upon the basis of manhood rather than upon the basis of hereditary or other class privilege. That we are still at the beginnings in both these matters is clear enough.   Even fundamental rights are not too secure as yet, and the spirit of democracy is still engaged in the struggle against privilege.   But we have definitely entered upon the struggle, and we have entered upon it specifically as members of the secular state.

Why the public schools in the United States are increasingly secular.   In the District of Columbia, the territories, the Indian reservations, and the insular possessions, public education comes under the provision of the Federal Constitution that forbids the Congress to make any law concerning an establishment of religion.   The full force of this prohibition was not at first recognized, for government funds were appropriated for the support of Indian schools under the control of religious bodies, some Catholic, some Protestant.   From this patronage of churches, however, the government has already partly withdrawn, and complete withdrawal is in sight.

In the States of the Union public education is under State control, and is therefore not subject to the federal prohibition of an established church.   Some of the oldest States had at the outset of their history what amounted practically to a State church. But they have moved away from such entanglements, and the younger States have commonly begun their career with constitutional bars against them. At the present time the separation of the state from the church is axiomatic throughout the Union.

But the application of the axiom to the public schools has not been easy or uniform. The constitutions, the statutes, the court decisions, and the administrative precedents of the different States differ greatly from one another. Nevertheless, a general trend, an unambiguous one, is discernible: The States participate less and less in anything that is specifically recognized by the people as religion.

Before we ask for the reasons of this trend, let us glance at a single specimen of the change in question. The Ordinance for the Government of the Northwest Territory, promulgated in 1787, that is, the territory northwest of the Ohio River, contains this clause: "Religion, morality, and knowledge being necessary to good government and the happiness of mankind, schools and the means of education shall forever be encouraged." Here, it is clear, the state has the distinct intention of teaching religion, or of seeing that it is taught. But the constitutions of the States that were carved out of this territory show a progressive modification of this intention until, in some instances, no trace of it is left.

The first modification is in the constitution of Ohio, which was adopted in 1802: "Religion, morality, and knowledge being essentially necessary to the good government and happiness of mankind, schools and the means of instruction shall forever be encouraged by legislative provision, not inconsistent with the rights of conscience." In 1851 the statement is changed still further: "Religion, morality, and knowledge being essential to good government, it shall be the duty of the general assembly to pass suitable laws to protect every religious denomination in the peaceable enjoyment of its own mode of public worship, and to encourage schools and the means of instruction." Thus, first the rights of conscience are brought in as a limitation; then the ground of the provision is narrowed to the needs of good government, no reference being made to any other value in religion; finally, the duty imposed changes from encouraging schools in which religion shall be promoted to protecting religious denominations in their own modes of worship.

Indiana puts into her constitution in 1816 only this shred of the original statement in the Ordinance of 1787, "Knowledge and learning generally diffused through a community being essential to the preservation of a free government," followed by regulations respecting school lands. In 1851 the statement is changed to read as follows: "Knowledge and learning generally diffused throughout a community being essential to the preservation of a free government, it shall be the duty of the general assembly to encourage, by all suitable means, moral, intellectual, scientific, and agricultural improvement." Michigan in 1850 makes the list still briefer: "The legislature shall encourage the promotion of intellectual, scientific, and agricultural improvement." The various constitutions of Illinois have no trace of the original declaration of 1787. The Minnesota constitution, 1857, declares: "The stability of a republican form of government depending mainly upon the intelligence of the people, it shall be the duty of the legislature to establish a general and uniform system of public schools." Here at last not even morality is mentioned, and intelligence is declared to be the main support of republican institutions.

Though these items cover only one phase of the movement in a limited part of the country, the impression that they convey of a change toward secularism correctly represents a general shift in most of the States of the North and West. What is the explanation? Not any general decline of religion during this period, but the clash of competing religious bodies between which the States determined to be neutral. If the teaching of religion in the public schools produces a wrangling community or school district, the State follows the clear dictate of practical wisdom when it removes the divisive object out of the schools. The whole experiment in popular government would be imperilled if the schools should become class schools. They must be, at all cost, schools of the whole people.

A convenient example of the practical logic that has just been referred to is the contest between Catholics and Protestants over public school funds in the State of New York in the forties. In the law of 1813, which established a system of public instruction, there was a clause that provided for distributing the funds for the City of New York among benevolent, religious, and educational associations that maintained charity schools. As a result, some eight or ten religious societies received subsidies. In 1824 the legislature gave to the common council of the city authority to designate the societies that˙should thus share in the public funds. The scheme produced constant friction, particularly because the Catholics felt that they did not secure their proper share. A chief Protestant beneficiary was the "Public School Society," which maintained what amounted to a chain of public schools without public supervision. The Catholics desired to be put substantially upon a parity with this society. A petition addressed to the common council failed after a long debate. An attempt to secure relief through the legislature likewise failed. At last the question was carried to the electorate itself. The result was a law that no school shall receive any portion of school moneys in which the religious doctrines or tenets of any Christian or other religious sect shall be taught, inculcated, or practised.[1]

Another specimen of friction and of the way of removing it comes from within the original Northwest Territory. As early as 1842 Cincinnati was agitated by complaints that text-books used in the schools contained passages that were obnoxious to Catholics, and that Catholic children were required to read passages from the Protestant Bible. This agitation kept up for twenty-seven years, when Catholic members of the board of education, aided by certain liberals called "freethinkers," passed a resolution that prohibited the reading of the Bible in the schools. Some citizens applied to the superior court for a permanent injunction to prevent the enforcement of this regulation. The court, by a divided vote, granted the petition,

[1] For the history of this most interesting case see the classified Bibliography, Division G, first and third paragraphs.

but an appeal was had to the supreme court, which reversed the decision and upheld the right of the board of education to make the regulation in question.

This right had been attacked on the ground of the Ohio constitutional provision of 1851, which has already been quoted: "Religion, morality, and knowledge being essential to good government." This, argued the petitioners, not only requires religious instruction in the public schools, but specifically Christian instruction based upon the Bible. This was inferred from the historic connection of this clause in the Ohio constitution with the Ordinance of 1787. The framers of this Ordinance, it was said, could have had in mind none but the Christian religion. Opposing counsel pointed out that the Christian religion as thus understood is the Protestant religion, which is essentially sectarian, and that the use of the Bible contemplated by the petitioners is a distinctly Protestant use. Consequently, it was argued, the petitioners practically maintain that Ohio has a state religion. Therefore counsel for the board of education labored to show that the State of Ohio, like the United States, has no religion, Protestant or Catholic, Christian or other.

In the superior court, two of the three judges assented, each in his own way, to the proposition that the State of Ohio has a religion. "We are led to the conclusion," says one of them, "that revealed religion, as it is made known in the Holy Scriptures, is that alone that is recognized by our constitution." The dissenting judge, however, declares that the only way in which neutrality between the sects can be maintained in the schools is by excluding religious instruction altogether. "To hold that Protestants have a right to have their mode of worship and their Bible used in the common schools, against the will of the board of education . . . is to hold to the union of church and state, however we may repudiate and reproach the name."

The opinion of the supreme court coincides with that of the minority member of the superior court. It denies that the Christian religion is a part of the law; it denies altogether that the state has a religion. It is true, runs the reasoning, that religion is necessary to good government, as the constitution

says, and the state must have the best religion, but the best
religion is to be had, as the constitution indicates, by keeping
hands off—by protecting all forms of religion, so that, through
their own interactions and conflicts, the best may come to light.[1]

The difficulty of maintaining in law the distinction be-
tween religion and sectarian religion. There is a large
mass of opinion among religionists and educators to the effect
that since church and religion are not the same, the separation
of the state from the church does not imply that the state or
its schools must be non-religious. The warring sects hold much
in common; why should it not be taught in the schools?
Some court decisions support this conclusion. For example, in
the celebrated Edgerton case, the supreme court of Wisconsin
held that the use of any version of the Bible as a text-book in
the public schools is sectarian instruction, yet one of the judges
took pains to say that the decision of the court does not hinder
the use of passages of the Bible for the purpose of moral instruction, or even for inculcating the broad principles of religion that are common to all the sects.[2]

As a matter of pure theory the distinction between religion
and sectarianism can doubtless maintain itself. In the administration of schools, however, there are factors other than
those contemplated by the theory. These additional factors are:

(1) The teacher, who is almost certain to have received his
religious training from a sect. No teacher, it may be said,
can teach with conviction what is common to the sects without more or less leaning toward or away from something in
some of the sects. By the position of an emphasis, or by silence
with regard to some point, if not by positive assertion, a particular tint is sure to be given to the instruction. As a matter of
fact, is there, or can there be in real life any such thing as a
colorless religion? Is not the notion an abstraction? Actual

---

[1] *The Bible in the Public Schools. Arguments in the Case of John D. Minor
et al Superior Court of Cincinnati. With the Opinions and Decision of the
Court* Cincinnati, Robert Clarke & Co., 1870; *Board of Education. Opinion
and Decision of Supreme Court of Ohio in J. D. Minor vs. Board of Education.*
Cincinnati, 1873; see also 23 *Ohio State Reports*, Granger, 21–254.
[2] 76 *Wisconsin Reports*, Conover, 177.

religion, the sort that one feels and acts out, is always a product of particular historical conditions, and it always involves particular social relations over which conflict is likely, even certain, to occur. How, for example, can any actual religiousness be entirely indifferent to priests? How can one steer a middle course between reverence for them and hostility toward them? If one assumes an attitude of simple non-recognition, is not this itself hostility?

(2) The parents and the board of education that represents them. We must reckon with the possibility of religious sensitiveness on the part of persons who have not studied the philosophy of religion, and are not trained to see or feel the religious affinities between sects. The control of the schools rests ultimately in plain citizens like these. One group of them easily becomes distrustful toward religious teaching by a teacher who belongs to a competing group. Moreover, the most strictly non-partisan teaching that can be achieved is likely to be unsatisfactory by reason of what it omits.

(3) The ecclesiastical organizations. Most of them maintain a ministry that is jealous for the doctrines of its particular church, and likewise apprehensive of encroachments from some other church. Moreover, several churches claim to be *the* church. The direct consequence of the claim to exclusive authority as teacher of religion is this: Insistence that any religious teaching that is given in the public schools be supervised by the authority-possessing church, the only alternative being the exclusion of all such teaching. Many Protestants, accustomed to think of the content of a doctrine without special regard to the problem of doctrinal authority, fancy that the public schools might teach in peace the doctrines that are held in common by Catholic and Protestant. But this would be Protestant teaching! It would be so because it would assume the Protestant position of liberty in teaching and in learning. Catholics will not accept any such plan. From their point of view any religious teaching whatever that is done without Catholic authorization contains an implied denial of the Catholic doctrine of authority.

It is conceivable that Protestantism, because of its tendency toward religious liberty, that is to say, toward appreciation of common humanity as against all sectarianism, might, if left to itself, unite upon some plan for teaching religion in the public schools. But under existing conditions the law has to regard Protestantism in its totality as a sect over against Catholicism as another sect. If it seems anomalous, even absurd, that a state that is built upon liberty and equality should forbid itself to teach religious liberty, we should remind ourselves that our loyalties are manifold, that they are not matters of logic merely, and that they win many of their greatest victories not by might nor by power, but by spirit.

Catholic dissatisfaction with the public school system. The doctrine of infallibility, as formulated by the Vatican Council, declares that the Pope, when he speaks with authority, is infallible in all matters of faith and morals. The Catholic Church as teacher, accordingly, claims exclusive prerogative in everything that is included under the category of character-formation. In strictness, then, the state has no right to teach morals. But can the teaching of morals, or can character-formation be separated from the ordinary instruction of an elementary curriculum? The Catholic answer is that the young pupil, knowing that his schooling is intended to prepare him for life, gets from his school experience an impression of what is important in life. If the school is silent upon the great issues of religion and morals, this silence itself tends to give religion and morals a secondary place in the child's outlook. Therefore the Catholic contention is that religion and morals must be taught in continuous connection with the usual common school branches.

Two things follow: First, the parish school, and second, dissatisfaction toward the public schools. This dissatisfaction manifests itself in various ways. In repeated instances the reading of the Bible in the schools has been complained of on the ground of its sectarianism. In some cases, after the use of the Bible has been discontinued, the schools have been condemned as "godless." But the most common complaint is that Catholics are obliged to pay taxes for the support of schools to which they cannot conscientiously send their children. Hence the oft-renewed agitation for a division of the school funds whereby parish schools shall be compensated for teaching the common school branches.

Premising as before that something more than logic is involved in the adjustment of our differences (as witness the very great extent to which Catholics find it possible to use the public schools, after all), we may well notice that, in strict logic, there is a profound contrast, which amounts to opposition, between the theory of education that prevails among Catholic thinkers and that which underlies education in the modern secular state. The theory of the modern state is that it has a right to educate the children as a necessity for its own safety and progress, and as a means of promoting the common welfare. Hence compulsory education laws. On the Catholic side, when the right to educate is in question, the emphasis is upon the parent rather than the state. Inasmuch, however, as the parent is required to obey the church, the Catholic theory may fairly be said to be this: That the church alone has a right to control the culture of mind and of character. That is, from the standpoint of theory alone, accommodations and adjustments in actual practice being ignored, Catholicism has not yet assimilated the educational philosophy of the modern state.

The demand for division of public school funds with parish schools. The argument for partial support of parish schools by taxation runs to the effect that these schools, while accomplishing their religious purpose, fulfil also the ends of the state by teaching such subjects as reading, writing, arithmetic, etc., and that the state may properly pay the parochial school for teaching these subjects, especially as Catholic taxpayers are debarred by conscientious scruples from using the public schools.

If the problem could be reduced in reality to such simple terms as buying a certain amount of knowledge of this or that, it would be easy enough; the state would simply examine in certain subjects, and pay a stipulated amount for every pupil who reaches a prescribed grade. But the educational purpose of the state is not as meagre as this. The state desires to express *itself* to its children. A democracy must transcend class consciousness, must support and develop the sense of human equality, must train the different elements of the population to co-operation by early habituation of children, and by early awakening a consciousness of citizenship, of *common* citizenship, and of what it means. Can a parish school, which is a class school, accomplish this? The very purpose of a parish school is, primarily and predominantly, to cement together a particular group within the state. It causes children of this group to associate with one another, not with children of other population-groups. And within this closed society the state never speaks in its own person, least of all with its own authority.

It is an obviously sound axiom of administration that wherever public funds go, public control should go also. But a practicable method of public control within a parish school has never been devised. Nor is one likely to be discovered. For the teacher in such a school is appointed by and is answerable to the ecclesiastical power—is an agent of this power and not at all of the state. The act of teaching is here an act of the church, not the joint act of state and church, nor a mixture or alternation of acts first by the church and then by the state. There is, in short, no sphere within a parish school in which the state could act of its own authority; it would be able to act at all only by invitation, permission, or compact.

Public appropriations for parish schools would therefore mark a sort of one-sided union of church and state, one-sided because, though it would assure the church of its sectarian aims, it would not assure the state that its children will receive a broadly social training. That any large number of citizens should be conscientiously unable to use the public schools is deeply to be regretted. That these citizens have shown their faith by paying, here and there, for a second set of day schools is a matter for admiration. But this is the cost to them of religious conditions that divide citizens instead of uniting them. The public should not pay the cost of that which separates citizens from one another. Not only so; it should be a settled part of public policy to keep the public schools so richly attractive, so broad, humane, and responsive to community need, that they will continue to be, but in growing measure, schools of the whole people, the great mixer and democratizer of our heterogeneous population.

How some Protestants would have religion taught in the public schools. The dissatisfaction of the Catholics touches the public school system as such, the basal principles of it. Protestants, as a rule, accept these principles, but there is considerable Protestant unrest over the way in which non-sectarianism works in actual practice. Many claim that the schools can teach religion and yet remain unsectarian, and the point is made again and again that, though the necessity for religious education is as broad as the nation, the present provisions for it are relatively narrow. In the first place, a considerable proportion of the children receives no religious instruction at home or through Sunday schools. In the next place, the amount of instruction given by the Sunday school to its pupils is pitifully small. In the third place, the quality of the teaching in Sunday schools is unsatisfactory. Are we not, then, actually in danger of becoming a non-religious people?

Moved by such considerations, many Protestants are strenuous to retain or to introduce Bible reading in the public schools. A smaller number calls for specific religious instruction in these schools. The nature of these proposals requires careful scrutiny.

(1) *The ground for demanding Bible reading in the schools is ambiguous.* The argument shifts back and forth between the value of the Bible as literature, and its value for religious guidance. It might seem ungracious to suggest that effort is being made to introduce religious teaching under the head of merely literary study. Yet one can hardly help seeing in the background of this whole agitation the distinctly Protestant emphasis upon the Bible as the authoritative word of God. It is unlikely that the agitators for Bible reading would be satisfied to have the Bible treated in the schools exactly like other literature. No; a distinctive, unique reverence is expected, and

even worship in direct connection with the Scripture reading. In short, it is proposed to make the state schools an agency for propagating a distinctly Protestant attitude toward the authority of the Scriptures.

(2) *Protestant agitation for religion in the schools has not sufficiently considered that in the eyes of the law Catholic and non-Catholic versions of the Bible alike, and Protestant as well as Catholic worship, are coming to be regarded as sectarian.* The crux of the matter is the Catholic claim to exclusive religious authority. This claim is, of course, sectarianism. But, justly, or unjustly, Catholic citizens take the ground that to deny this authority, or even to practise religion without recognizing it, is also sectarianism. Here, in fact, the population is cut in two, and the courts, quite naturally, attempt to keep the schools neutral as between them. Therefore any version of the Bible whatever will have only a precarious standing in the schools if a parent chooses to object to it as sectarian. The same is true of worship. It must be either Catholic or non-Catholic, and therefore open to objection from one side or the other. Objection is not always made, to be sure. In communities that are fairly homogeneous in religious population, the schools often practise religion and teach it without producing friction. But growth of a community in size and in heterogeneity of race and of religion commonly puts an end to the old acquiescence in a particular type of religion in the schools, whereupon we face the alternative of introducing more types upon a plane of mutual equality, or else of excluding all.

(3) *Undue hopes are entertained as to the religious effect of listening to the reading of Bible passages.* Again we hear a faint echo of the old Protestant conviction that in the very words of the Scriptures God speaks directly to each individual. Without doubt mere listening to elevated sentiments well phrased has some effect upon the listener, especially if the words reinforce something that the pupil learns in other ways also. That is, Bible readings might be significantly fitted into a genuine plan for religious education, and such readings in the day school might happen to add something to the effectiveness of religious teach-

ing in home or in Sunday school. But of themselves, as mere fragments, by chance related or not to other parts of a system, they cannot be regarded as having the educational significance that the vehemence of the agitation often seems to assume.

(4) *Plans are lacking for the preparation of public school teachers for the teaching of religion.* No one can think that religion can be taught by mere words regardless of the religious character and convictions of the teacher. No one who thinks in educational terms can suppose that the effective teaching of religion requires no specific preparation therefor. How, then, shall we assure ourselves of the personal and professional fitness of public school teachers in this matter? What shall be the tests? What shall the normal schools add to their curriculum? Merely to state these questions is to expose the educational shortsightedness of the agitation for teaching religion in the schools. Imagine the state undertaking to prepare, test, and supervise teachers of religion! In the interest of religion itself we should deny that the state is competent to teach it.

What a democratic state can contribute to a socialized religious education. The considerations to which we have just attended may seem at first sight to isolate the state from religion, and to strip and impoverish the human spirit, instead of enriching it, in the schools. It would be so if religion were identical with either dogmatism or ecclesiasticism. For both are in their inmost nature sectarian; they have always divided Christians from one another. If we should identify religion with them the schools would have to be secular not only in the sense already defined (that is, that they leave the organization of religion altogether to private initiative), but also in the sense that state education and religious education would pursue divergent rather than convergent aims. The schools, giving ultimate value to the broadly human, would have a tendency to promote a secularistic life in distinction from the religious life as thus conceived. But nothing of the kind will be implied if we advance from dogmatic and ecclesiastical standpoints in religious education to a fully social position. When we bring religious education under the conception of the democracy of

God, we have a socially unifying aim to which everything that is truly democratizing and humanizing in state education contributes. For example, a public school that causes pupils of several racial groups to mingle with one another as neighbors, and to realize their unity in a common devotion to the flag as a symbol of liberty, promotes thereby the precise aims that socialized religion would have in a similar situation. In a certain school upon the Pacific coast the pupils of Caucasian extraction, though their daily life is surrounded by prejudice against Mongolians, have become convinced disciples of equal opportunity for Chinese pupils, and have even become protectors of Chinese children against aggression from "Americans." If an exactly parallel phenomenon were to occur in a Sunday school we should spontaneously think of it as a triumph of Christian education.

The interest of a socialized religious education in the public schools is not that they should teach religion in addition to reading, writing, and arithmetic, but that they should teach democracy, and that they should do it thoroughly. To "teach" democracy, it need hardly be argued at this stage of our discussion, means to develop intelligent democratic attitudes, activities, habits, and purposes—in short, to make the pupils democrats.

Here lies the acutest part of the problem of moral instruction and training in the public schools. Real educators are chary of proposals to "introduce moral education" into the schools. It is there already in every piece of work that the pupils are led to do thoroughly; it is there in everything that produces loyalty to the reasonable rules of the school; it is there in the co-operative life of schoolroom and playground; it is there in customs and measures that make for community consciousness and for political idealism—it cannot be introduced, it can only be improved. The improvement for which we most need to strive, about which anxiety is most nearly justified, concerns, not a set of standard virtues that are the same under tyranny and under liberty, but measures for leading pupils to have as their own the great purposes of democracy, which are not only humane, but also constructive and aggressive.   The problem of morals in the schools melts into the problem of creating ambition for a sort of society that is partly prefigured in our historic national ideals, but is still for the most part unachieved.   Give us public schools that develop active interest in human welfare, passion for the basal rights of man as man, faith in the capacity of men for unselfishness, and the habit and purpose of co-operation— give us public schools like these, and social religion will look upon them as doing God's will even though they do not name his name, but only that of his children.

The appropriate policy for socialized religion with respect to the state schools, then, is neither to curb their influence because they are secular, nor to induce them to take over worship or instruction in religion as such, but to get them to realize more and more the possibilities of government of the whole people, by the whole people, and for the whole people, and to provide ever better and better training of intelligence and of will with reference thereto.   Ultimately all the schools may be expected to provide, as some do now, training in both remedial and preventive philanthropy.   In addition they will become nurseries of political progress, not indeed by being tools of political parties, but by constantly recalling attention to the human values that furnish the only ground for the real settlement of political questions.

The specific educational functions of free religion in a free state.   To organized religion there will remain the educational privilege of inclusiveness and of prophecy.   How long states will assume that national selfishness and self-will are politically legitimate, no one can say, but as long as they do, as long as the sociality of the state is arbitrarily limited to a race or to a territory, religious education will have the function of humanizing the state.   In the name of the God of the whole earth, who is the Father of all men, the church must reveal the large sociality that takes in the self-governing state but transcends it.

Just so, the great social problems of individual destiny, the destiny of friendship and love, and the destiny of the race it-

self—problems of the meaning of life that call for the unflinching eye and the resolute heart—will remain to the churches as
voluntary associations.   There are depths of human need that
the state does not undertake to sound.   There are valleys of
experience for which it provides no companion or guide.   There
are heights of self-sacrifice to which it does not venture to point.

Through every social problem, moreover, whether it falls
under the purview of the state school or not, there runs the common human need for inspiration, for the divine inbreathing of
hope, for uncompromising love, for far-sight, for letting go the
half-gods in a great and ultimate faith in Fatherhood and
Brotherhood.

To the churches that have caught a glimpse of this educational horizon falls the task of experimenting and agitating
with a view to a permanent system of democratic religious instruction and training for the children of the whole nation.   Religious education for the whole people must be provided by the
churches at their own expense.   Buildings, equipment, trained
teachers, scientific supervision—all these must be had.   No
mere spurt or spasm will accomplish all this; we must enter
upon a long campaign, only the beginnings of which we ourselves can live to see.   The campaign will be expensive in point
of financial cost, of loyal labor for a distant goal, of hard study
and patient experiment, of disappointments, of deferred hopes,
of strains between friends.   But no one who knows the genius
of the Christian religion will imagine that the love that loves
to the uttermost can be otherwise than costly either to God or
to those who would be godlike.

CHAPTER XVIII

THE DENOMINATIONAL DEPARTMENT OF RELIGIOUS EDUCATION

The emergence of religious education within denominational consciousness. The fact that Sunday schools are universal in a denomination, or that improvements in them are actively labored for, does not of itself prove the presence of the idea of religious education in the denominational consciousness, much less of thought-out standards and policies for education as distinguished from other operations. As long as Sunday school teaching is controlled by the tacit assumption that it is a branch of expository preaching or of evangelistic appeal, there is little about it that is distinctive of education. Under these conditions such a simple, rudimentary educational process as habit-formation—to take a single example—is scarcely undertaken at all. Habits may be talked about, exhortations about them may be plentiful, but the actual habit-forming process is not under conscious control. This example may stand for many facts. The Sunday school, under these conditions, is a school chiefly in a germinal sense, practically all that is specifically and technically educational not yet having come to clear consciousness.

The lack of denominational educational consciousness in the immediate past is revealed and typified by the fact that in several large denominations the functions of a department of religious education are only now being differentiated from those of a denominational publishing house or society. That a denomination should have educational principles and policy; that the duty of carrying them into the whole denominational life should be committed to a corps of educational specialists; and that the Sunday-school publications should become organs

266

for such principles and policy under the guidance of these specialists—this is new to the old-line publisher, and it is new to the Sunday schools that are his patrons.

As each of our cities has a department of education that is not confused, say, with the police department, or with the street department, and as every enlightened board of education seeks the services of an expert educator as superintendent of schools, so the unmistakable trend in the religious denominations is toward a distinct educational consciousness expressed in a department that employs expert and technical service. The idea of the "technical," with its basis in the "scientific," has come only slowly, it is true, into control even of the public schools; in many parts of the country it has not yet arrived at clear consciousness, but is subordinated to office-holding designs, or to ignorant economy. We must not be surprised when we meet like inertia in the churches. Official positions and financial costs will create problems and difficulties. But already the movement of specializing toward the expert and the technical has begun on a denominational scale in several of the bodies. We may confidently expect that advances in religious education will be made in the future not merely school by school, but also denomination by denomination, thousands of schools going forward simultaneously.

Unifying the educational work of a denomination. A sure sign of the infancy of educational consciousness on the denominational scale is our habit of identifying departments of religious education with departments of Sunday schools. What, then, of young people's societies and other organizations of the young, and what of denominational academies and colleges? The purpose of all these, as far as it is defined at all, is educational in a broad, if not a technical, sense. The specific ground of their existence is expectation of religious results. But clarity of purpose, policies appropriate to the purpose, and efficiency in executing it, have been generally lacking. We have already noticed the waste in local societies through overlapping, duplicating, and scattering. This evil could be cured through whole denominations if they had a unified educational department.

That the general board of a young people's society should be an independent department of a denomination, or even an outside body without responsibility to the educational authorities of the denomination, is as anomalous as would be, in the public schools, a department of physical culture that is not responsible to the superintendent of schools or to the board of education.

As to denominational academies and colleges, it is not unfair to say that, though they are interested in both education and religion, they have rarely conceived of *education* in religion as their central function and the reason for their existence.   There has been lack of a definite conception of religious education as a specialized undertaking based upon laws of growth and therefore requiring both continuity and technical care.   Administrators who sincerely desire to promote Christian character have believed in technical proficiency and continuity anywhere but here, and they have rarely been ready to pay the cost of it.   Instead, they have added inexpensive non-educational religion to expensive non-religious education.   The most usual methods of doing this are the maintenance of unsystematized, discontinuous preaching; supporting either shoddy Bible study because of its religiousness, or a sound department of Bible under the supposition that instruction in the Scriptures is religious instruction or even religious education; transferring the religious functions of the institution to student Christian associations, with their immature leadership; and resorting to occasionalistic, high-pressure revival meetings.

One element in the situation is, of course, the increasing difficulty of meeting the educational standards of state institutions.   Into new courses, new buildings, and new laboratory equipment, money and thought have been forced to go.   Religion has had no like force that it could bring to bear upon administrators.   Hence it has tended to become, as far as administration is concerned, an appendage of education, or an accompaniment of it, and not a too expensive one.

A final reason why the educational resources of each denomination have not been unified into a scheme of religious education is the inherent difficulty of constructing such a scheme upon the basis of a pre-social interpretation of the Christian religion. How can a college that awakens its students to the liberty of science advise the same students at the same time to take the intellectual attitudes of dogmatic religion? How can a college that opens the eyes of its students to law and growth and continuity in nature, in history, and in the mind of man, represent the religious experience as a separate, independent, and discontinuous thing? If an attempt is made to cultivate both, it is practically certain that two different sets of men will do the cultivating, that the religious work will be set off by itself and isolated, and that the religious appeal will tend toward occasionalism and toward emotions split off from academic interests.

But when the Christian religion is conceived as the purpose to co-operate with God in building democracy, it offers a unifying and organizing, not dividing, principle for education. All the legitimate work of a college can be brought under this purpose. All of it will be vivified when it receives this baptism. The dawdling of students in our colleges; the childishness that clings to them after they have become grown men and women; the dilettanteism of alumni associations; the lack of positive content in college loyalty; the administrative drifting, and the atrophy of social will in the professor's marooned specialty— this is our academic tragedy. This is the educational worldliness from which we must be converted.

Here is the unique opportunity of the college that is willing as an institution to confess Christ. Let it conceive its whole mission in terms of the democracy of God. Let it test its curriculum, its administration, its budget, its alumni by their contributions to social welfare, social justice, and world society. Let it dare to be different from other colleges by having a focalized social purpose, whereas their purposes are dispersed and foggy. Let it consciously serve a cause, a radical cause that appeals to the idealism of youth. And in all this let it not assign God to any compartment of the mind, but assuming that "where love is God is," let it teach its students to find communion with him precisely in social relations with men, in the social task, in all the study that prepares for it, and in the inspiration that impels to it.

One can imagine the entire educational machinery of a denomination coming under the control of this unifying purpose. One would then behold a sight as inspiring as it would be new—the Sunday school, the societies, the academies, and the colleges all marching together toward a single goal. What an immeasurable, unprecedented contribution to society would accrue if even one Christian body should thus organize its educational powers. But to do it an educational department would be necessary, a department that could command the services of experimenters, writers, editors, promoters, and administrators; that could have access to all the educational agencies of the denomination, and that could be to each of them a medium of denominational stimulus and of denominational support.

Producing teachers and leaders. In a denominational policy like this nothing is more vital than to provide real educators, and nothing is more difficult. For the push is toward specialization, the technical, the ascertainably efficient, not toward mere proclamation, exhortation, or agitation, which are far easier. The task that is before us is nothing less than to provide a continuous supply of skilled workers through the whole department, from the humblest lay teacher in a Sunday school to the corps of professional experts who guide the entire denomination.

(1) *Training the unpaid lay workers in the parish.* "Teacher training" is too narrow a term for what is here intended. For officers of a Sunday school, as well as teachers, require help. Nor is the Sunday school all. The church school must include, as we have seen, all the work for children and youth, and therefore the work of parents and of various leaders of groups. Hence, the training division or department of the school will touch perhaps the major part of the adult active members of the parish. To suggest that this mass of laymen should be trained by the church for genuine skill as educators will perhaps cause some persons to smile at the visionariness of the proposal, and others to frown in dismay at the crushing responsibilities that would fall upon church administrators. I have no desire to

conceal the degree to which church life will have to be transformed if this vision is to be realized. Sunday and week-day meetings to which church members are now invited for their own spiritual refreshment will to a large extent be converted into periods for instruction and drill in the specific duties of church workers. Instead of "attending the church service," one will give the church service, and study how to give the best. Worship, as a result, will have more point, and more firm attachment to daily living. The desultoriness of miscellaneous sermonizing, too, will give place to continuity, system, and the urgency of immediate needs.

To convert a listening church into a working church is not the matter of a day or of a season but of a generation. Many an experiment must be made, not every one of which will succeed. Advance will not be steady or even all along the line. We must use half-measures as a means to better ones. We must honor any layman's best, however imperfect it may be. But, granted this spirit of tolerant, patient practicality, a policy of constant pressure toward skilled churchmanship will in one generation produce a new type of churchman.

The content and the methods of training courses for different sorts of lay workers in religious education cannot here be discussed in any detail. The most that is permitted is a hint or two as to some fundamental conditions of efficiency.

First, The possibility of developing a body of skilled non-professional religious educators grows out of the fact that both the motive for study and the material that most needs to be studied lie within the sphere of the domestic instincts, particularly the parental. Between instinctive fondness for children and Christian love for mankind there is entire continuity. Training in the motive to teach, then—and this is the corner-stone of the whole enterprise—will consist in bringing the parental instinct into action, whether one is a parent or not, and in developing instinctive attachments into an intelligent Christian purpose to transform society into a family of God. Stated in another way, the basis of the best training is the intelligent focussing of one's Christian experience upon the social will of God as it applies to children and youth.

Second, This experience of God in an intelligently developing fondness for children is to be had primarily through one's own interactions with particular children, not through child-study generalizations made by other persons.   The material for study is first of all living beings, and only secondarily books.

Many a training class, reversing this order, has gotten as far as the book, and then stopped.   Labor was put upon definitions and laws under the supposition that somehow the knowledge of them would constitute knowledge of children, but in the end these formulæ did not even introduce the student to real children, but remained mere lumber in the attic of the mind. No; observation of children is fundamental.   It needs to be guided, of course, for the most effective observation, as has been said, is that which puts definite questions to nature.   But in this case the questions that most need to be asked are not the critically analytical ones of the theoretical psychologist (such as the precise number and the classification of the instincts, the precise nature of imitation, or the part played by motile images in the growth of intelligence), but broader questions as to children's conduct, particularly how they act in given social situations.   For the objective point throughout is to be able to make such changes in social situations as will produce desired changes in children's social attitudes, purposes, and habits. Not that we need to be shy of academic generalizations, but that we should follow the rule of good teaching that formulæ are to be brought in when the pupil already has something that needs formulating.   The end of our teaching in the training class, moreover, is not the achievement of a sound generalization, as it is in much academic teaching, but ability to regulate the social relations of children so as to get certain social results. Of course the professional educators who are back of this training of laymen will control their own thinking in some measure by finer distinctions and more details of a technical kind, but what the rank and file of the lay educators require is the more homespun sort of wisdom.

Third, In accordance with the well-worn maxim that we learn by doing, practice in educational processes or part-processes is fundamental in the training of lay educators. We must rid our constituency of the naïve superstition that teacher training consists in laying in a stock of ideas about teaching. Ideas are, of course, essential to skill, which is ability to get a specific result by means of knowledge. But skill is achieved by the fusion of doing and thinking into one. Training for the church-school worker, then, will not be isolated from the actual work of the school. The school itself will be his immediate object of study, and his relation to it as a student will be that of an apprentice. Observation and practice, then, which we may call the laboratory method, will assume the primacy that the text-book now holds.

Fourth, The fallacy of outline courses must be exposed and abandoned; that is, the attempt to cover a wide area in a short time by making the instruction very thin. This is not the way to gain even abstract knowledge, much less to gain skill. "One thing at a time, and this done well." The acquisition of firm control in a single process is not only important in itself; it has also an outreaching influence. It is almost fascinating to witness the general transformation in the attitude of a teacher who, having conquered his faults in a particular process, now knows that he can deliberately get the results that he aims at. Such an experience carries a teacher a hundred times further toward general skill than committing to memory abstract formulæ for the whole of good teaching.

Therefore, if the time available for training during any one season happens to be short, we must not on this account dilute the contents of the course. Whether the time be long or short, let the work be intensive, and let the standard be demonstrated improvement in some actual educational process, whether story-telling, preparing lesson plans or schemes of questioning, keeping records, making reports, conducting worship, teaching one's own child his first prayer, or merely discovering the cause of inattention on a particular occasion.

(2) *The opportunity of the college to produce lay leaders of parish education.* Granted the social view of collegiate education, as outlined in a preceding section, there are three points at which

the college may be expected to touch the problem of religious education in a positive way. *First*, the college will promote by educational methods the immediate religious growth of its students. *Second*, it will include in its curriculum a study of the church as a social institution. This study will concern both the aims and the methods of a socialized church, and its general result will be to send the students back to their home churches qualified to support progressive measures, and to initiate and lead them.   *Third*, this elementary study of the church will awaken some of the students to the possibilities and the attractions of the ministry as a life-work, professional specialization in religious education being included. Though a college offers no specifically professional training, it may nevertheless perform the extremely important service of a selective agency for the ministry. Such colleges, however, as offer professional training in preparation for high school teaching may not unreasonably be asked to lay the foundations for the profession of religious education also.

Postponing for a moment the problems of professional training for religious education, however, let us glance at the possibilities suggested under the second of the just-mentioned heads. There is a common complaint that college experience, even high school experience, not only does not increase the loyalty of young people to the church but actually cools their ardor.   The usual interpretation of this cooling process is that the intellectual life has been cultivated at the expense of the religious life.   The remedy that is usually offered, accordingly, is the cultivation of a personal religious life *alongside* the intellectual life.

Underlying this prescription and the diagnosis that precedes it are several assumptions that require scrutiny. On what ground can we assert that the churches, as they now are, furnish the one natural sphere for the religious life of educated men and women? Is it certain, then, that growing indifference to his church on the part of a collegian connotes decline in his personal religion? Is it not just possible that some part of the difficulty grows out of the fact that while his religious outlook widens and his religious capacities increase, the church seems to him to be static? What does the church do to show him that it is not so? What assurance have we that students really understand what the church is and does? Should we expect them to come back to their home churches to repeat over and over the things that they did when they were just emerging from childhood? If not, what church work is there that calls for the collegian's trained powers, and how can he learn what this work is and what it requires?

The answer to these doubts is this: *First,* a large part of the trouble grows out of the student's sheer ignorance of the churches, neither the churches nor the college having provided him with the information that his growing mind requires. Rather, when he famishes for information he is given exhortation. *Second,* least of all has the college or the church revealed to him the place and the possibilities of the church as a social institution that has a contribution to make to the general social movement. *Third,* personal religious life has been cultivated too much upon the plane of individual status, and not enough upon the plane of a social purpose held in common. A purpose to build a democracy of God, rather than dogma or emotional experiences, should be the basis of religious fellowship in the college. *Fourth,* the particular church work in which by far the largest number of laymen is systematically engaged, namely, religious education, calls most naturally for educated leadership, yet the college student, instead of having his eyes opened to the nature of religious education and to the possibility of skilful service in it, is allowed to think of it in terms of the poor teaching that he himself received in the Sunday school when he was a child.

The obvious way to deepen the religious life and the church loyalty of college students, then, is to give them opportunity to study religion as social purpose, the church as an instrument of possible social advance, and religious education as an opportunity for educated laymen to help transform the church itself! At the present moment our real problem is less that of adjusting the student to the church than that of opening in the church a highway for the social aspirations that are already present in the minds of the thoughtful.

There are the best of academic reasons why a course on church life 'or on religious education should include not only general principles, but also sufficient details of process to enable the student to judge a specimen of teaching and to begin teaching. If the college of yesterday cherished the notion that close contact with particular facts is non-essential if only generalizations are well defined, the college of to-day assumes that, even in the interest of a vital grasp of general principles themselves, specimen facts, at least, need to be observed and analyzed by the student himself, not merely described by the professor or by the text-book. Therefore a consciously close relation of a college study to a life purpose or a foreseen duty reinforces the study itself. Hence, collegiate study of religious education should make the student acquainted with the actual materials used in the church school, with the actual processes employed, with the actual problems of administration. He should see them all with eyes that are wide open to the great social principles that are involved, and to the general underlying laws of teaching. That is, the best college teaching of religious education, even if no specific professional training is undertaken, will nevertheless prepare the student to be a leader in the actual educational work of the church.

That insight into the principles and the methods of a socialized religious education will bring inspiration to do the work itself, let no one doubt. Our idealistic young people bless us when we show them a way in which to make idealism effective. The hard part of the problem is not with them, but with college administration on the one hand, and with church administration on the other. Without uncharitableness, and without blame for limitations for which historical excuses can be made, we may say that the inertia of institutionalism in the administration of both college and church is the chief obstacle that stands in the way of a supply of lay leaders in religious education. There are notable instances of colleges that have already begun to follow the gleam, but many are faltering, compromising, or delaying. Too many of our college authorities have not half freed themselves from the pre-social view of the functions of a college. Most administrative officers are half paralyzed by the sleeping sickness of educational conventionality. Even religious colleges have not taken pains to relieve the individualistic squint with which students interpret to themselves the meaning of the Christian religion. Otherwise more, many more, of the colleges would be eager, would vie with one another, to introduce students to such an intensive study of religion and of the church as would produce intelligent and aggressive laymen.

On the other hand, what is more certain to rob the church of skilled lay service than the discovery on the part of collegians that their minister is cold toward their progressive ideas, their fresh enthusiasms, their discontent with things as they are, and warm only toward repetition of things as they have been? There are ministers, and the number is growing, who really lead their people forward and not merely 'round and 'round a circle. But there are others who neither lead forward nor support laymen who are willing to take burdens of leadership upon themselves. Concerning these ministers the greatness of the cause calls for plain speaking. I speak not of hypothetical possibilities but of repeated occurrences when I say that it is folly, if it is not treason to the church, for a minister so to receive a young collegian who is eager to take part in aggressive religion as to make him feel isolated, not understood, suspected of being "unspiritual," religiously suppressed. It should be regarded as a clerical scandal for a minister to discourage such reforms in the Sunday school as are universally approved by competent authorities. If we can excuse in the aged some inability to desire change, we can also retire the aged from leadership. But what shall we say of the minister who, before the age for retirement comes, will neither take the trouble to become a competent leader in parish education, nor seek out competent leaders, nor welcome the services of those who, having caught a vision of better things, desire opportunity to serve?

(3) *Producing professional workers in religious education.* It is obvious that the unpaid parish workers whom we have

thus far considered must have guidance from professional leaders, that is, those who receive pay for their service on the ground of its expert quality and on the ground of the time, labor, and expense required to become and to remain an expert. The term "expert" must be interpreted liberally. In the infancy of the reform of religious education it cannot mean the finished craftsman, but only the one who, using such opportunities for study and for experience as actually exist, is more ready than others to make wise experiments in reconstruction. In this class we must place, or be able to place, the pastor, the parish director of religious education, the employed lay parish worker, the writers and editors of lessons and of material for teachers, the secretarial force of the denomination's central department of religious education, and teachers of religious education in colleges, theological seminaries, and training-schools for professional lay workers.

First, A denomination that does not trifle with its own spiritual life will pursue the policy of producing as quickly as possible a generation of pastors who are competent when they enter upon their ministry to lead their parishes in religious education. More than one denomination already requires every candidate for the ministry to pass an examination in this subject. This shows which way the wind is blowing. But it is of itself little more than a straw, for a meagre smattering of information suffices to meet the present requirement. The theological seminaries are somewhat generally increasing the amount of their instruction in this subject. But if we ask whether they are now ready to supply the churches of the country with pastors who are competent to guide their parishes in the reconstruction of religious education—competent, not in the sense of accomplished and mature craftsmanship, but in the sense of knowing how to begin and how to keep on learning— we must confess that no denomination has yet brought its seminaries to this standard.

The seminaries, like the colleges, are hampered by pre-social views of their educational function. They are divided in their curriculum and in their methods between a desire to make their students accomplished and a desire to make them efficient. Much, very much, has still to be done, too, upon the theory both of Christian experience and of the church as a social agency. But certain parts of the issue are clear. It is fair to put these two questions to any seminary: Are you ready, and are you equipped in faculty and in library, to utilize the church's experience in religious education, and the resources of educational science as these bear upon education specifically in religion? If so, have you so organized the requirements that you make of your students, and the motives that you bring to bear upon them, that your graduates go out, as a matter of fact, equipped as beginners in the professional guidance of religious education in a parish?

Second, A denomination that is educationally awake will apply the same principle to the curriculum and the methods of training-schools for professional lay workers, such as deaconesses, pastor's assistants, parish visitors, Sunday-school superintendents, and missionaries. These schools, in fact, having fewer educational traditions to hamper them, have outstripped the seminaries in this respect. Great possibilities of specialized professional lay service are appearing upon the horizon. If a really scientific training in the educational branch of Christian work gets a footing in the training-schools three things are likely to happen: Much unspecialized and relatively ineffective parish work will give way to specialized and effective reconstruction of parish education; professional standards in this department will react upon other departments, so that they too will require and receive specialized skill; and opportunities thus opened will attract into the ranks of the professional lay workers a larger number of able, ambitious, and well educated candidates.

Third, A denomination that sees the full truth that religious education is properly a specialized operation, to be guided by scientific insight as well as inspired by religious motives, will have to put the training of its directors of religious education and of its editors and secretaries in this department upon a footing corresponding to the best practice in the preparation of superintendents of public education. It is true that most of our superintendents of public education have not had the best preparation; boards of education are still obliged to employ the effectively handy man, the faithful routine man, or the one-sidedly progressive man where a real educator is needed. Just so, the denominations must utilize in positions of educational power many a man who, though facilities for adequate professional training are still very scarce, and only yesterday did not exist, has demonstrated in semi-technical ways a capacity for leadership. But meantime men of this type see, and the denominations must see, that these positions are bound to become more and more technical. The ministry is to become differentiated into at least three specialties, the pastorate, missionary service, and education, and each will require, say, three years of training governed strictly by foresight of the particular functions of each. Already events have occurred in more than one denomination that make it practically certain that the editorial and administrative branches of Sunday school departments will yet be put wholly upon this technical basis. As to the directorate of religious education, one sign of the times is that the men and women who form the Department of Church Directors in the Religious Education Association have adopted as a qualification for active membership a three years' theological course that includes religious education, or else a two years' course in an approved school of religious pedagogy.

Fourth, A denomination that commits itself to these policies will discover that one of its chief difficulties concerns a supply of competent teachers of religious education in colleges, theological seminaries, and training-schools. It goes without saying that a college or seminary professorship of religious education implies capacity for research as well as for teaching. Large library facilities, and a school of religion in which principles may be practised, demonstrated, and discovered by experiment also loom before us as ultimately indispensable. In all these respects we are in the first beginnings. We have to make our way without precedents; heavy costs have to be added to institutional budgets; correlations with other departments of instruction and research have to be created, and meantime the field is calling aloud for results. Some of these problems will be opened still further in the next chapter. Already, however, it should be plain that the denominational problem reaches all the way from the Sunday school to the theological seminary and the university.

The denominational department of religious education as an agency for social reconstruction. The conception that we have now reached is that, just as the present denominational department of foreign missions reaches its hand down to every local society, outward to every mission field, and upward to the recruiting and training of missionaries, so the denominational department of religious education should stimulate the thinking of layman and minister alike, and should guide and organize practice in both the teaching of children and in the teaching of their teachers. But there are various possible ambitions for such a department within the scope of this general statement, as: Ambition to be the exclusive purveyor of printed matter for the Sunday schools of the denomination; ambition to fix a particular curriculum upon the whole denomination; ambition to develop denominationalism by drilling children in it; or, in contrast to all these, and in necessary opposition to them, ambition to make of the entire denomination a devoted and trained force for the Christian reconstruction of society in the large. An intense, firmly knit denominational consciousness can be neither approved nor disapproved until we know to what it devotes its energies. If it merely feeds itself, and then uses its ensuing strength to feed itself again; if its great contribution to the world is an invitation to join the denomination, then the best that can be said for it is that it represents social development, but arrested development. When the great social devotion comes, these half-gods will go. And the central function of a department of religious education is to awaken the great devotion. Therefore denominational consciousness will be quickened into interdenominational consciousness, community consciousness, world consciousness. This will be done through the social content of lesson material; through provision for the practice of social service; through community religious enterprises, such as teacher training, in contrast to merely denominational enterprises; through encouragement to experimentation and variety as against uniformity; through participation of denominational leaders in great non-denominational movements for educational and social advance. Such a department of religious education makes for denominational strength, but not for denominationalism. It makes, rather, for the democracy of God.

CHAPTER XIX

BEYOND THE DENOMINATIONS

The value of denominational variety in religious education. We are now to consider the need of organizing religious education upon a basis broader than that of the denomination. The implication will be that there are some important things that denominations as such are not best qualified to do. Lest this implication should be interpreted as depreciation of active denominational loyalty, let it be said in advance that some important ends are best attained through free variation. We may think of the history of each religious body as an experiment in social religion, and of the educational work of each as an experiment in religious education. Now, in a matter as complicated as this, a variety of experiments, each bringing some particular factor or method into the foreground, has its own value. At a later point in our discussion, Part V, we shall see how, as a matter of fact, several types and tendencies in Christian education have sprung up, each having something to contribute toward the effective socialized type that is the objective point of our present aspiration. It is not to be supposed that we can invent education any more than we can invent family life. In both matters we have, rather, to reflect upon what already exists in order to find elements worthy to be built into a fairer structure, as well as to discover what to avoid. We learn to educate by educating. It is by following out various ideas that their value or their lack of value is demonstrated. In fact, the "trial-and-error method" of learning applies not only to a rat that is finding out how to get the cheese, not only to a child who is adjusting himself to the laws of family life, but also to educators who desire to know how best to educate.

The verdict of history upon the denominational phase of the Christian religion is likely to be that in the narrower loyalties men received a training in free co-operation that was an essential preliminary to the wider co-operations that lead on to a just world organization. Hence, the part of wisdom is not to lower the intensity of denominational loyalty, but to socialize its content ever more and more. The reform of religious education needs a background, not of denominational sloth or half-heartedness, but of active devotion to whatever educational ideal seems vital from the denominational point of view. "Devotion to an ideal" means, of course, something more than speeding up the machinery of a routine, something more than a prejudice charging into battle, something more than conceited complacency; it means, rather, the sort of conviction and of earnestness that goes with the open eye, the eye that discriminates between ideals, that recognizes Christliness beyond the pale, yes, that looks ever for discrepancies between one's social practice and the Christian ideal. Denominational loyalty like this will contribute to the wider organization of men, not hinder it. But such devotion will draw upon extradenominational resources. To these let us now turn.

A common social purpose tends to create common organs for itself. To the extent that any denomination teaches the Christian principle of social justice and of world society, it creates a psychological necessity for organizations of the Christian consciousness more broad than the denomination. An individualistic religion, whether of the sacerdotal, or of the dogmatic, or of the experiential type, can express itself fully within the walls of a sect. Its interest in the world at large is to get men inside the same walls. But when one has the social mind of Christ one's ambition is to give effect to it wherever and however one can in all the world by combining with any man who is willing to go any distance, great or small, in the same direction. The achievement of a social interpretation of the gospel leads right on toward the achievement of interdenominational union of effort. Love has to produce organization, both because love makes men want to be in one another's company, and because it gives them a common purpose to do a large work. One can easily witness in the Federal Council of the Churches the contrast between the inhibiting effect of doctrinal sensitiveness and the emancipating effect of social purpose. The delegates can heartily agree, for example, to work for a weekly rest day, though they cannot agree upon the scriptural basis for Sunday observance.

A social theory of religious education is bound to have its eyes turned toward the wide organization of religious education itself. Without at all overestimating the clarity or the unity of social purpose in the Religious Education Association, one can nevertheless see that the fundamental source of its peculiar influence is its social spirit and outlook. Here is a society that does not publish text-books, that does not control any curriculum, that founds no schools, that has no authority over or official entrance into any school, that was not founded by the denominations, and is not supported by their funds but chiefly by contributions from individuals belonging to the underpaid salaried classes; yet this society has touched with a quickening hand almost the whole of Protestant religious education in this country and to some extent in foreign lands. It has been able to do this, in the first place, because of the social, co-operative spirit that was growing within the denominations. The organization was a practical necessity because, scattered through the religious bodies, there was a large and growing number of educators who had begun to conceive education in more social terms than those of dogma or of ecclesiasticism, even in terms of the needs of modern society. Hence it comes to pass that the deliberations that have taken place under the auspices of the Association have almost constantly placed side by side problems of social advance and problems of educational organization, method, and material. If nothing more had been accomplished than to furnish a clearing-house of ideas for all sorts of workers in religious education, the social significance would have been large. But there is here, in addition, nothing less than the forerunner of a unified educational consciousness among the Protestant bodies.

What administrative organs this consciousness will produce cannot be said as yet. The Sunday School Council of Evangelical Denominations, founded by the voluntary action of denominational editors, publishers, and secretaries, may possibly become a sort of federal legislative council for determining common policies, standards, and methods within a restricted group of denominations. Inasmuch, however, as each body that is represented in the Council has what amounts to a veto power upon all acts, the policies that can be agreed upon will be shaded toward an average or toward a mimimum; they will not represent the best that the more progressive denominations are already prepared to do.

Another interdenominational body, the Federal Council's Commission on Christian Education, has begun to consider important special problems. Here is an agency that might conceivably do much to promote the socializing of religious education, particularly through some close connection with the other social activities of the Council. Yet we have to recognize the significance of the fact that socially hesitant denominations have equal rights with socially progressive ones in the Federal Council, and that religious education is the point at which social hesitancy is most likely to become social obstruction.

The oldest of all the interdenominational societies in the field of religious education, the American Sunday School Union, is devoting its energies chiefly to founding new Sunday schools of an entirely conventional type. The International Sunday School Association, which touches directly the largest number of schools, and could conceivably lead in reform, is not only subject to the same limitations upon progressiveness as the Sunday School Council, but its policy has been so distinctly and for so long a time controlled by religious conservatism that does not think in either social or educational terms, that the Association, instead of leading in the reconstruction of religious education, has had to be painfully won to the cause. The momentum of this conservatism has been lost, and the engine has now been caught upon a dead centre. Yet here is a vast amount of machinery for interdenominational co-operation, machinery that is too valuable to be thrown upon the scrap-heap, or to be kept at the less significant operations. It used to be the proud boast of Association leaders that under its guidance nearly all the Protestant Sunday schools of the country, and many in foreign parts, studied the same lesson on Sunday. This was interpreted as a marching together of the forces of Protestantism. The bursting of this fancy through more careful analysis of the educative process does not rebuke the notion that Protestantism might really march together, nor does it forbid the International Association to organize the marchers. But concrete social goals are necessary. Bible study is not the goal, but only a means thereto. If the religious earnestness that has always characterized this old society should turn to the social significance of the gospel, and the social ends of religious education, there is no knowing what contributions to the wider organization of Christian forces might result.

The basis for the wider organization of religious education is a common purpose to do the will of God in establishing the democracy of God upon earth. Without denying social value to unions formed upon a narrower platform than this, and without impatience with ancient shibboleths that say nothing of mercy, or of justice, or of world society, we must nevertheless see that nothing but love is a sufficient organizing principle—not our reasonings about love, but the act of loving, and the purpose to go on loving to the uttermost. When we conceive religious education as having the function of inspiring the young with this Christian purpose, and of training them in methods of making it effective in the world, then religious education will create for itself organs as broad as the purpose.

This principle is illustrated in the Missionary Education Movement. Here is an organization that is doing educational work for and in many denominations as their common organ. If I mistake not, this is the nearest approach that has yet been made to an effective, working union of several denominations. It has come to pass almost silently, and now that it is here it has the "feel" of a natural and simple part of every-day life. What has made this possible? The clarification of the missionary motive as that of outgoing, sacrificial love. Denominational differences do not keep us apart when we ask, What are the conditions of child-life or of the life of women, or of the life of men in central Africa or in western China, and what can we do to improve these conditions? In short, the foundation for a wide and effective organization of religious education is precisely the socializing of the content and purpose of our religion.

The wholesomeness of independent criticism and propaganda, and the unwholesomeness of anything like a denominational educational trust. Anthropologists tell us that one great reason of the backwardness of the native tribes in the interior of Africa is that they have had so little intercourse with other peoples. Historians are accustomed to point out the quickening of the mind that comes from contact of one civilization with another. It is not less true that every religious denomination requires for its own health plentiful contact with standpoints and practices other than its own. Religious inbreeding connotes, in the natural order of things, religious deterioration. There is not a denomination to which independent agitation and propaganda of religious education reaches that has not cause to be thankful for it. This is true even from the standpoint of denominationalism except when it assumes the position of infallibility. Independent criticism, independent publications, fresh experiments—these enable me to see, as I could not by looking at myself, just what I am doing, and how I can better attain my present ends. But independent agitation has the added value of helping me to revise my ends. Unless I claim infallibility, I must be ready to revise them, and I ought to be thankful for stimulation to clear thinking and deep feeling with respect to them.

A denominational department of religious education that endeavors to be self-sufficient is bound to injure its own cause. Any combination of denominations that undertakes to build walls that shall keep out everything that has not been produced within the enclosure will fail, of necessity, to provide the best possible. Love must keep open house to ideas as well as to persons. It must receive as well as give. No group of denominational leaders is wise enough to prescribe the uniformly best course of lessons, or the uniformly best lesson publications, or the uniformly best schemes for teacher training for even one denomination. There is no uniformly best for schools and conditions that are not uniform. And if the uniformly best for to-day could be discovered, to-morrow it would no longer be so, but would be at some point or other a hinderance to the best.

Beyond all this we need to keep in mind the history of publishing houses that have enjoyed a monopoly, or anything approaching it, within a given ecclesiastical market. When business processes and religious officialism blend, the possibilities of confusion are immeasurable. Such a combination is, on the whole, as deceptive as desire for riches. Not that religion and business should be kept apart from each other. The crux of the matter is in the monopolistic tendency; it is in the pursuit, in ecclesiastical business, of economic policies that are socially objectionable anywhere. If we unite such policies with religious education, we must curtail its social purpose from the outset, and we subject it to the necessity of endless compromises.

The inference, which is confessedly harder to put into practice than is the policy of the closed market, is that religious education will get on most rapidly toward its social goal when a variety of influences has access to every church school. The problem of adaptation to particular local conditions should be kept constantly alive. The study of what other schools are doing should be steadily encouraged. The habit of openness toward new ideas and methods and materials, from whatever source appearing, and some capacity for judging them, should be one of the aims in the training of teachers and of leaders. Such a policy will not only enable schools here and there to do more excellent work; it will react favorably upon the denominational or interdenominational publishing enterprise itself. Greater acuteness and foresight in the securing of material, greater attractiveness in the presentation of it, and greater business skill in manufacturing and selling will be the effects.

The participation of universities in the making of religious

educators. When religious education acquires the purpose of taking a definite part in the evolution of society as a whole, and when, in order to fulfil this purpose, we undertake to lift the teaching of religion from the plane of traditional routine to that of a scientifically controlled process, we obligate ourselves to cosmopolitanism of intellect as well as of heart. To make it effective, we must go on to assume the university attitude of freedom, of scientific method, of eagerness for new knowledge and for the widest organization of knowledge. In the preparation of leaders the top round of the ladder will not be the training-school (under whatever name it goes), but the school or combination of schools (under whatever name) that has the university's range of instruction, together with the spirit of research and facilities therefor.

The course of recent events leaves no ambiguity as to the manner in which this requirement is to be met, namely, by combining the work of a department or school of theology with the work of a university department of education. The school of theology will contribute, in general, an intensive study of religion and of its works; the university department of education will contribute to outlook upon education and to inlook into the psychology of it. To be more specific, the range of opportunity for one who desires to become a technically accomplished specialist in religious education may be expected to include the following:

(a) The history of religion.
(b) The psychology of religion.
(c) The philosophy of religion.
(d) The sociology of religion.
(e) The general history of education.
(f) The special history of religious education.
(g) The psychology of education.
(h) The religious life of children and youth.
(i) Observation and analysis of the teaching process in the day school.
(j) Observation and analysis of the teaching process in the church school or school of religion.
(k) The general principles and methods of school administration.

(*l*) The special methods of administration in religious education.
(*m*) Closely supervised practice in religious education.
(*n*) Provision for experimental study of religious education.
(*o*) The philosophy or general theory of religious education.

All these courses, it is assumed, will be on the university level both with respect to standards of admission and of study, and with respect to standards of scientific thoroughness. The order in which the items are named is not intended to indicate anything as to the arrangement of a student's program, but only certain relations between the department of education and the theological school. The relation here suggested between the various courses is that of close intertwining, or even of something still more intimate. They are all related to one another as are the organs of the human body when it lives and breathes. We have here no mechanical juxtaposition of pieces of knowledge, but the unity of a single purpose realizing itself in a complex world. In the light of this purpose, it would be incorrect to think of the courses in the department of education as fundamental, while those in the school of theology are accessory. The courses in religious education, and in the study of religion, not only make a direct attack upon data that are unconsidered in the department of education (note, for example, *b*, *d*, and *h*), but the practical methods in religious education, being controlled by the all-pervasive aim of promoting religious growth, do not merely apply what has been learned in day-school experience. The impossibility, too, of ranking religious education as a particular under a general conception of education that makes no analysis of the religious life might seem to be obvious enough. In addition, the theory of religious education tends, on the whole, to be more inclusive than educational philosophy that lives in constant contact with the restrictions of state education.

From all this it will appear that the whole curriculum for the advance of learning and for the preparation of the highest experts in religious education must be lifted above denominationalism. Our task is never that of making merely denominational applications of non-religious educational theories and methods.   We must carry the unsectarianism of science into our analysis of what is specifically religious. Psychology, sociology, and experiment must speak in their own tongue with respect to the most intimate things in religious experience, often with respect to matters upon which denominations are sensitive. If a denomination chooses to maintain a theological school in which these things are promoted with hearty unreserve, this denomination proves thereby that it is passing into the larger society; it is losing its life and gaining life.

PART V

EXISTING TENDENCIES IN CHRISTIAN
EDUCATION VIEWED FROM THE
SOCIAL STANDPOINT

CHAPTER XX

THE ROMAN CATHOLIC TYPE

The purpose, scope, and spirit of Part V require a word of advance explanation. The purpose is to set in high relief the theory that has already been expounded. In accordance with the principle, expressed at the beginning of the first chapter, that theory arises within practice and is continuous with it, I intend to show that the new educational point of view is, as a matter of fact, arising within the churches. Like other new inspirations, it has to struggle for utterance, oppose traditions, and be opposed. It has to be refined in the furnace of experience before it fully reveals its own nature. Into the ecclesiastical furnace, then, let us take a look, seeking there for facts that illustrate, either by similarity or by contrast, tendencies toward a social view of religious education.

Some differences between Christian bodies will have to be mentioned, and in some instances discrimination will have to be made between tendencies that co-exist in the same body. But no general survey of denominational types or tendencies will be offered, nor will our evaluation of a particular educational thread constitute a judgment upon any church as a whole. Indeed, the spirit of this analysis is not that of seeking to give or to withhold credit, but rather that of seeing facts simply as facts. Of course I shall make no concealment or even pretense of reticence as to my own attitudes; in view of what precedes, any such attempt, even if there were a motive for it, would be futile. But I trust that to be possessed of a conviction will not debar either author or reader from the recognition of facts or of typical tendencies within facts.

Presuppositions of **Roman Catholic education.** No Christian body is more insistent upon education as a primary function of the church, and no one has proved the depth of its educational convictions by greater sacrifice, than the Catholic Church in the United States. No other church holds with such unanimity a definite, logically articulated theory of religious education, nor exhibits greater consistency in practice. This utter coherence is due primarily to a firm grasp by the entire hierarchy upon certain presuppositions. They may be conveniently expressed as follows:

(1) *Education is the transmission of a completed faith, not participation in the evolution of a faith.* In Catholic education changes in method may occur within limits presently to be indicated, but the purpose and the content are assumed to be fixed and uniform for the whole world to the end of time. Repetition, reproduction, prevention of change within the scope of religion—this rather than experiment, new enterprise, or discovery, is the spirit.

(2) *The basal process in this transmission is intellectualistic.* The term "intellectualistic" is here used because dogma is made to precede and govern life. The processes of intelligence are not employed primarily for defining an experience or a purpose that the pupil already has or is in process of forming, but for defining something entirely antecedent to such experience and purpose, and intended as a control thereof. Archbishop Ireland puts the matter thus: "Nor is mere intellectual instruction sufficient for the religious education of the child. Intellectual instruction is necessary; *it is the fount from which all else will flow.* But the child must be led as by the hand to put into daily practice the truths with which its mind has been saturated."[1] How intellectualistic this notion of a preliminary mental saturation is we shall see vividly when we examine the methods employed for accomplishing it.

(3) *Both dogma and rules of conduct are to be imposed upon the pupil by authority. This authority, moreover, is lodged in*

---

[1] Bernard Feeney, *The Catholic Sunday School* (St. Louis, 1907), page x. The italics are mine.

living men who announce and administer penalties for non-conformity.[1] Authority as teacher, authority to command what is to be believed and done, descends in orderly gradation from the Pope to every priest. There is always a living voice that can declare the end of the matter in everything that concerns faith and morals.[2] This authority is not limited to the declaration of general principles, but it goes on to hearing confessions, imposing penance, and granting or withholding absolution; to permitting or forbidding participation in sacred rites held to have the greatest potency; finally, to control of the keys of eternal life. Whatever the method of teaching employed, then, however gentle, however free from painful restrictions, 'round about the whole are the adamantine walls of psychic compulsion. Within these walls whatever is said and done has within it the implication, the atmosphere, of a government that is in no sense responsible to the governed.

Much Protestant education, too, has attempted to impose the Christian faith by authority, but with an educationally important difference. When authority is lodged in the Bible rather than in a living teacher, variant interpretations of the authority itself are possible. The Bible is powerless to prevent them, or to punish, even so much as by a threat of withdrawing spiritual privileges, any person who falls into error. Consequently, Protestant teachers, all in all, instead of wielding power, use persuasion, or seek a rational and essentially free assent. As a rule, children know that inside the velvet glove there are no fingers of steel.

Within Protestantism, consequently, there is more unreserved

[1] "If . . . by 'independence of mind' is understood unrestrained liberty of thought in religious matters, it must be admitted that the *Ratio Studiorum* and the whole Institute of the Society [of Jesus] are uncompromisingly opposed to it, and that the Jesuits always endeavored to suppress it. For they are bound by their profession, and fully determined to uphold, defend, and propagate revealed religion, as taught and interpreted by the Catholic Church. In this they do not differ from other religious orders, nor from any consistent Catholics.' Article, "Jesuits" by R. Swickerath in Monroe's *Cyclopedia of Education.*

[2] According to the Catholic theory, *no one but the Church has a right to teach morals at all.*

lodgment for the educational doctrine of interest, and there is readier assent to conforming material as well as method to needs that appear in the pupil's own experience. The position of Catholicism is that the child must be conformed to the material and to the teacher who officially transmits it. "The position which the director holds in the Sunday school is supreme. He is the prime mover in everything. All that is done is inaugurated by him. He is the '*forma totius gregis.*' The whole machinery is guided by his touch, or rather, the entire mechanism is in a manner of his creation. He is not only the rudder, but his at the same time is the firm hand thereon."[1] "As to the director, and this is as it should be, a step cannot be taken in any path without confronting him. The children, to use the scholastic phrase, are the prime matter; the director and the teacher the substantial form which gives the Sunday school its individual existence."[2]

Such a Sunday school, considered as a society, is an autocracy, a benevolent one no doubt, but yet an autocracy, and by this primarily must its capacity for social education be determined. It is the purpose of Catholic education, the very kernel of it, to perpetuate and make universal an autocratic government of religious and ethical thinking and of religious and moral conduct. That this is the very antipodes of the aspiration for a democracy of God is obvious enough. And the opposition does not cease at any supposed boundary between the spiritual and the temporal. Such boundaries are mere conventions; the facts show no such separation. For no laws of spiritual life are clearer than the interconnectedness of soul and body, the continuity of the ethical with the political, the suffocation of the higher life by economic injustice. Moreover, even if the existence of these spiritual laws should be denied, the fact would remain that autocratic authority over matters of faith and morals includes the authority to determine autocratically what constitutes a matter of morals. In short, Catholic educa-

[1] E. A. Halpin, *The Method of the Catholic Sunday-School* (New York, 1904), p. 12.
[2] *Ibid.*, p. 40.

tion not only cannot be education for democracy; it cannot fail to educate against democracy.

The particular aims of Roman Catholic education. The characteristic aims follow so directly from the presuppositions that little more than an enumeration is necessary.

(1) *To fix in the mind of the child church doctrine and tradition.* "The modern Sunday school, they say, was originated in 1781 by Robert Raikes. That is, of course, the Protestant Sunday school. Non-Catholics have imposed the name on us all, yet the difference between their work and ours is exceedingly great. Our Sunday schools should be called catechism schools or classes. We teach catechism. They teach, or explain, or— God knows what—the Bible. Their Sunday school is a Bible class. Ours is a catechism class. . . . The Bible holds a place in our schools, but not that which belongs to the catechism." [1]

(2) *To produce observance of particular rules with respect to religious devotions and with respect to conduct.* Children are told just what to do in church and elsewhere, and they are minutely drilled in doing it. They are not left with general principles or ideals, the applications of which they must work out by their own thought and experiment, but with rules that specify the very thing that is to be done or avoided, and with the habit of doing it already formed. Thus it is that the Church seeks to perpetuate itself unchanged.

(3) *To fix the spirit and habit of full, unquestioning obedience to the Church.* In view of what has been said of the autocratic character of Catholic education, it will be sufficient at this point merely to indicate that the subjects of autocratic rule can be, and are, trained to believe in, obey, and support it with unwavering conviction. How to produce such obedience was one of the great and successfully solved problems of the founders of Jesuit education. Loyola the soldier did not abandon militarism when he turned from war to the Church; he merely transferred the sphere of his militarism to the human spirit. In the Society of Jesus he raised an army of perfectly regimented minds. They,

[1] Halpin, p. 2.

in turn, have found in teaching their supreme opportunity for producing a like regimented Church.[1]

The fundamentals of method in Roman Catholic education. It is not by any subtle trick, or ingenious device, or mysterious influence that Catholicism secures these results, but by the persistent and organized use of simple and obvious methods.

(1) *Habit-formation by drill processes is the pervading essence of the whole.* The laws of habit, let it be remembered, apply to much more than overt acts. Attitudes as well as particular acts can become habits, and attitudes include shades of feeling. We can acquire an habitual interest in one thing, so that we notice it when it is present, and an habitual indifference to another, so that its presence goes unnoticed. We can acquire hard and fast associations of ideas, so that A always brings up P, which is agreeable, while B always recalls Q, which is disagreeable. In this way we can go on to form a habit of thinking thus or so of anything, and such an intellectual habit may become so firm that the habitual conclusion has the force of a self-evident presupposition. Conscience, taste, and in fact standards of judgment in every sphere can become petrified as habits. A habit of self-limitation—or of submission to the will of another, can become so ingrained as to seem second nature. It is by the continuous use of this principle that Catholic education gets its results. It is a system of habit-formation. Let us, then, glance at two or three phases of the process.

(2) *Hence the great prominence of memory drill upon verbal formulæ.* The great propositions of the faith are not reserved

---

[1] Now and then the question is asked how the Roman priesthood is kept in intellectual subservience to the papacy. How came it to pass that modernism, for example, was so easily suppressed? Why were there not more martyrs to it, at least? Especially, what kept modernism from raising its head at all in this country, where freedom of thought is supposed to be breathed in the very atmosphere? How can educated men who have come into contact with modern historical and scientific knowledge remain so unaffected by it? What can induce them to abjure the right to think for themlseves? The major part of the answer is that the Catholic system of education is organized, from the infant class to the theological seminary, under the all-pervading aim of producing obedience as a permanent frame of mind. On the whole, the system secures what it seeks. It produces genuine obedience, not merely the pretense of it; actual conformity in thinking, not duplicity or self-division except now and then; submission so complete as to be practically painless.

until the child has a religious experience that requires them for
its expression; they are not reserved even until the child can
understand them. A beginning of habituation and of conformity is possible even in advance of understanding and of
experience. "In the primary Sunday school grades, the main
object is to indelibly fasten on the memory the truths of faith,
and to impart such explanation as the young mind is capable
of receiving. It might be said that it is mere surface work.
The chief task lies in giving the child a memory grasp of Catholic
doctrine. It is an all-important achievement. It is essential.
One need not care, for the very young, how parrot-like may be
their knowledge; a pervading familiarity with the text is the
beginning of all after knowledge, and without it there is danger
of inaccurately obtaining it, which is pernicious in the extreme,
and which is worse than ignorance. It is better not to know
in these momentous matters than to misstate."[1] Since exact
conformity is the end sought, the stress is never removed from
the verbal forms in which the Church has clothed her teachings.
That is, habit-formation, not independent judgment, remains
the essence of the method to the very end. "Children, unless
they know their catechism *verbatim* may be said to have no
knowledge of it whatever. They have not laid that foundation
without which any superstructure, durable or fair to look upon
is, if not absolutely impossible, at least so difficult as to demand
superhuman effort."[2]

(3) *Expression from the pupil takes the form of reproduction
of what he has been told rather than that of "free self-expression."*
If we desire free self-expression from the pupil, we place him
in a situation that is likely to call forth a spontaneous reaction that is of worth, one that will help him to find himself, and
then we let the reaction come—we do not prescribe it, require it,
or even tell the pupil in advance what we hope for. Hence pupils' opinions, likes and dislikes, approvals and disapprovals,
become a part of the learning process. Or, if the situation
presents a problem for solution, rather than an object to be
appreciated, the pupils' work will show doubts, guesses, tenta-

[1] Halpin, p. 19.   [2] *Ibid.*, 24.

tive inferences, very likely dissent from the teacher, but also the joy of discovering something for oneself. This brief and partial statement is sufficient to illustrate the methods of self-expression. Now, when we examine the work books of pupils from carefully managed Catholic Sunday schools, we find little of this, but much telling back of what the teacher or the text-book has told. The purpose, in fact, is not discovery, not train-ing the pupil to see for himself whether or not the truth is as it is said to be, not the solution of problems by the pupil. The Church has already solved his problems, and she now un-dertakes to transfer ready-made solutions to him. Hence the pressure of the school upon him is toward the most accurate possible reproduction of what he has been told.[1]

(4) *Gradation of material, in the proper sense of "gradation" does not exist, but rather fuller and fuller treatment of the same outline, with some change from sensuous to logical modes of impression.* Pupils are graded to the extent of being arranged in five, six, or eight age groups. The grouping is determined to some extent by the pupil's changing relations to the Church, as his first communion and his confirmation. But for all ages the essential content of instruction is, as has been indicated already, the catechism. *The catechism is the curriculum.* It is, of course, not at all a transcript of a child's spiritual growth, but a thought structure built by adults to meet certain strains felt by adults. Moreover, the order in which it is presented is not determined by freely picking out the parts that have the closest relation to experience at this or that age, for the main outline of the whole is presented at every age. One writer, after saying that during each year of his Sunday school life each child should study or review in regular succession "at least all the fundamental truths" of his religion, recommends that in all the grades the same topic be studied each Sunday, the dif-

---

[1] That this is characteristic even of higher classes is clear from Halpin's description of a class in Higher Catechism. The same principle of method prevails in the specific training for the priesthood also. When we act upon the assumption that the function of reason is to confirm conclusions already held as final, we may, indeed, grow in logical nimbleness, but it is the nimble-ness of habitual co-ordinations that have merely extended their range and thereby solidified themselves.

ference between the grades being simply one of simplicity and extent of the material. This is called a "graded system," whereas it is in fact a uniform system.[1]

At first this abstract material is presented to a considerable extent as something to say in connection with a particular religious act which the teacher takes pains to have the child perform, or as a statement of the meaning of some sensible object connected with worship. Later the catechism meets the pupil as a system to be grasped as one interconnected whole.

The early, and in fact never-ceasing association of dogmas with sensible objects and with particular acts of devotion is undoubtedly effective for the purpose for which it is used. The sense of reality that attaches to the impressive sights and sounds within the church, and to the acts that one does there, attaches also, under the laws of habit, to the formulæ that are used in connection therewith. What I and the other worshippers are doing, what the priest is doing, what the pictures, statues, and vestments signify—as far as I think of this at all (and the teacher sees to it that I do think of it) I think of it in the terms that are drilled into my mind by repetition. This is what it all is to me. To a considerable extent, even methods that are relatively external and mechanical have this result. But when spiritually minded teachers, by personal example, and by careful control of conditions, produce in their pupils the emotions of awe and of mystery, some real penitence, some real joy in forgiveness, some fear of penalty and some sense of security from it, and withal the comfortable realization that we know how to be safe in life and in death, then pupils tend to identify their very selves with the system that imposes itself upon them.

[1] P. J. Sloan, *The Sunday-School Director's Guide to Success.* New York, 1909.

CHAPTER XXI

THE DOGMATIC PROTESTANT TYPE

Within Protestantism various educational types coexist.
It is not possible to speak of "the" Protestant type of religious education as we have done of the Catholic type. For not only are there many sorts of Protestantism, but within each Protestant body, at least within the larger bodies, variety, ferment, fresh experimentation are characteristic, and consequently at times the strain of conflicting convictions. Catholic education is a close-knit system; Protestant education is a conglomerate, several different types being found side by side, even within the same denomination. To speak of "the dogmatic Protestant type," therefore, or of the other types that will engage our attention in the following chapters, is not to characterize any denomination by a single educational tendency. It will be necessary to draw examples from the practices or from the official utterances of this or that body, it is true, but the reader should bear in mind that in each instance a single item has been taken from a group of jostling tendencies. It should be noted, moreover, that such terms as "dogmatic," "ritualistic," "evangelical," and "liberal" are intended to be descriptive only; they are not epithets that carry either approval or opprobrium. For the purpose is not to judge theologies or forms of ecclesiastical life as such, but only to understand the educational tendencies and affiliations that belong to them.

Comparison of the dogmatic Protestant type of religious education with the Catholic type. Protestant education is dogmatic when it is controlled by these presuppositions: That there is a finite, historical organ that exercises divine authority upon earth; that this authority imposes upon men a changeless faith which it is the function of religious education to

304

transmit; and that education transmits it primarily in the form of certain propositions. That this educational point of view exists in large Protestant areas needs no argument, nor is the affinity with Catholicism at all obscure.

(1) *There is affinity with Catholic education to the extent that external authority is propagated by intellectualistic drill processes.* As in Catholicism, so in much Protestantism, we find drill upon set formulæ, as of a catechism; the persistent use of doctrinal rather than descriptive terms for experience, both the experiences recorded in the Bible and those of present-day Christians; and a tendency, which will be exhibited in some detail in a subsequent section, to bend the curriculum as a whole to the outlines of a dogmatic system. If this were the end of the matter, an educational appraisement of it would be easy. But Protestant dogmatism, even of the most rigorous sorts, includes in its doctrines certain views of the church, of the Bible, and of the religious life that involve decisive modifications.

(2) *But the Protestant abnegation of all claims to infallibility on the part of the church changes the relation between teacher and pupil from that of commanding and obeying to that of helping and being helped, which makes for democracy.* The Protestant teacher, just because he is Protestant, obligates himself to regard the pupil's interests and modes of mental assimilation. If Protestantism tends to prize unduly a winsome personality in a teacher, nevertheless the social tendency even of this is toward friendliness between equals.

(3) *The ascription of authority to the Bible rather than to the church turns attention to a literature that is predominantly a transcript of life rather than a body of doctrine. Therefore Protestant emphasis upon Bible study tends to counteract Protestant dogmatism.* The Catholic writer, quoted in the last chapter, who contrasted the teaching of catechism with the teaching of the Bible, did not exaggerate the difference. The Bible is educationally as different from catechisms as the affection of a mother toward her baby is different from the law of the state that forbids a mother to let her offspring starve. And the more objective our study of the Bible becomes, the more it gives the pupil

an impression of moving among men like himself. The desire of a teacher to make a passage interesting or vivid lures him toward· precisely the features of it that the pupil can appreciate through his own experience and observation. It is true that dogmatism, phrasing in its own way whatever it touches, and insistent upon illustrating its own convictions by ancient life that was unconscious of them, tends constantly to depress the vitality of Bible study. But its insistence upon the Bible as the very word of God in due time reacts in the interest of life.

(4) *The intellectualism of dogmatic teaching is further modified by efforts to induce a personal religious experience.* The most dogmatic Protestant teaching, in the same breath in which it assumes that certain beliefs are essential to the Christian life, warns the pupil that he can be spiritually dead even though his beliefs are perfectly correct. The Catholic child is .taught that he can be saved by conformity; the Protestant child is told the exact contrary. The Catholic child is told that God is present in the mass; the Protestant child is told that God's presence is to be discerned in the heart. We shall presently discover that dogmatic Protestantism is restrained from reaping the whole educational advantage of its belief in Christian experience. But we can see at once that to teach the pupil to establish a direct relation between himself and· God, a relation the nature of which the pupil himself judges, is to turn attention once more away from dogma and authority toward life that can easily take a democratic form.

Protestant dogmatism cannot accept whole-heartedly the principle of gradation of the material of instruction. We have seen that Catholic education repeats the main outlines of Catholic dogma from department to department of the Sunday school. This is necessary because the end to be attained is utter habituation of the mind. Protestant dogmatism tends in the same direction, but for the reasons that have just been given, is not so thoroughgoing. Here is the meaning of the half-acceptance, half-rejection of graded lessons by certain Protestant bodies. The fundamental idea of gradation is that the pupil is to grow from within; dogmatism desires the pupil to conform increasingly to something that is without. Growth from within presupposes freedom, and it invites variation. To provide for growth is to furnish changing sorts of food as capacity for assimilation changes; it is to feed spontaneous interests as they arise. Habit-formation is involved here, of course, but also the free variation toward which dogmatism is necessarily apprehensive. True gradation of material aims to call into play whatever capacity for judgment and discovery the pupil has, and by exercising this capacity at its various levels of growth to bring it finally to maturity. Whole-hearted dogmatism like that of the Catholic Church will have none of this; the modified dogmatism of some Protestants fears and opposes it, but from no defined or definable educational standpoint that can satisfy the other demands of Protestantism even of the dogmatic type.[1]

No official body has been at greater pains to state the issues here involved than certain committees that reported to the General Assembly of the Presbyterian Church in the United States of America, in 1913. Let us ask, then, what conceptions of education are here expressed or implied, first premising on our own part that our quest is not to determine the educational status of an ecclesiastical body, but solely to understand educa-

---

[1] The Sunday-School Committee of the General Synod of the Evangelical Lutheran Church in the United States of America, in a report made in 1913 criticises "the forced pedagogical theory that the child itself is the centre around which the teaching of the Bible must adjust itself at no matter what sacrifice of truth. We strongly advocate a system of graded lessons," the report continues, "but the whole spirit and the doctrinal position of our Church is against a system of grading which seeks merely to interest the child by fanciful and far-fetched interpretations of Scripture, by attempting to catch the child by making the stories of the Bible simple myths, by extra-biblical lessons from nature, from life, from history. . . . We are persuaded that in the Church, as in the family, strong Christian men and women are made of the children, not by giving them always what they want and what will entertain them, but what they need." See *Proceedings of the General Synod*, 1913, pp. 114–117. The real issues here involved would have been far more sharply drawn if the report had been a little more accurate and a little more thorough in its contrast between the theory that "the child itself is the centre" and the theory that children are best educated by "giving them what they need." What we have here is first, a misleading caricature of the doctrine of interest, with no recognition of any truth at all in it, and second, an ambiguous reference to what children need. If the ambiguity were cleared up, "what the children need" would turn out to be, of course, some adult point of view to which the children are expected to conform.

tional tendencies that are inherent in a certain type of Protestant thought and practice.   First, then, we find approval
of graded lessons.   The Standing Committee on the Board of
Publication and Sabbath-School Work "heartily approves of
the general plan of graded lessons for use in churches preferring
them to the Uniform Series."[1]   But a conviction is expressed
that "the present lesson helps in the graded system may be
substantially improved," and the following principles are offered
for guidance in a proposed revision of certain parts and new
publication in others:

> (1) Simplicity of expression and clearness of definition.   (2)
> Complete harmony, in all exposition and definition, with the sys-
> tem of evangelical faith accepted by our Presbyterian Church;
> and especially with regard to the divine inspiration of the Scrip-
> tures as the supreme revelation of God, the deity of Jesus Christ
> as God in the flesh, coequal with the Father and coeternal, the in-
> herent sinfulness of human nature and the consequent need of a
> spiritual regeneration, and the atoning merit of Christ as a Saviour
> from sin.   And, further, that in the use of extra-biblical lessons, the
> honor of the Scriptures be maintained in this way: Where so-called
> "nature studies" or "stories" are used in the earlier grades (be-
> ginners, primary and junior) they are to be used in connection
> with definite selections of Scripture, and then only in the form
> of pictures or emblems to illustrate moral or spiritual truths;
> and that in the use of biography or history, or ethics or social
> science, a definite portion of Scripture be used as a basis of the
> lesson, the biography or historical event or principle of ethics
> or of social science being used to illustrate the Word of God and
> confirm its fundamental teachings.

The last clause is an almost exact reproduction of the scholastic conception of education.   Each study is conceived of,
not as an unforced exercise of intelligence and conscience upon a
given piece of human experience, not as a means of developing
judgment and power to discover, but as a means of illustrating

[1] Report presented to and approved by the General Assembly at Atlanta,
May 21, 1913.

and confirming certain fixed teachings—in this case certain interpretations of Scripture.

The relation between "complete harmony" with the accepted system of evangelical faith and the theory of gradation is revealed more distinctly in another report made to the same General Assembly by a Special Committee on Graded Lessons.

> We recommend the revision of the Beginners', Primary, and Junior Lesson Helps so as to express with greater clearness the fundamental Scripture doctrines. . . . (1) The Scriptures as an authoritative revelation from God. (2) The sinfulness of human nature and the need of regeneration. (3) The atonement offered by Jesus Christ.

Here we have a perfectly explicit proposal to teach the indicated dogmas to children from four to twelve years of age. The child is to be bent to the material by a process of reiteration as in Catholic education.

The committee goes on to express dissatisfaction with the view of religious growth that is stated in one of the books for teachers; the view, in a word, that the child's spiritual life may be made continuous, so that conversion, as it is ordinarily understood, will not be necessary. Inasmuch as the committee intimates that this *may* occur under favorable conditions, though only through the regenerating work of the Spirit of God, we might expect the committee to indicate some possible conception of how the divine Spirit might use the educative process as a whole. Instead the committee desires to have incorporated in the "Forewords" and in the instructions to teachers "suggestions on the best methods of leading scholars to Christ." The tendency here manifested to *add* religious appeal to educative processes instead of making these processes themselves, all of them, religiously vital, is an inevitable corollary of the intellectualistic, because dogmatic, approach to the curriculum. When teaching is conceived primarily as instruction in dogmas, something has to be added, of course, in the interest of religious living. To this dualism in religious education it will be necessary to return in a later section.

The dogmatic Protestant type tends to separate religious life from religious instruction. We have just now touched upon an instance in which, after recommending that certain dogmas be taught to children of four to twelve years, a committee advises also that the teachers be instructed in "the best methods of leading scholars to Christ." Here "coming to Christ" is treated as a thing by itself, and not involved in religious instruction as such. This type of educational thinking goes on, moreover, to separate training in the duties of the Christian life from both instruction and coming to Christ. "Surely," says the committee, "the prime object of the Sunday school is to lead the scholars to Christ the Saviour, and then to train them in the Christian life with its privileges and duties." "And *then*" to train them in the practice of religion. The entire scheme includes, it now appears, three stages or parts: *First*, drill in the dogmas; *Second*, leading to Christ; *Third*, training in Christian living. Here we have simply one thing added to another—first beliefs that are not acts of consecration, then a kind of omnibus surrender to Christ, then Christian living in the world.

In the background of this scheme is the fundamental assumption that knowledge or thought is a thing *per se* that is to be applied by the will, which is another thing *per se*. Moreover, the will is taken as a general or abstract entity apart from the particular desires and purposes that spring up in one's experience of human society. Hence the great choice of Christ, the major loyalty that is aimed at, is treated as an event or experience by itself, and duties to one's fellows as a distinct and subsequent thing.

If these underlying assumptions of dogmatic religious education are mistaken; if thought itself is a phase of active adjustment to the conditions of life, so that religious beliefs held antecedently to religious living are only pseudo-thinking; if, further, the will comes to itself in and through particular social interactions, not antecedently thereto, then, if we are to have a vital and organically unified religious education, we must begin with the formation of a social will through the performance of particular social acts out of which may grow Christian social habits; we must go on to make these practices thinking reactions—a discriminative, foresighted, information-seeking Christian faith; through practice of the lesser consecrations we must develop power for the larger ones, and through the experienced validity of the Christian purpose in social action, we must reach the heights and the depths of Christian belief. Leading pupils to Christ will then no longer be separated from, but fused with, leading them into Christlike social living. Thus the pupil's social experience under the leadership of Christ will be no "and then," no department of religious education, but the very lungs with which religious nurture draws in the breath of its life.

Social tendencies of the dogmatic Protestant type of religious education. Any complete inventory of the social tendencies of the type of religious education that has now been described would have to include a survey of the social content of the systems of doctrine that are in control in various denominations or Sunday schools. What level of sociality is reflected in the idea of God that is taught to the children? In the conception of sin? In the notion of the kingdom of God? In the particular duties that are inculcated? In the standards of church life? Obviously such a survey is impossible in this place. The most that can be done is to analyze social tendencies that are inherent in the dogmatic point of view as it is held in common by various sorts of Protestants, and in practices that are common.

(1) *Teaching the child that he stands in direct relations to God, that is, relations not necessarily mediated by priest or by church, tends to liberate the mind from all tyrannies, spiritual and political.* This teaching as to the accessibility of God is, of course, not distinctive of any single type of Protestantism; it is a common Protestant conviction. It is mentioned here in connection with the dogmatic type of Protestantism because, as a matter of fact, dogmatism here limits itself, actually renounces the absolutism, which in practice is the autocratic rule, that characterizes Catholic education. When we tell a child that he can carry everything in his own way directly to a God who will fully under-

stand, we invite a human being to think of everything from the divine point of view that develops in his own mind as he prays. From the judgments that thus arise the church and its dogmas have no ultimate immunity. To peoples and classes that have been touched by this Protestant teaching, God is a refuge and strength against all oppression. The struggle for liberty, religious, political, or economic, is sanctified; it becomes, not the impiety of mere revolt against social order, not the letting loose of class hatred, but a solemn consecration to the eternal purpose of the world. The possibilities that lie open in this direction are, however, seriously limited by other parts of the dogmatic scheme.

(2) *But the lack of social deliberation tends to isolate the individual, and to open the way for individualistic conceptions of duty.* The dogmatic type of education causes the pupil to become orthodox by a process of habituation, not by the give-and-take of a group of inquiring minds. Real deliberation of a social sort upon doctrine was finished in some council of long ago. The individual of to-day can make his complete response to instruction, can become and remain orthodox, without a single act of co-operation with anybody.

This tendency to isolation does not stop with beliefs. For dogmatism teaches duties also by authority, either the authority of a command that is supposed to have been directly revealed, or that of an inference drawn from an authoritative doctrine. The result is a set of rules or of sentiments where there should be training in the analysis of social relations and in co-operative work for improving them. One can hold the rule or feel the sentiment in isolation. Hence, in part, the amount of non-cohesive, non-co-operative, socially ineffective goodness among church members.

Nor is this the end of the matter. In the absence of social deliberation upon the meaning and the ends of life, there is no adequate check to self-deception with respect to the issues involved in our social conflicts and in our social aspirations. Many a man who is devotedly religious is stiff-necked in social relations simply because in early life he was taught rules when he should have learned the lesson of conferring with one's fellows whenever their interests are involved. Christians of this sort are accustomed to stand upon their rights, that is, upon precedents that give them some individualistic advantage; therefore such Christians let social wrongs also follow precedent. It is not uncommon—is it not in the natural order of things?—for stiff economic and political conservatism to be united in the same person with intense dogmatic religion, and to find support therein.

(3) *To make the Bible the practically exclusive source of material is to keep the attention of pupils fixed upon predemocratic social conditions.* Through the material of the curriculum we lead the pupil to notice and appreciate standards of human goodness, and to think of these standards as the will of God. If, now, the curriculum takes its instances of goodness from tribal relations, and from life under monarchical nationalism; if the virtues of the warrior are often to the fore, while the virtues of a free citizenship have not as yet even dawned upon the horizon of the good man's hopes; if loving-kindness must still express itself almost exclusively in the narrower personal relations,and in relief, while causes of wide-spread woe remain unguessed and unsought for; if social justice, though hot against those who profit by the exploitation of human beings, sees no way to endow the exploited with civil authority to control the conditions of the common life; if the democratic spirit, as far as it is present at all in individuals, finds no way to organize itself politically, or even to conceive of a civil state through which it could utter itself—if the curriculum has such a limited outlook upon Christian character, how can it present, without stammering and without ambiguity, the fully Christian ideals of a democracy of God?

It is true that even the crude social conditions of early Hebrew history and legend yield nuggets of gold for the religious teacher. Nothing, perhaps, more effectively assists in the analysis of certain simple relations between individuals, and of certain relations within the family, than some of the Old Testament stories. There is, moreover, no absolute break between the virtues of a hospitable sheik, or those of a generous-hearted mountain chieftain, and the virtues of a citizen when he votes to tax himself for the improvement of the public schools. Nevertheless there are two unescapable limitations upon the Old Testament as curriculum material for the development of intelligent Christian purpose:

(a) The characters and the incidents of the Old Testament that can be used to advantage have to be selected out of a mass that contains, because of the level of the whole, much unusable material. Even in circles that are controlled by the doctrine that every word of the Bible is infallible divine revelation, such selection has already gone far. There is discreet hesitation to take upon Christian lips many a word and sentiment that are said to be the word and the sentiment of God. There is a tacit understanding that tender minds shall be shielded from much of the moral crudity from which Yahweh is not represented as shrinking at all. But the selection must be much more rigorous than it is at present if the formation of really Christian standards of life and really Christian conceptions of God is to be our dominating purpose.

(b) Even the Old Testament worthies with whom we are glad to have the children keep company, will have to be used negatively, as well as positively, that is, to point what is not Christian as well as what is. So will their notions of Yahweh illuminate the character of God by contrast. Their virtues and their faith in God both reflect the social assumptions of their time. It is by measuring these men by the standards of their time, in fact, that we learn how great they were. When we idealize them as though they were true Christians we gain nothing, and we lose an opportunity for making Christian standards clear by contrast with these earlier and lower levels of society. It is necessary to be on our guard lest pre-Christian conceptions of God become a part of a child's faith when he listens to the beautiful Old Testament stories. In fact, only in the greatest utterances of the greatest of the prophets do we find the distinctively Christian consciousness of God emerging.

The spirit of Jesus, in short, is the social standard by which everything else in the Bible is to be weighed and measured. The *spirit* of Jesus. Here a distinction is necessary· with respect to the educational use of the New Testament. Jesus, too, died without having witnessed a single instance of political enfranchisement in the democratic sense. Apparently he did not foresee the possibility that brotherhood should achieve a non-paternalistic expression in the civil state. We look to him in vain for political wisdom—that is, guidance with respect to how to organize the good will in an effective social order. So obvious is this that our leaders have many times warned us that Jesus was not a teacher of economics or of politics or of sociology, just as they have warned us also that following Jesus is not the same as imitating him, as with respect to celibacy, for example. The social leadership of Jesus resides in his spirit of social good will, his simple appreciation of every one as a neighbor, his trust that God, who is love, will not let us go until we have become a brotherhood. Here brotherly love is all one with faith and hope.

The most daring and the most unflinching social teaching will never cease to look back to Jesus. But if it *sees* Jesus it will look, with him, to the future. It will breathe his spirit, but it will not stop with his words. "I have yet many things to say unto you," the Fourth Gospel reports him as saying, "but ye cannot bear them now." The spirit of Jesus is so forward-looking, so creative, so inexhaustible that the Bible cannot possibly be a sufficient text-book of Christian living. To tie religious education down to it, as dogmatism desires to do, would make us like those who are ever learning but never able to come to the truth—ever learning to love, but ever permitting the social order to defeat love.

CHAPTER XXII

THE RITUALISTIC PROTESTANT TYPE

Fundamental characteristics of the type. By the ritualistic type of Christian education is meant that which lays particular emphasis upon the pupil's relation to the church as a society that worships by prescribed forms. Though this characterization lacks the precision of an exact boundary-line, and though it does not suffice to describe the whole educational life of any Christian body, it does, nevertheless, identify a particular tendency that exists in various bodies. In the Protestant Episcopal Church, to take the most obvious example, we find religious education conditioned fundamentally by the fact that every baptized infant is, by virtue of his baptism, a member of the church. It follows as a matter of course that the aim of religious nurture is to help the child to realize increasingly the meaning of this already existing relation, and to perform more and more the acts that it entails, until the full stature of a churchman is reached. The meaning of the whole is set forth briefly in the creed, and it is expanded in the catechism. The acts are predominantly those of worship as it is prescribed in the prayer-book. Acts of churchmanship broaden out, of course, into ecclesiastical enterprises like missions, and the part of the creed that refers to the church expands into an interpretation of ecclesiastical history. Here, then, are two currents that flow side by side—training in a definite set of religious acts, and instruction in a definite set of beliefs. Rather, here are two phases of a single process for leading the pupil into greater and greater participation in a religious fellowship. For doctrine is presented specifically as church doctrine, not as a reasoned philosophy, not even as exegesis of the Bible.

316

Let us call these two phases of churchmanship doctrine and worship. Each is susceptible of variant interpretations that lead to variations in educational practice. Thus, on the side of doctrine there may be a close approach to the dogmatic type of religious teaching, or there may be wide divergence from it. Teaching of catechism that insists upon the literal truth of traditional doctrines moves toward dogmatism; but when doctrines are treated as symbols of the church fellowship, or as mental pictures that assist in producing a devotional frame of mind, the movement is away from the dogmatic type. All in all, the ritualistic type tends to exalt the organic life or fellowship of the church, and for this reason great latitude with respect to theological thought becomes natural. Therefore the educational tendency that we are now considering takes far less concern for the orthodoxy of the pupil than for his religious practices.

On the side of worship the variations range all the way from the mass, an act wrought by the priest for the people, to the cultivation of the evangelical type of conversion, in which the individual realizes God without priestly intervention. The church as teacher, accordingly, may take the attitude of an authority that requires conformity because it is the official agent of God upon earth, or that of a group of friends who would share their treasures with children, or it may take an intermediate position like that of the family, a group with common interests that are pursued in common, a group that educates precisely by the community of the younger and the older members.

Some educational advantages of the ritualistic point of view. (1) *The church and its services offer material of instruction that the pupil can experience as present and concrete.* The church building and its furniture, to begin with, meet the pupil as a visible expression of religion. Here is the font at which he was baptized, for example. It becomes, in due time, a means of teaching him that he is a member of the church and a child of God. Here is the sanctuary that contains the cup out of which he will drink at his first communion; here is where the bishop will sit when he comes to confirm *you.* So with a large number of objects. In this way the church building and its furniture can be used also for introducing some analysis of the parts of the morning and the evening service. The prayer-book itself then becomes another piece of concrete material, interesting, if for no other reason, because it is associated with pew and kneeling-stool and chancel, but interesting also because it now becomes a guide to things that are to be done by the child himself. Next comes the use of the Christian festivals—the Christian year—as concrete teaching material. The day schools have only begun to realize the educational possibilities of our national festivals, but the Christian festivals have been effectively used for centuries as a method of popular instruction in Scripture story and church doctrine.

(2) *Small children are fond of action and of repetition.* When to the sensuous impressiveness of a churchly interior, music, vestments, processional, and responsive actions of priest, choir, and congregation, we add opportunity to take an active part in the whole, important conditions of a child's interest are met. This is true even if the part be nothing more than standing or kneeling or saying "Amen" at the right point. Here are prayers to be committed to memory because they are to be used. One must learn to find the place in the prayer-book because it too is to be used. Repetition also fits in with children's spontaneous ways. Children are sometimes said to be little ritualists by nature. They want the favorite story told again and again, and they prefer to have it unchanged.[1] They enjoy repeating nonsense rhymes. They invent and hand down from one generation of children to another essentially ritualistic ways of conducting parts of their plays, as "counting out." They devise secret symbols and artificial languages to be used among themselves. They like to repeat the same evening prayer, and to turn it into a singsong. The explanation of this fondness for ritualism is to be found chiefly in the fact that the recurrence of a familiar thing to which one has been able to make

---

[1] I was once telling to two children, aged respectively three and five, a story that they had already heard, when I inadvertently changed the word "kind" to "good." Instantly the younger child interposed "kind" with some vehemence, and the five-year old seconded the amendment vociferously.

adjustment in the past produces a sense of being equal to the occasion. In a small child's world there are so many things that are uncontrollable and unpredictable, so many confusing situations, that there is positive satisfaction when he can know "just what comes next." To master a religious ritual, consequently, brings satisfaction even regardless of the particular significance of the content.

(3) *Many adolescents welcome symbols for longings that they are not as yet able to understand.* When adolescence approaches, one may react from that which is familiar and ordinary, desiring something different and fresh. But now an entirely contrary tendency is likely to set in, a tendency which, though it is the opposite of childhood's liking for the familiar, nevertheless reinforces the influence of the ritual. For adolescence not seldom brings idealistic longings that crave expression though they cannot as yet define themselves. Symbols offer one mode of expression, especially symbols that are stately and sounding, but not too literal. What is ancient, somewhat apart from the common day, to be used in common but not to be too familiarly talked about—this offers, so to say, a large and dimly lighted room in which the adolescent self can walk forth with other souls without being too closely interrogated as to who or what it is.

(4) *The assumption that the pupil is already a member of an important group that includes adults can be used as an incentive to study and to social growth.* Under ritualistic presuppositions the pupil will not be treated as a mere individual, or merely as one of the social class "children." Teaching will rarely if ever consist exclusively in bringing together a child mind and a piece of abstract information. Interfused with every process and with every piece of material will be some relation that is to be fulfilled between the pupil and the group to which he belongs. A direct motive for fulfilling it will grow out of the fact that he belongs to the same society as the most dignified adult. The church is "our" church, the pastor is "my" pastor as much as anybody's. The creed is what "we" believe much more than it is what "I" believe. If this did nothing more for a child than

give him some little sense of his own dignity, or produce a little genuine reverence, it would be worth while. But it can be used by the teacher as an interesting approach to various parts of the subject-matter. Just as the expectation of going on a journey next week through a given part of the country makes the geography of it all alive to a child, so the prospect of having a new part with grown-ups in their enterprises makes the enterprises themselves significant, even enables a child to feel motives that might have had no other entrance into his feelings. But more than this; the teacher can use the child's social connection with adults in the church as specific material for the teaching of social relations and for the development of particular social habits. Much of the peculiar power of the family in social education might conceivably be achieved by a warm and well organized church fellowship.

Some pitfalls of ritualistic education. We have seen that ritualistic tendencies in education have two phases, teaching of creed and catechism, and training in worship. In both directions dangers appear.

(1) *When the meaning of the church fellowship is found in an ancient symbol instead of in a common, forward-looking purpose, there is danger that instruction will be either dogmatic, or else of the shallow, memoriter sort.* Before me lies *A Fundamental Catechism*,[1] intended for children from six to twelve years of age, which has precisely the marks, already stated in earlier chapters, of the dogmatic type of teaching. Here is what purports to be knowledge, but it is pseudo-knowledge as far as it enters at all into the minds of children of six to twelve years. "How did God make all things? Ans. God first thought about making things, and then willed to make them, and then he made them. . . . What do we call making things out of nothing? Ans. Making things out of nothing we call creating." Again, there is the dogmatic inability to accept the principle of gradation of material, the same dogmatic formulæ being offered for children all the way from six years to twelve. Finally, there is the characteristic dogmatic insistence upon particular words. "The

---

[1] By H. H. Oberly. Published by Thomas Whittaker, New York, 1908.

teacher should see that the lessons are learned according to the exact words." That is, instead of using words because one has something to say, the child employs them in such a way as to produce a verbal mental habit that prevents thinking.

One might go on to ask: What in general is understood by "learning" the Ten Commandments, the Lord's Prayer, and the Apostles' Creed in any of our churches? What is the educational significance of finding a class of catechumens letter-perfect in them all? How much does it assure in the way of an intelligent Christian purpose held in common? In short, under dogmatic and ritualistic auspices alike the very form of catechetical instruction and its intellectualistic presuppositions prove to be inadequate for Christian education that has as its dominating motive the inculcation of a forward-looking, world-transforming social purpose. Without doubt the incorporation of the missionary interest into church education is enlarging the mental horizon and stimulating the social will. But the relation between missions and the ancient creeds is rather tenuous at the best, so that the tendency is to add giving to catechizing rather than to regenerate the catechizing itself. Moreover, as long as the exposition of the Christian faith retains the dogmatic form, the missionary purpose itself will lack social breadth, missions themselves being a measure for propagating the catechism, and for getting men into churches as sectarian as ours at the home base.

(2) *Training a child in prescribed, indefinitely repeated acts of worship as the main constituent of churchmanship provides for the perpetuation of the church as a particular society in the community and the world, but not for the reconstruction of the community or of the world.* In non-ritualistic circles the training of children in precise forms of worship is looked upon with considerable distrust. What is desired, it is said, is inner life, not outward ceremony, however seemly. There is fear that the ceremony, being punctiliously insisted upon, will be substituted for the states of heart and will that it is supposed to express. Ritualistic education can easily reply that the children under its care show at least as convincing signs of rever-

ence and of real appreciation of the content of church worship as children otherwise trained. Moreover, psychology is likely to be called as an expert witness to the truth that outward "expression of the emotions" may actually help to produce the emotions themselves. Finally, it may be said that the common worship of every organized communion sooner or later takes on definite, characteristic forms, to which children, as a matter of fact, become habituated, so that the real issue is not that of inner life *versus* outer form. We have to choose, rather, between different sorts of inner life, and between different sorts of outer form.

Neither the *pro* nor the *con* in this debate reaches quite to the bottom of the problem of social education in and through the churches. A ritual has direct social significance. For a liturgy does not merely relate the worshipper to some particular idea, or merely remind him of God. Even when it does these things ineffectively it nevertheless relates the worshipper to other worshippers, binding them all together in a common social consciousness. It does this, not only or chiefly by bringing them together within four walls, but by causing them to do and to say many things in unison. There are fraternities, like the Freemasons, that appear to maintain their existence chiefly by the unifying power of a ritual. There is no room for doubt that training in ritual worship is an effective method for producing in children a genuine group consciousness, each child being carried beyond self-regard and self-will by each common act. Of social training, as of learning arithmetic, it may be said that we "learn by doing" more than by listening. We learn "togetherness" by doing some particular thing together over and over again.

The ritualistic type of religious education thus furnishes a means for the perpetuation of the church as a particular society within the community. A distinctive form of worship, repeated every Sunday, produces in the worshipper a sense of being himself religiously distinct from the mass outside his church. This sense of distinctness easily passes into a positive sense of obligation, and into firm loyalty. It would be difficult to discover an educational instrument that is better adapted for producing a close-knit, self-perpetuating ecclesiastical consciousness.

But the point of its social strength is also the point where danger of social limitation and defect appears. For the problem of the Christian religion is that of transforming the community's whole social life into a brotherhood. A particular religious fraternity within the community, though its doors be wide open to everybody, is not, and cannot be, the solution of this problem. The social education of the child must have a horizon that reaches far outside of church consciousness. He must be trained to community "togetherness" not merely ecclesiastical "togetherness." Loyalty *to* the church must fuse in his consciousness with loyalty *of* the church to the cause of social welfare, social justice, and world society.

This might conceivably be accomplished in part through a ritual. But the content of it would have to be rich in social suggestiveness. To be thus rich, it would have to approach the problems of to-day and of to-morrow in terms that are not too ancient. The simple truth is that we cannot adequately express our own sense of the social will of God in terms derived from the outworn social standards of centuries ago. How, for example, can we bring ourselves to pray heartily for "the poor" in the ancient terms? The existence of poverty suggests to us, or ought to, a different line of reflection, a different sort of stimulus. We need modes of worship that will make it uncomfortable for us to carry "the poor" to the Lord when we the worshippers are carrying the product of the laborer's industry in our own pockets! Nor will the offering of our worldly substance as a part of the ritual suffice. Into worship itself must go the sword of the Spirit, the sword of the social justice that is love.

CHAPTER XXIII

EDUCATIONAL TENDENCIES OF EVANGELICALISM

Personal religion as experience of reconciliation with God. The term "evangelicalism" will be used in this discussion in the restricted sense of promoting personal religion conceived as experience of one's reconciliation with God. Evangelicalism takes the standpoint of personal experience as distinguished from doctrinal correctness, from correct church relations, from ritualistic performances, and from correct acts or "good works." Reconciliation is thought of, not as our achievement, but as divinely wrought for us and within us, and requiring of us only surrender of self-will and acceptance of the will of God. The emphasis is upon an experienced reversal of one's status before God, and a corresponding reversal in one's course of life.

To produce contrast-effects like this the conditions of stirring emotions must be created. The people have been gathered into great assemblies where the arts of social suggestion have been employed, often with skill. The dreadfulness of sin, the hopeless outlook for the sinner, the sufferings of Jesus on our behalf, the readiness of the Father to forgive, the happiness of the pardoned sinner, and his release from the thraldom of evil desires and habits—these are the most characteristic themes. They have been reinforced by appealing music, personal testimony of converts, individual urging, and the sight of others yielding to these persuasives. So much has religious emotion been focussed upon this one point that "having a personal Christian experience" has been understood in large circles as meaning "having a conversion experience." The remainder of life has anchored itself in the assurance that at some particular point in time "the great transaction" has been completed.

The impossibility of continuously maintaining the emotional

exaltation of the revival, and the limited response to the revival appeal, have necessitated much softening down of these contrast-effects in the every-day life of the churches. The typical appeal now becomes to "decide for Christ," and highly colored emotions are declared to be non-essential. Here we find a shift of emphasis from God's acts in us and with respect to us, to our acts with respect to him and his purposes. What here remains as characteristic of evangelicalism is little more than the teaching that to be a Christian one must at some particular instant cross a line that separates the saved from the unsaved.

Some social consequences of this point of view. Looked at as an abstract theory, the standpoint of such a personal religious experience, as far as it is held out as a privilege of every one, and not as an arbitrary divine bestowal, may be said to contain a germ of religious democracy. As a matter of fact, insistence that all men are sinners, that all are subject to the same condemnation, that all must meet the same conditions of salvation, and that the attitude of God is "Whosoever will," has been an appreciable social leveller. Revival meetings are notably democratic in tone. If wealth or privilege retains any aristocratic prerogative in them, it must be by some subtle rather than overt control. Moreover, the thought that each of us stands in direct, indefinitely modifiable relations with God, not merely in some fixed social status, has been an immeasurable inspiration to self-development. It has brought out the innate powers of multitudes of plain men. It has stimulated education. Long before our States reached a conviction that the public school system should reach all the way to the university, or even to the high school, ministers were successfully appealing to farmers, mechanics, and shopkeepers to found and support academies and colleges and to send their sons thereto.

Theoretically evangelicalism transcends also certain other tendencies to spiritual aristocracy that have long had a place within Christianity. No longer are the favors of the divine presence regarded as a prerogative of a few saints who can give themselves to contemplation and to austerities while the mass of the people walks upon the lower level of formal compliance with a few external requirements of the church. No; the plain man, too, can walk in heavenly places in this life, and he can converse out of his own experience upon the highest themes.

All this is true theoretically, and to some extent in practice. But the tendency toward democracy that is unquestionably here is partly defeated by the effort of evangelicalism to promote a uniform experience among human beings who are not uniform. Attempts to standardize religious emotion have failed even in religious bodies in which these attempts have been unresisted. But in the meantime, individuals who by virtue of temperamental traits or of a favorable conjunction of circumstances happen to have had the standard evangelical experience, have become a spiritual aristocracy. They are the ones who have indubitably "got religion"; they are the ones who have something to talk about in the experience meeting; and consequently a tacit discount is placed upon experience of other types. Thus we have a superior religious class alongside the religious commonalty, and between the two there often exists an emotional difference that interferes with the formation of unified group purposes.

The place of children in the thought of evangelicalism. Not only are adults not all capable of the experience that evangelicalism has prized; this experience is also practically inaccessible to young children without forcing'them toward religious morbidity. The conversion experience is distinctly a thing of adolescent and adult life. Here, then, is another tendency to religious stratification. If church membership is reserved for those who have had the standard evangelical experience, then what is the religious and ecclesiastical status of young children who are under the church's care? Unmodified evangelicalism has no workable conception of a present Christian life for them, or of membership in the Christian communion.

A movement that exalts the love of God as evangelicalism has done is bound, of course, to take a warm interest in children. It is bound to find ways to teach religion, whether consistently or not. In fact, the churches that have been foremost in the

Sunday school movement are the ones that have been most strongly impregnated with evangelicalism. They have looked upon the Sunday school theoretically as an agency for converting the young. But they have stretched the term "conversion." Their observation of children has shown the inapplicability of the term in its strict evangelical sense to the younger pupils, and to a large extent even to adolescents. The churches have been forced by realities to conceive the Sunday school more and more as an educational enterprise. The acclimating of the term "religious education" during the last twenty years is an interesting index of this movement. Religious thought with respect to the young is crystallizing, even in evangelical circles, around the idea of religious growth—growth that does not necessarily presuppose an antecedent conversion.

Wherein, now, can such religious growth be conceived to consist? Can it be included within the notion of religious experience, and if so, how? The close association of evangelicalism with dogmatism produced as a first conception of the pupil's growth that of increase in his knowledge of the Scriptures. But this did not satisfy the presupposition that religion is an experience of God. Evangelicalism, with all its emphasis upon the Bible, could not rest here. The child's knowledge, even of the Scriptures, must not be left as a thing by itself; it must somehow be wrought into an integral life that can move on from level to level as the child's years increase. Again and again effort has been made to meet this demand by adding evangelism to religious education. But this has not met the situation because it ignores the principle of growth. Child evangelism is itself something *per se* interjected into the course of teaching and training, and entirely independent of the principle of growth.

Gradually there is dawning a realization that our social experience is a sphere for communion with God, that here children can share religion with adults, and can grow in religion without any forcing whatever. Here the bond of union between adults, and between them and children, is the same; it is neither uniformity of doctrine, nor yet the emotional experience of reconciliation, but rather the experience of a *purpose of reconciliation*, the purpose to live a common life as brothers, and in so doing to live a common life with the Father.

This is not only an inclusive conception, inclusive of individuals old and young, inclusive of all churches as far as they are really brotherhoods, inclusive of all the good will beyond the churches; it is also a theologically reconciling conception. The notion of sin and of release from it, the notion of individual reconciliation with the Father, and the notion of a life that is from above, are not only not smothered; they are filled with the most poignant content. The waste of life because we are not brothers, the waste of health, the poverty, the broken homes, the stunted and distorted minds, the quarrels, the oppression of class by class, the riots, the wars, the pessimism—all this in the midst of which we live, a part of which we are, is the world sunken in iniquity. When in such a world we take as our own God's purpose of reconciliation we do not escape the experience of condemnation and of repentance, or the necessity for a saving faith. For we have natural tendencies to selfishness, greed, and revenge, all of which must be overcome; we have to extricate our will from a social complex in which we profit at the expense of our fellows; we have to face the suffering of the world as a consequence in part of our own neglect; we find necessary not only stern self-discipline, but also faith that is robust enough to face unflinchingly this, the most stupendous, the most oppressive, the most tragic problem that the mind of man has conceived.

This social experience of God in his world—God in all love, and in all that wins us to the love way—makes the love of the Father and the love of the neighbor one experience. This is a religion of the heart. It will tax all the emotional resources of evangelicalism. It will still single out each individual, and it will go on utilizing the values of mass suggestion. But it will not separate emotion from study or from action. And because it will maintain these three in vital unity, it will obliterate the gulf that has existed between child and man, between religious education and religious experience.

The Sunday school as an evangelistic agency. What has just been sketched might be called a socialized evangelicalism. It conceives religion as experience, and specifically as experience of reconciliation, but it holds that reconciliation lies in the purpose to reconcile, and that three parties are involved, myself, my neighbor, and God. It holds, further, that the inner rectification of the heart, and the outer act of establishing a just society, are phases of one and the same reconciling process. Religious experience is here no longer separated from the social relations and enterprises that a child can appreciate. On this basis the Sunday school can still be—it must be—an evangelistic agency. But its effectiveness as such an agency will depend to some extent upon reconstructing existing conditions and methods.

(1) *Unambiguous standing within the religious communion should be made possible for every child.* This cannot be done until child religion is conceived in terms of a growing purpose. A recent writer in a magazine that is published in the interest of the religious life of boys treats the Christian experience as if it must have its beginning in the bluntness of a conscious life choice. He speaks of a *day* when we choose to take religion in earnest, of an *hour* when the gospel must be deliberately accepted or deliberately rejected. "The choice of life," he says, "cannot be broken up into little bits."[1] Here we have a mechanical rather than a vital mode of thought concerning the things of character. The successive acts in which a will grows are thought of, not in terms of growth but of accretion, or as so many mutually external bits which are merely juxtaposed or heaped up. The same type of thought appears in those who hold that every child must be on one side or the other of a fixed line that separates the saved from the unsaved. Parents whose affection makes it impossible for them to set up any such mechanical division between their own offspring, especially between young children, often fail to see the incongruity of ascribing anything of the kind to God.

A social conception of God and of our reconciliation with him

---

[1] "Conversion," by H. R. Mackintosh. *American Youth*, August, 1913.

will recognize every affectionate pulse-beat as divine. Religious education will seize upon every impulse to generosity, to justice, and to co-operation as an occasion to make the pupil realize that just here he is in fellowship with the church and with the Father. This fellowship will involve mutual recognition, the child recognizing the church as a society in which he must grow, and the church recognizing children as already within itself, yes, as its very self in process of growth. This recognition, to be most effective, will need outward signs and specific methods of calling to remembrance. Just what changes this will imply in the rules of various denominations need not here be specified, nor is it necessary to suggest particular occasions on which adults and children may well celebrate together their unity in the Christian purpose. It is enough to point out that overt acts of co-operation, and overt recognition of one another, are essential alike to the child and to the adult.

(2) *The undue extension, and consequent weakening, of the term "conversion," should be resisted.* When the religious life of small children is thought of in terms of status rather than in terms of growth, the tendency is to extend and dilute the meaning of the conversion whereby the status is supposed to be established. If the term is to be applied to persons whose will is still relatively inchoate, lacking sharp edges and definite moral attitudes, what shall it mean when adults are called upon to repent and be converted? Obviously, if adults and young children are both included under the term, its essential and irreducible meaning will be found in the infantile mind that shows signs of piety. Have we not here a large part of the explanation for the indefiniteness that has come to characterize the evangelistic appeal to adults? And of the degradation of statistics of conversions—as though one who holds up a hand, or signs a card, or shakes hands with an evangelist is to be counted as a converted man! In the interest of child religion and of adult religion alike, this tendency should be resisted. Small children are simply not capable of viewing life's problems in the perspective that is implied in an intelligent life choice.

But they are capable of responding to love, and of sharing with adults in the work of reconciliation—they are capable of growing in the love way.

(3) *If a "decision day" is observed, it should respect the principle of growth, with its corollary of gradation.* The *reductio ad absurdum* of Sunday school evangelism is found in Sunday schools that once a year interrupt and lay aside the educational process in order to make an appeal to all pupils above seven years of age to make an immediate decision for Christ. There are schools in which the same little children sign decision cards year after year. The trouble with this is not that there is too much evangelism, but too little. For the meaning of the supposed decision is washed out and faded by the indiscriminateness of the method. It should require no great depth of either psychological or religious insight to perceive that when the same appeal for decision is put before a child of eight and one of sixteen before whom the vista of life is opening emotionally and intellectually, there is religious incongruity that is likely to interfere with the vital processes of both. The will grows; it, as well as the intelligence, requires gradation of educational process and material.

Moreover, to ignore on decision day the growth of will that has been going on through the regular processes of instruction and training is to run the risk of making personal religion abstract or sentimental or bafflingly mysterious. Why ask a child to begin the religious life when he has already taken many steps in it? How can teachers assume that Christian purpose is lacking when the whole tendency of the preceding Sunday school experience has been to produce and clarify such purpose? The most that decision day can be expected to do is to produce more or less of a climax in a process that has been going on for years. This climax, too, will differ from department to department. If decision day could be changed in substance and in name to "fellowship day," the purpose of which should be realization of our fellowship with one another, with Jesus, and with the Father in a common purpose of social reconciliation, then every grade in the school could celebrate the festival in its own way. The social longings of adolescence could be met by confirmation or its equivalent in the way of public confession by the pupil and recognition by the church. A parallel, but simpler and narrower, declaration of standpoint could be made by each earlier department or grade, and recognition by the church through the department could correspond to the recognition of adolescents as full members. The whole would constitute a joyous-solemn calling to mind of what it is that unites these pupils and their teachers to one another in the church and in the school, with appropriate measures for enabling each pupil, in a manner appropriate to his age, to realize that this is *my* purpose, and that this is *my* church.

There is reason for questioning the social tendency of decision-day methods that cause pupils to exaggerate the differences that exist between them. There are schools in which certain pupils, whose expressions of religious interest have been more prompt or more free than those of other pupils, have been put forward until they have become "forward." The worst of it is not that these few children become priggish, but that religion is misrepresented to the mass of the pupils. It is misrepresented because their own religiousness goes relatively unrecognized, and because religion itself here becomes sponsor for a kind of aristocracy.

The sum of the matter is that every day should be a day of decision for every pupil according to his capacity for decision. That is, the whole of religious education should have its roots in social acts, relations, and purposes that grow from more to more continuously. Not that the socializing of the will can be expected to proceed with even pace through all stages of growth. The curve of mental as well as of physical growth is irregular, and so is the curve of social interest. We are to expect rapid increase here, slower increase there, with only approximate conformity of the individual to any age scale. The general growth of social interest that comes with adolescence may well be taken advantage of to secure the crystallization of social purpose that has long been forming, that is, to cause the pupil to realize, as never before, the fellowship of

purpose that constitutes the church. But the realization
of this fellowship should be part and parcel of the whole scheme
of religious instruction and training in all the grades.

(4) *Whatever is vital in the "evangelistic department" of
Sunday school organizations should be taken up into the regular
plan of instruction and training, and "child evangelism" should
cease.* The reason for an evangelistic department, a child
evangelist, and evangelistic mass meetings for children grows
out of the presupposition that the Sunday school, in its regular
and systematic work, will teach Bible or catechism rather than
develop Christian purpose in children. Let us make the presupposition untrue! When we do so, we shall realize that
evangelistic meetings for children, especially those conducted
by strangers who use high-pressure methods that ignore the
laws of growth, are not only unnecessary, but also injurious.
They are injurious because the impression that they make upon
children as to the nature of the Christian life is untrue. It is
as untrue as would be the presentation to healthy children of a
bottle of medicine to make them grow. The Christian life
cannot be truthfully separated, with either child or adult, from
the social issues that constitute the difference between the mind
of Christ and the love of the world. To draw the child's mind
away from these issues as they appear before him in his own
inch-by-inch experience, and as the faithful Sunday school
teacher has to recognize them, into a relatively abstract or
sentimental contemplation of himself or of Christ, is to counteract, not to supplement the sound work of religious education.

(5) *Greater emphasis should be placed upon the content of the
Christian purpose.* In morals and religion alike we are under
the influence of traditions that unduly exalt the form of life as
against the content. We are not seldom urged to be conscientious, or to be true to duty when if we followed the advice,
we should obey an ignorant and sometimes injurious sense of
duty. We are advised to surrender to God before there has
been adequate inquiry into our idea of God. The value of surrender to God depends upon the character of the God to whom
we surrender. We are invited to come to Christ when it is not

decisively clear what this means in terms of actual social living. The nature of God and the mind of Christ must be expressed in these terms in all our teaching. The divine presence and the divine nature are to be discerned in the love between men that the pupil can actually witness and take part in. Here is the application within religious education of evangelicalism's insistence that religion is an experience. Children can have the experience because they can appreciate love and form a personal will to love. But this will to love must learn to discriminate. It must be trained to take notice of the conditions of human life; it must learn what are the causes of welfare and of illfare; it must define social issues as they arise, but always with eyes for the distant as well as the immediate good. This is evangelistic teaching, the teaching of the good news that is for all the world, the pressing home to the individual pupil of the insistent love of God.

CHAPTER XXIV

EDUCATIONAL TENDENCIES OF LIBERALISM

The notion **of religious freedom.** For the purposes of the present discussion religious liberalism may be defined as the attempt to incorporate freedom into religion. Not freedom from religion, but freedom in religion, is the idea. As religious repression has taken the two main forms of control of thought and control of worship or of ecclesiastical life in general, so the effort at liberation has been directed chiefly toward untrammelled thinking and a rationally regulated life, worship included.

The demand for religious subjection has always presented itself as a command of God addressed to men, whereas it has always been a command of some men addressed to others in the name of God. The essence of dogmatism is its demand that I shall take as divine revelation what other men have already judged to be revelation. To submit to this demand is to submit to men, not God. Just so, when the church prescribes exclusive modes of worship or rules of conduct, what happens is that some men presume to decide these things for others. Hence the central tendency of liberalism has been to clear up the confusion of mind whereby human opinions have been given the force of divine revelation, and human judgments the force of divine commands, and to show, instead, the inherent naturalness and reasonableness of religion. This clearing-up process is going on actively in many ecclesiastical circles, orthodox as well as heterodox.

The result of resisting sectarian restrictions upon the mind, and of falling back upon what is broadly human as the sphere in which to trace the thoughts of God, varies according to the position of the emphasis. When liberalism places its emphasis upon sound knowledge, how to maintain religious zeal becomes a problem. The very narrowness of dogmatism seems at times to produce religious intensity that has power with men, whereas the liberal thinker tends not seldom to become an onlooker rather than a doer. On the other hand, however, breadth of thought tends with some persons toward a more or less mystical realization of the all-encompassing divine life. Here is warmth of feeling, not mere pointedness of thought. But, all in all, the attempt to incorporate freedom into religion tends to replace the rejected authority not so much by sound knowledge, or by mystical delights, as by the affirmation of ethical principles as the mind of God. When liberalism insists upon being positively religious as well as open-minded, it has nothing that it can substitute for simple goodness. Dogmatism encounters the danger of substituting orthodoxy for kindness, and ritualism the danger of substituting institutional conformity for social breadth. But liberalism has no cloak with which to conceal the irreligion that is in all unkindness, all neglect of human needs.

Liberalism instills ethical principles, not by authority, but through reflection. Hence the tendency to habituation by drill processes is less in evidence than it is in either the dogmatic or the ritualistic type of education. Moreover, since reflection is a process in which one acts as an individual, a process in which one must resist gregarious tendencies, for the time being at least, liberalism is less inclined than is evangelicalism to mass movements that sway men by suggestion rather than by inciting them to think for themselves.

Here, then, are three points in which liberalism has obvious significance for a theory of religious education: The effort to develop in each person an individual or independent attitude in all religious matters; the awakening of thought as contrasted with mental habituation; and the fusion of rightness toward God with rightness toward men. Before we attempt to weigh the social significance of all this, let us pause to consider some phases of the relation between religious freedom and the general cause of human liberty.

Can there be religious emancipation within aristocratic or plutocratic society? It is possible to think of liberal religion in terms of the individual rather than of society. If the civil state protects me from distraint of person and of property on account of religion, and if I use my own ability to think, resisting all ecclesiastical dictation, am I not then free indeed? What is religious emancipation if not just release from ancient ecclesiastical restraints?

The youth of our colleges are often warned not to think of freedom as merely negative, the mere absence of restraint. We say to them: "You cannot be really free until, *first*, you acquire ability to resist your impulses and to organize yourself upon a plan that you deliberately approve, and until, *second*, you acquire purposes large enough to furnish outlet for your powers." With equal truth a *third* thing might be said: "You cannot be free until you are enlisted in the cause of freedom for all. For the *you* that requires to be organized, and that requires outlet for its powers, is social in nature, fundamentally so. Moreover, as long as you remain an acquiescent, non-protesting member of a society that oppresses your fellows, you must either close your eyes to injustice or else bribe your heart by the advantages of silence. In either case the wheel of inequality passes over your soul, grinding it into the dust. Oppression makes its beneficiaries as well as its victims unfree."

It is quite possible to exercise negative religious freedom without finding adequate religious self-expression. The negatively free mind may be most conventional, most swayed by the interests with which it is socially and economically bound. It may be a contented member of a religious set or clique. It may be so tied to the past as to resist the truly free religion of social justice. As a matter of fact, the era of our attempt to unfetter religion finds various fundamental rights of man as yet unachieved, and as yet there is no sufficiently clear demonstration of the essential relationship between the different kinds of freedom. In a society that does not yet secure to masses of children the health that the community possesses the means to bestow— in such a society what is religious freedom after all, even for one whose own children are healthy?

The right to think, and to worship according to the dictates of one's own judgment does indeed occupy a basal position in the general emancipation of man. But the structure of liberty consists of much more than foundation-stones. Release from restraint is release of power that insists upon giving effect to itself. In this case, what effect? To throw off the yoke of spiritual subjection must ultimately mean getting into action for larger, deeper spiritual ends. It must mean that we are ready to wrestle as never before with the god of this world.

In short, within a social system of aristocratic or plutocratic privilege, positive religious emancipation is possible only on condition that we enter into the divine purpose to do away with privilege and set up democracy. Religious liberalism has not failed to give signs that this is the law of its inner life, for it has been foremost in opposition to slavery. In general, too, the liberal mind can be relied upon to see through the obfuscations whereby autocracy of many kinds constantly strives to justify irrational force by reason. Going forward in the same path, emancipated souls will find still fuller religious life, still fuller realization of God, in the struggle for social justice and a world society. Emancipated souls must find this, or else, their freedom being merely negative, their religious life will be bound hand and foot by social orthodoxy.

The educational problems of liberalism. All the queries that have just been raised as to the relations within liberalism between reflection and action on the one hand, and between individual independence and social justice on the other, are educational problems. I shall now set them forth as such, with a hint or two toward solutions.

(1) *Liberalism opens the way to the most vital materials and methods of instruction, but it encounters the danger of intellectualism.* It is of the essence of external religious authority to discourage too curious prying into facts with respect to the human bearers of the supposed divine prerogatives. History is relatively non-essential, at least history as inquiry, for dogmatism is fully ready to formulate all that is religiously essential in the past. Similarly, dogmatism is satisfied with a relatively narrow range of subjects for study. Why, for instance, should one

study religions other than one's own? Why should one be religiously concerned to understand the world movements of the present, since a completed faith was once delivered, and only once, to the saints? This intellectual attitude liberalism exactly reverses. It is interested in the human as such, partly for the sake of avoiding human error, partly because the human as such is looked upon as revealing divine guidance and meaning. Therefore, the further we can trace down the human elements in history the better; the more we know about other religions the better for our own.

This spirit meets the interests of pupils without reservation, for it brings human action into the foreground, and encourages curiosity. There is less tendency to flatten out things in the interest of a formula. Moreover, methods of pupil self-expression can be adopted with less reserve. For, whereas dogmatic teaching fails of its purpose unless it gives the pupil's mind a particular set, liberalism is most concerned that the pupil should weigh facts, and do some real thinking of his own, even if his thoughts do not reproduce those of his teacher.

On the other hand, so much of the struggle for religious freedom has centred around the right to think, and the adoption of sound methods of investigation has necessitated so much revision of biblical interpretation, that liberalism has formed an intellectual habit that, carried into religious life, becomes intellectualism. The place that intellectuality occupies in the campaign against restraints and against historical errors is different from the place that it holds in the promotion of vital religion. The mental operation that is chiefly required for religious growth is the discriminative appreciation of values. This involves, of course, observation of facts, some understanding of the past, and some rational foresight; it involves some generalization of the standpoint from which one judges life and duty; but here the main work of intelligence is to clarify one's desires and purposes so that revision may be made, and to discover means whereby one's life purposes may be carried out. The achievement of a broad outlook, then, or of ability to prove or defend one's position by sound knowledge is at most a single part, and that not the central part, of religious instruction.[1]

(2) *Liberalism makes for ethical clarity and breadth, but it easily fails of ethical fervor.* Holding to the ideal of a rationally ordered life, as distinguished from one that is ecclesiastically prescribed, the liberal would avoid, on the one hand, drifting with the currents of conventionalism and, on the other hand, being swept off his feet by floods of mass emotion. The attitude of ethical reflection has the value of contributing to clarity and breadth of purpose, and not seldom to steady loyalty to a principle through thick and thin. But, on the other hand, reflection has the effect of inhibiting impulses, and of postponing or resisting rather than of initiating action. Now, a locomotive engine must of course have a throttle, but it must have steam also. Human impulses must be regulated and redirected, but yet the inner fire is what moves life up the grade of progress. Religious education must include provision for cultivating religious fervor.

[1] Some years ago a liberal-minded clergyman of orthodox affiliations, convinced that catechetical instruction should be revived in Protestantism, and finding no printed catechism that suited him, undertook to write one. Here are some of the questions and answers that resulted:

"1. *Q. Apart from the things which you believe, hope, or imagine to be true, what do you know ?*

A. I know that there is a world, and that I live in it.

2. *Q. How do you know that there is a world ?*

A. I know that there is a world because I can touch, taste, smell, see and hear.

3. *Q. How do you know that you live ?*

A. I know that I live because I think, feel and will.

.   .   ..

23. *Q. Since God made you to love these things, does he compel you so to do ?*

A. No; though God has made me in order that I might love the good, the true, and the beautiful, He made me able to love or to hate, to choose or to refuse, that so my love may be my own free offering to Him. This liberty is God's highest gift to me, and I must take heed that I do not prove unworthy of His trust.

24. *Q. How may we know God ?*

A. We may know God through our own moral character, our conscience, and our best aspirations and hopes; through nature and the beauty of the world which he has made; through the better impulses of all men, and the enlightened understanding and holy living of the best men; through the Bible; and through the life and teachings of Jesus Christ."

This was intended for pupils from ten to fifteen years of age. The obvious assumption is that what the clergyman regards as fundamental in his own thought-system is fundamental in religious instruction and therefore should come first.

(3) *Liberalism cultivates respect for man as man, but it does not so readily appreciate institutional organizations of the good will, such as the church.* It is not to be wondered at that those whose liberties were wrested from the church by hard struggle should show little inclination toward ecclesiastical harness. But respect for man must go on to become love for man, and love must go on from being a sentiment to become a policy of action, and love as a policy of action requires machinery for co-operation and for continuity. Liberalism should go on to free men's hands and feet as well as heads—free them not only in the sense of getting them loose, but also in the sense of getting them into exercise. It would seem as though the next step is to transform ecclesiastical institutions into organs of a freedom that is more complete than free speech, even the freedom of love in co-operative action.[1]

(4) *These three positive educational tendencies of liberalism can be reinforced, and the correlative defects avoided, by identifying religious freedom with the positive purpose of the democracy of God.* When religious instruction has as its definite goal the formation of an intelligent and thoroughly Christian social will, the menace of intellectualism will be removed. It will be removed, not by letting down intellectual standards, not by putting fences around inquiry, but by putting knowledge into its natural and proper relation to life. It is, I believe, the uniform experience of teachers and of educational institutions that, all in all, students show the greatest intellectual zeal when they are conscious that the knowledge that they seek has a bearing upon their wider purposes.

Ethical clarity and breadth, moreover, can best be promoted

---

[1] The ecclesiastical limitations of negative freedom are clearly apparent in the following words of ex-President Eliot: "The genuine Unitarian values so highly his liberty of thought and his freedom from all bonds of traditional and gregarious opinion that, as a rule, he is not willing to attempt the imposition of his own opinions on anybody else, not even on his children. He is rarely interested in foreign missions except on their medical and anthropological side, and he makes a poor propagandist at home; for he is apt to hold that nobody ought to be or become a Unitarian except a person whose own mind and will work in such a way that he cannot help being or becoming a Unitarian." (From a pamphlet, *The Education of our Boys and Girls*, published by the American Unitarian Association.)

in the presence of live social issues. There is, to be sure, a more or less popular notion that in order to see a moral issue clearly one must be outside it, must be able to look at it without feeling it. But this is at most only a half-truth. There are matters, such as music and poetry, in which we do not even begin to understand until our feelings are engaged. So, in moral instruction nothing so effectively shakes pupil and teacher out of moral conventionality as to face the actual, present struggle of men for justice, and especially to take some part in it. "I never thought of this before" is the common experience when moral reflection steps out from the social aloofness of generalities into the concreteness of a moral world now in process of creation. When we get into the struggle to put love into effective action, when we insist upon getting results, then two things happen: We love with a new fervor, and we see the nature of the issue as we never saw it before.

It is then that the necessity and the possibilities of the church fully dawn upon us. The church is necessary as a preacher of *radical* good will, which is human participation in a divine love that, though it may be repulsed, will not be defeated. The church is necessary as a fellowship of those who, aspiring to this radical good will in their own conduct, need the support of like aspiring souls. The church is necessary as a champion of the "forlorn hopes" of society, the social causes that the "practical" man regards as visionary. The church is necessary, finally, as an educator of children in these ideals and practices. It is the only institution of large scope that we can have any hope of inducing to teach democracy in this thoroughgoing fashion. Liberalism needs the church for the achievement of liberty itself.

CLASSIFIED BIBLIOGRAPHY

A

THE NEW SOCIAL CONSCIOUSNESS MANIFESTING ITSELF IN GENERAL
THEORIES OF EDUCATION

Bagley, W. C. *The Educative Process.* New York, 1910. Part I, "Functions of Education."

Cubberley, E. P. *Changing Conceptions of Education.* Boston, 1909.

Dewey, J. *Democracy and Education.* New York, 1916.

Dewey, J. and E. *Schools of To-morrow.* New York, 1915.

Earhart, L. B. *Types of Teaching.* Boston, 1915. Chapter XI, "Socializing Exercises."

Graves, F. P. *A Student's History of Education.* New York, 1915. Chapter XXVII, "Present Day Tendencies in Education."

King, Irving. *Education for Social Efficiency.* New York, 1913.

——, *Social Aspects of Education.* New York, 1912.

MacVannel, J. A. *Outline of a Course in the Philosophy of Education.* New York, 1912.

McMurry, F. M. *Elementary School Standards.* Yonkers-on-Hudson, 1913.

Monroe, P. *A Text-Book in the History of Education.* New York, 1915. The last four chapters analyze the educational inheritance of the present generation.

O'Shea, M. V. *Education as Adjustment.* New York, 1905. Chapter VII, "Adjustment as Affected by Social Organization."

——, *Social Development and Education.* Boston, 1909.

Perry, C. A. *Wider Use of the School Plant.* New York, 1911.

Scott, C. A. *Social Education.* Boston, 1908.

Smith, W. R. *An Introduction to Educational Sociology.* Boston, 1917.

Snedden, D. *Problems of Educational Readjustment.* Boston, 1913.

B

THE SOCIAL INTERPRETATION AND APPLICATION OF THE CHRISTIAN
MESSAGE

The indispensable source for those who desire to keep abreast of both thought and action in this field is Ward, H. F., *A Year Book of the*

Church and Social Service in the United States. New York, 1916. New editions are to be expected from time to time. This little book sketches the history of the social service movement in the churches; describes the organization and gives a directory of the social service departments of the various denominations and of the Federal Council of Churches; describes methods and programs of work; quotes the official utterances of the denominations; gives a directory and description of extra-ecclesiastical agencies for social service, and contains what is probably the largest, most thoroughly classified and annotated bibliography of the subject, including a large variety of pamphlet material.

1. *The General Conception of the Christian Message and of the Christian Experience*

NOTE.—The intention here is merely to reveal a type of thinking. The list is not representative in any other sense. For a fuller list, see Ward's *Year Book.*

Brown, W. A. *Is Christianity Practicable?* New York, 1916.

Coe, G. A. "Contemporary Ideals in Religion." *Religious Education,* XI (1916), 377–387.

Fremantle, W. H. *The World as the Subject of Redemption.* New York, 1892.

Henderson, C. R. "Christianity and Social Problems." Chapter XI of *A Guide to the Study of the Christian Religion,* G. B. Smith, editor. Chicago, 1916.

King, H. C. *Theology and the Social Consciousness.* New York, 1902.

——, *The Moral and Religious Challenge of Our Times.* New York, 1911.

Macfarland, C. S. *Spiritual Culture and Social Service.* New York, 1912.

Mathews, S. *The Individual and the Social Gospel.* New York, 1914.

——, "Theology and the Social Mind." *Biblical World,* XLVI (1915), 201–248.

Rauschenbusch, W. *Christianity and the Social Crisis.* New York, 1907.

Strong, J. *My Religion in Everyday Life.* New York, 1910.

——, *The Next Great Awakening.* New York, 1913.

Ward, H. F. *Social Evangelism.* New York, 1915.

2. *The Christian Approach to Particular Social Conditions and Problems*

NOTE.—This list also is intended to be merely typical. It is sufficient to indicate the change that has begun to take place in the practice of the Christian life, but for an adequate list of particular activities and programs and books, see Ward's *Year Book*.

Atkinson, H. A. *The Church and the People's Play.* Boston, 1915.

Balch, W. M. *Christianity and the Labor Movement.* Boston, 1912.

Coleman, G. W. *Democracy in the Making.* Boston, 1915.

Douglass, H. P. *The New Home Missions.* New York, 1914.

Earp, E. L. *The Rural Church Movement.* New York, 1914.

Elwood, C. A. *Sociology and Modern Social Problems.* New York, 1913.

Faunce, W. H. P. *Social Aspects of Foreign Missions.* New York, 1914.

Forbes, E. S., editor. *Social Ideals of a Free Church.* Boston, 1913.

Gladden, W. *Applied Christianity.* Boston, 1891.

——, *Christianity and Socialism.* New York, 1905.

Gulick, S. *The Fight for Peace.* New York, 1915.

Hoben, A. "American Democracy and the Modern Church." *American Journal of Sociology*, January, 1917.

Jefferson, C. E. *Christianity and International Peace.* New York, 1915.

Lynch, F. *The Peace Problem.* New York, 1911.

——, *Challenge: The Church and the New World Order.* New York, 1917.

Macfarland, C. S. *Christian Unity at Work.* New York, 1913.

Men and Religion Movement, Messages of. 7 vols. New York, 1912.

Nearing, S. *Social Religion.* New York, 1913.

Rauschenbusch, W. *Christianizing the Social Order.* New York, 1912.

Smith, S. G. *Democracy and the Church.* New York, 1912.

Strayer, P. M. *Reconstruction of the Church.* New York, 1915.

Tippy, W. M. *The Church, a Community Force.* New York, 1914.

Trawick, A. M. *The City Church and its Social Mission.* New York, 1913.

Vedder, H. C. *The Gospel of Jesus Christ and the Problems of Democracy.* New York, 1914.

Ward, H. F. *Poverty and Wealth.* New York, 1915.

——, *The Social Creed of the Churches.*

Ward, H. F., and Edwards, R. H. *Christianizing Community Life.* New York, 1917.

C

CHANGING CONCEPTIONS OF RELIGIOUS EDUCATION

For conservative types of thought, see the volumes of *Proceedings of the International Sunday School Association*, published under various titles by the Executive Committee, Chicago; also Sampey, J. R., *The International Lesson System, the History of its Origin and Development.* Nashville, 1911. Compare "Christian Training and the Revival," in King, H. C., *Personal and Ideal Elements in Education.* New York, 1904.

For all phases of the reform movement in religious education, consult the files of the magazine *Religious Education*, and also the volumes of *Proceedings of the Religious Education Association* that preceded the magazine. Several valuable summaries of current movements will be found in the "Annual Surveys" presented at the conventions of the Association and printed in the above named publications. Consult also the files of the *Biblical World.*

Certain beginnings of the reform movement in Great Britain are evidenced by the papers and resolutions of a conference called by the British Sunday School Union. See Johnson, F. (editor), *Bible Teaching by Modern Methods.* London, 1907.

On education with reference to the coming world order, see the numbers of *Religious Education* throughout the year 1917. See also Ballantine, W. G., *Religious Education for the Coming Social Order.* Pamphlet, Boston, Pilgrim Press, 1917.

A composite picture of present points of view can be had by referring to articles in Nelson's *Encyclopedia of Sunday Schools and Religious Education.* 3 vols. New York.

Two recent utterances on the relation of religious education to democracy are: Winchester, B. S. "The Churches of the Federal Council and Week-Day Religious Instruction," a report made to the Federal Council at St. Louis, December, 1916, and published in the *Proceedings of the Council;* and a pamphlet by Athearn, W. S. "Religious Education and American Democracy," Malden, Mass., 1916.

D

TEXT-BOOKS THAT HAVE GROWN OUT OF THE SOCIAL CONCEPTION OF THE CHRISTIAN LIFE

In this list only such texts are included as seem to conceive of Christian education as a process of socializing conduct, purposes, and thought, in the spirit of Jesus. Many lessons that enforce social duties are contained, of course, in texts that presuppose one or another presocial conception of Christian experience, but these texts are not mentioned.

An extended annotated bibliography of *Graded Text-Books for the Modern Sunday School,* printed in 1914, can be had upon application to the Religious Education Association, 1032 East 55th Street, Chicago. For the latest list in each of the graded series, write to the various publishers of lesson systems. The almost constantly growing lists of the Association Press, of the National Board of the Young Women's Christian Associations, and of the Missionary Education Movement should be consulted also.

Text-books of social religion adapted to classes of adults and of older adolescents are relatively numerous; texts for early and middle adolescence are rare; for most of the years below adolescence non-existent.

1. *For Classes of Adults and of Older Adolescents*

Dole, C. F. *The Citizen and the Neighbor.* Boston, 1884.

Douglass, H. P. *The New Home Missions.* New York, 1914.

Edwards, R. H. *Christianity and Amusements.* New York, 1915.

Faunce, W. H. P. *Social Aspects of Foreign Missions.* New York. 1914.

Henderson, C. R. *Social Duties from the Christian Point of View.* Chicago, 1913.

Jenks, J. W. *The Political and Social Significance of the Teachings of Jesus.* New York, 1911.

Kent, C. F. *The Social Teachings of the Prophets and Jesus.* New York, 1917.

Kent, C. F., and Jenks, J. W. *The Making of a Nation.* New York, 1912.

——, *The Testing of a Nation's Ideals.* New York, 1914.

Mathews, S. *The Individual and the Social Gospel.* New York, 1914.

——, *The Social and Ethical Teaching of Jesus,* Chicago, 1913.

——, *The Social Gospel.* Philadelphia, 1910.

Nordell, P. A. *The Modern Church.* New York, Scribner Completely Graded Series.

Rauschenbusch, W. *The Social Principles of Jesus.* New York, 1916.

Richardson, N. E. *The Liquor Problem.* New York, 1915.

——, *International Peace.* Pamphlet. New York. Federal Council of Churches, 1915.

Soares, T. G. *Social Institutions and Ideals of the Bible.* New York, 1915.

Strong, J. *Studies in the Gospel of the Kingdom.*

——, New series: *Studies in Social Progress.* Published periodically by the American Institute of Social Service, New York.

Taft, A. B. *Community Studies for Country Districts.* New York, 1912.

Trawick, A. M. *The City Church and its Social Mission.* New York, 1913.

Ward, H. F. *The Bible and Social Living.* New York, etc., 1917. International Graded Lessons.

——, *Poverty and Wealth.* New York, etc., 1915. International Graded Lessons.

——, *The Social Creed of the Churches.* New York, 1912.

Ward, H. F., and Edwards, R. H. *Christianizing Community Life.* New York, 1917.

2. *For Classes in Early and Middle Adolescence*

Gates, H. W. *Heroes of the Faith.* New York, Scribner Completely Graded Series.

Hunting, H. B. *Christian Life and Conduct.* New York, Scribner Completely Graded Series.

Jenks, J. W. *Life Questions of High School Boys.* New York, 1908.

Weston, S. A. *The World as a Field for Christian Service.* New York, etc., International Graded Lessons.

3. *For Younger Pupils*

Cutting, Mrs. Charles, and Merrett, C. C. *God the Loving Father and His Children.* New York, Scribner Completely Graded Series. For primary pupils.

Dadmun, F. M. *Living Together.* Boston, 1915, the new Beacon Series. For primary pupils.

Everyland. A magazine intended to widen the social outlook of children toward children of other races. New York. The Missionary Education Movement. Adapted to primary and junior pupils.

Rankin, M. E. *A Course for Beginners in Religious Education, with Lessons for One Year for Children Five Years of Age.* New York, 1917. Scribner Completely Graded Series.

E

CURRENT PROGRESS IN THE ORGANIZATION AND METHODS OF RE-
LIGIOUS EDUCATION IN CHURCH, DENOMINATION, AND COMMUNITY

A reform movement in the organization and methods of religious education is more or less manifest in a multitude of publications, both books and periodicals. The present short list is intended simply to indicate the general direction of this movement. The reader should not fail to consult the files of *Religious Education* for articles not here listed. Whoever desires a complete picture of the situation in Protestant circles in the United States should consult in addition the reports of the Sunday School Council of Evangelical Denominations; the Sunday-school magazines published by the different denominations; the proceedings and the various circulars of the International Sunday School Association; the reports of the Sunday School Commission of the Federal Council; the reports of denominational commissions and departments of religious education or of Sunday schools; the teachers' books in each of the graded lesson series; the newer text-books for teacher training, such as the "Modern Sunday School Manuals" (published by a Methodist and Congregational syndicate), "The Worker and His Work" series (published by the Methodist Book Concern), and the handbooks on "Principles and Methods of Religious Education" (published by the University of Chicago Press); finally, the constantly enlarging lists of the denominational and other publishers of religious literature.

Typical of the endeavor to transform the Sunday school are the following:

Athearn, W. S. *The Church School.* Boston, 1914.
Cope, H. F. *Efficiency in the Sunday School.* New York, 1912.
——, *The Evolution of the Sunday School.* Boston and New York, 1911.
——, *The Modern Sunday School and its Present-Day Task.* New York, 1916.
Evans, H. F. *The Sunday School Building and its Equipment.* Chicago, 1914.
Frayser, N. L. *The Sunday School and Citizenship.* Cincinnati, 1915.
Gates, H. W. *Recreation and the Church.* Chicago, 1917.
Hartshorne, H. *Worship in the Sunday School.* New York, 1913.
——, *Manual for Training in Worship.* New York, 1915.
——, *The Book of Worship of the Church School.* New York, 1915.

Hutchins, W. N. *Graded Social Service for the Sunday School.* Chicago, 1914.

Richardson, N. E., and Loomis, O. E. *The Boy Scout Movement Applied by the Church.* New York, 1915.

The movement toward a community conception of the function of religious education is represented by the following publications. Much material will be added by the 1918 convention of the Religious Education Association, which is to take this as its topic.

Athearn, W. S. *The City Institute for Religious Teachers.* Chicago, 1915.

——, *A Community System of Religious Education.* Boston, 1917.

——, *Correlation of Church Schools and Public Schools.* Pamphlet. Malden, Mass., 1917.

Coe, G. A. "A General View of the Movement for Correlating Religious Education with Public Instruction." *Religious Education.* XI (1916), 109–122. See also other articles in this and the preceding volume of *Religious Education.*

"Co-operation in Christian Education." New York, Federal Council Report, 1917.

Wood, C. A. *School and College Credit for Outside Bible Study.* Yonkers-on-Hudson, 1917.

See also references under "Educational Relations between State and Church" in this Bibliography.

F

THE FAMILY AS AN AGENCY FOR SOCIAL-RELIGIOUS EDUCATION

Consult " A Brief Bibliography on Religious Nurture in the Home." Prepared and annotated by Moxcey, M. E. *Religious Education,* X (1915), 610–612, and add the following subsequent works:

Goodsell, W. *A History of the Family as a Social and Educational Institution.* New York, 1915.

Moxcey, M. E. *Girlhood and Character.* New York, 1916.

G

THE RELATION OF THE STATE TO RELIGIOUS EDUCATION

There is a long series of articles and allusions in the *Reports of the United States Commissioner of Education.* Of especial significance are the Reports of 1888-9, 1894-5 (the New York controversy), 1896-7 (statistics of religious exercises in public schools), 1897-8 (the New York controversy, etc.).

The United States Bureau of Education Bulletin No. 7 (1908) reports important judicial decisions.

On the New York controversy see also Bourne, W. O., *History of the Public School Society of the City of New York* (New York, 1870); a chapter in Burns, J. A., *The Catholic School System in the United States* (New York, 1908), and Hall, A. J., *Religious Education in the Public Schools of the State and City of New York* (Chicago, 1914).

The celebrated Edgerton case is reported in 76 *Wisconsin Reports*, Conover, 177. For the Cincinnati case, see 23 *Ohio State Reports*, Granger, 21-254, and the references already given in a footnote on page 255.

The constitutional provisions, laws, and court decisions are brought together in a convenient volume by Brown, S. W., *The Secularization of American Education* (New York, 1912). The same author brought the matter down to date in "Present Legal Status, etc.," in *Religious Education*, XI (1916), 103-108.

On the history of this matter in the Northwest Territory, see articles by Mayo in the *Report of the United States Commissioner of Education for* 1894-5.

On Massachusetts history see the first, second, and twelfth *Annual Reports* of Horace Mann, and *Report of the United States Commissioner of Education* for 1897-8.

On the Catholic position see a speech by Archbishop Ireland in *Proceedings of the National Education Association*, 1890, pp. 179 ff.; Burns, J. A., *The Catholic School System in the United States* (New York, 1908); O'Connell, C. J., *Christian Education* (New York, 1906); McQuaid, B. J., *The Public School Question* (Boston, 1876); McCabe, J., *The Truth about Secular Education* (London, 1906); articles on "Schools," "Education," etc., in the *Catholic Encyclopædia*, and the *Proceedings of the Catholic Education Association*, Columbus, Ohio.

A discussion that occurred in the National Education Association in 1889 is printed in the *Proceedings* and also separately under the title, *Denominational Schools* (Syracuse, Bardeen, 1889).

Arguments for entire separation of religious instruction from the public schools are contained in Mead, E. D., *The Roman Catholic Church and the Public Schools* (Boston, 1890); Spear, S. T., *Religion and the State, or the Bible and the Public Schools* (New York, 1876); Crooker, J. T., *Religious Freedom in American Education* (Boston, 1903); and

Harris, W. T., "The Separation of the Church from Schools Supported by Public Taxes" (*Proceedings of the National Education Association*, 1903).

On the controversy in Great Britain, see Riley, A., and others, *The Religious Question in Public Education* (London, 1911).

For practices and points of view in various countries, see Spiller, G., *Moral Education in Eighteen Countries* (London, 1909); Sadler, M. E., *Moral Instruction and Training in Schools*, 2 vols. (London, 1908); *Proceedings and Papers of the First International Moral Education Congress* (London, David Nutt, 1908); *Mémoires sur l'Education Morale* [the second Moral Education Congress] (The Hague, Nijhoff, 1912); also a volume of *Papers Contributed by American Writers* to the second Congress (Brooklyn, 1912).

Consult, on the whole topic, the indices of *Religious Education*, and see especially the number for February, 1911, and a bibliography (for free distribution) of "Instruction in Religion in Relation to Public Education," which was published in Vol. X (1915), pp. 613–624. Add to this bibliography the subsequently published article by Sheridan, H. J., "Religious Education and the Public Schools of Ontario," in *Religious Education*, XII (1917), 15–19, and the prize essay by Rugh, C. E., *The Essential Place of Religion in Education*. Published by the National Education Association, Ann Arbor, 1916.

On the relations between the public schools and the movement for week-day religious instruction by the churches, see *Religious Education*, Vol. XII.

H

THE SOCIAL CAPACITIES OF CHILDREN

On the instinctive endowment of man, see:

McDougall, W. *Introduction to Social Psychology*. Boston, 1909.

Thorndike, E. L. *The Original Nature of Man*, being Vol. I of his *Educational Psychology*. New York, 1913. A brief summary of original traits is given in his *Education*. New York, 1912, Chapter V. See also his *Educational Psychology, Briefer Course*.

Representative of the recapitulation theory are:

Bolton, F. E. *Principles of Education*. New York, 1910, Chapters IV, V, VI.

Fiske, G. W. *Boy Life and Self-Government*. New York, 1910.

Hall, G. S. *Educational Problems.* 2 vols. New York, 1911, espe-, cially Chapter IV, "The Religious Training of Children and the Sunday School," and Chapter V, "Moral Education."

Partridge, G. E. *Genetic Philosophy of Education.* New York, 1912. This work is an epitome of the educational theories of G. Stanley Hall. See especially pp. 50–58, and Chapter XII, "Religious Education."

On the limitations of the recapitulation theory, see:

Davidson, P. E. *The Recapitulation Theory and Human Infancy.* New York, 1914. Note his bibliography.

National Herbart Society, First and Second Year Books. Chicago, 1895, 1896.

Thorndike, E. L. *The Original Nature of Man,* being Vol. I of his *Educational Psychology.* New York, 1913.

For various points of view with respect to childhood religion, the conversion of children, etc., see:

Bonner, C. *The Christ, the Church, and the Child.* London, 1911.

Dawson, G. E. *The Child and His Religion.* Chicago, 1909.

Koons, W. G. *The Child's Religious Life.* New York, 1903.

Leuba, J. H. "Children's Conceptions of God and Religious Education." *Religious Education,* XII (1917), 5–15.

Mumford, E. E. R. *The Dawn of Religion in the Mind of the Child.* London, 1915.

Rishell, C. W. *The Child as God's Child.* New York, 1904.

Stephens, T. (editor). *The Child and Religion.* New York, 1905.

St. John, E. P. *Child Nature and Child Nurture.* Boston, 1911. An outline for study classes, with bibliographies.

I

THEORIES OF METHOD IN SOCIAL INSTRUCTION AND TRAINING

Bagley, W. C. *The Educative Process.* New York, 1910.

——, *School Discipline.* New York, 1914.

Cabot, E. L. "Methods of Ethical Teaching." *Religious Education,* VI (1911), 542.

Chubb, P. "Direct Moral Education." *Religious Education,* II (1907), 164.

Coe, G. A. "Virtue and the Virtues." *Proceedings of the National Education Association*, 1911; printed also in *Religious Education*, VI (1911), 486.

Dewey, J. *Moral Principles in Education.* Boston, 1910.

——, *Democracy and Education.* New York, 1916.

Gould, F. J. *Moral Instruction: Its Theory and Practice.* London, 1913.

Griggs, E. H. *Moral Education.* New York, 1904.

Healy, W. *Honesty: A Study of Causes and Treatment of Dishonesty among Children.* Indianapolis, 1915.

Kirkpatrick, E. A. *The Individual in the Making.* Boston, 1911.

——, *The Use of Money.* Indianapolis, 1915.

McMurry, F. M. *Elementary School Standards.* Yonkers-on-Hudson, 1914.

——, *How to Study.* Boston, 1909.

Moxcey, M. E. *Girlhood and Character.* New York, 1916.

Neumann, H. "Some Misconceptions of Moral Education." One of the *Papers by American Writers* to the Second International Moral Education Congress.

Palmer, G. H. *Ethical and Moral Instruction in Schools.* Boston, 1899.

Rugh, C. E., and others. *Moral Training in Public Schools.* Boston, 1907.

Shand, A. F. *The Foundations of Character.* London, 1914.

Sharpe, F. C. "The Development of Moral Thoughtfulness in Schools." One of the *Papers by American Writers* to the Second International Moral Education Congress.

Sheldon, W. L. *An Ethical Sunday School.* London, 1900.

Sneath, E. H., and Hodges, G. *Moral Training in the School and Home.* New York, 1913.

Strayer, G. H. *A Short Course in the Teaching Process.* New York, 1912.

Swift, E. J. *Learning and Doing.* Indianapolis, 1914.

Taylor, C. K. *The Moral Education of School Children.* Philadelphia, 1912.

Tufts, J. H. "How Far is Formal Systematic Instruction Desirable in Moral Training in Schools?" *Religious Education*, vol. III, October, 1908, p. 121 and *ff*.

On transfer of training, a bibliography of 68 titles will be found in Hewins, N. P. *The Doctrine of Formal Discipline in the Light of Ex-*

perimental Investigation. Baltimore, 1916. For statements of the problem, and for the chief points of view, see:

Bagley, W. C. *The Educative Process.* New York, 1910.

Colvin, S. S. "Some Facts in Partial Justification of the So-called Dogma of Formal Discipline." Pamphlet, *Bulletin No. 2 of the University of Illinois School of Education.* 1910.

O'Shea, M. V. *Education as Adjustment.* New York, 1905.

A symposium by Angell, Pillsbury, and Judd, in the *Educational Review,* June, 1908.

Thorndike and Woodworth. "The Influence of Improvement in One Mental Function upon the Efficiency of Other Functions." *Psychological Review,* VIII, 247–261; 348–395; 553–564.

INDEX

NOTE.—This Index contains the names of authors who are referred to in the text. For other names see the Classified Bibliography.

357